CHRISTIAN QUESTIONS
VOLUME 5

I0082249

HOW DO I STUDY THE BIBLE?

THE BEST BIBLE STUDY METHODS FOR CHRISTIANS

J. D. MYERS

REDEEMING
GOD.COM

HOW DO I STUDY THE BIBLE?
The Best Bible Study Methods for Christians
© 2025 by J. D. Myers

Published by Redeeming Press
Dallas, OR 97338
RedeemingPress.com

978-1-939992-78-9 (Paperback)
978-1-939992-79-6 (Mobi)
978-1-939992-80-2 (ePub)

Learn more about J. D. Myers by visiting RedeemingGod.com

JOIN JEREMY MYERS AND LEARN MORE

Take Bible and theology courses by joining Jeremy at
RedeemingGod.com/join/

WANT TO LEARN MORE?

If you have questions about how to study the Bible,
get them answered in the online course.

Learn more at RedeemingGod.com/Courses/

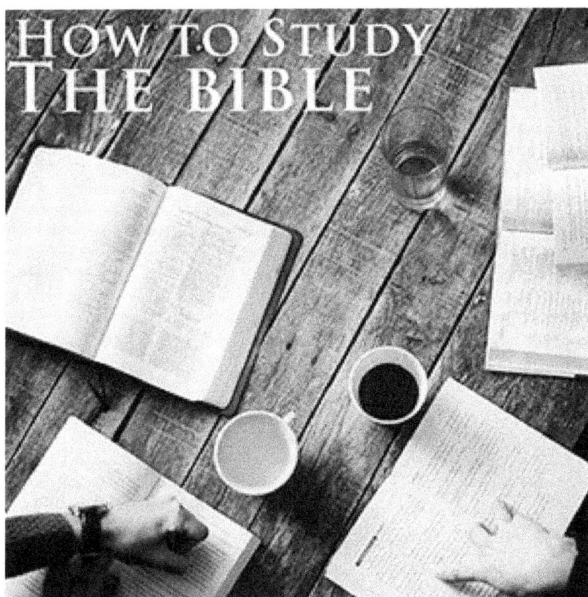

The course is normally $297, but after you join the
online Discipleship Group for $9, you can take this
course and all the others at no additional charge.
Learn more here:
RedeemingGod.com/join/

Other Books in the *Christian Questions* Series

Other Books by Jeremy Myers

Books in the *Close Your Church for Good* Series

All books are available at your favorite bookstore. Learn about each title at the end of this book.

There is absolutely nothing to compare [with the Bible] in all the other literature of the world. Its style is so simple and clear that a child can understand it, but its truth is so profound that we can explore the Book from childhood to old age and can never say we have reached the bottom.

—R. A. Torrey

.

TABLE OF CONTENTS

INTRODUCTION TO THE "CHRISTIAN QUESTIONS" BOOK SERIES

This "Christian Questions" book series provides down-to-earth answers to everyday questions. The series is based on questions that people have asked me over the years through my website, podcast, and online discipleship group at RedeemingGod.com. Since thousands of people visit the site every single day, I get scores of questions emailed to me each month from readers around the world. Many of the questions tend to be around various "hot topic" issues like homosexuality, violence, and politics. Other questions, however, focus more on how to understand a particular Bible passage or theological issue. For example, I receive hundreds of questions a year about the unpardonable sin in Matthew 12.

I love receiving these questions, and I do my best to answer them. But after I answer the same question five or ten times, I realize that it might be better if I had a ready-made and easily accessible resource I could invite people to read. This also provides the reader with a better explanation than I can give in a short email. For people who want the *full* experience, there are also online courses available for many of these questions at RedeemingGod.com/courses.

So the goal of this "Christian Questions" book series is to answer the questions that people send to me. Below is the current list of books in the "Christian Questions" series. Most of these are not yet published, but I include the list to show you where the series is headed.

What is Prayer?

What are the Spiritual Gifts?

What is Faith?

How Can I Study the Bible?

Why is the world so messed up?

Can God forgive my sin?

What is the unforgivable sin?

What is baptism?

What is the church?

What is repentance?

How can I evangelize?

Can I lose eternal life?

Why did Jesus have to die?

Should Christians keep the Sabbath?

What is demon possession?

How can I gain freedom from sin?

What is election and predestination?

Does God love me?

Why did God give the law?

Does God really want blood sacrifices?

What is sin?

What is the best bible translation?

Can I trust the Bible?

If you have a question about Scripture, theology, or Christian living that you would like answered, you may submit it through the contact form at RedeemingGod.com/about/ or join my online discipleship group at RedeemingGod.com/join/.

Several of the "Christian Question" books are available as free PDF downloads to people who join my online discipleship group.

Visit RedeemingGod.com/join/ to learn more and join today.

CHAPTER 1

THE ONE RULE

When I first learned to drive, I remember thinking that it was so much fun. I loved to drive as much as I could. Every chance I got, I would get in the car and drive somewhere—it didn't really matter where. I had my favorite roads and favorite streets, but it was all so new to me that I enjoyed driving everywhere.

The problem was that people kept hitting me. At least, that's the way I viewed it. When I first started driving, I was a little hesitant about going fast. I was driving at 25 mph when someone rammed into me from behind because they were going 65 mph. Yet when the police showed up, they said it was my fault! Apparently, it is reckless to drive 40 miles per hour below the speed limit on the interstate.

So I learned my lesson. I decided to speed up. I didn't want to get hit from behind again. But the very next week, I was driving along at 65 mph when I rammed into somebody who was only going 20 mph. So when the cops showed up, I told them it was the other guy's fault because he was going too slow. But the police officer still gave me a ticket. He said I was speeding in a school zone and could have killed somebody.

They made me attend a class where I learned all about speed limits and when not to go too fast or too slow. Then I went out driving again. But as I was driving along at the speed limit, someone came along driving in the opposite direction in my lane, and we had a head-on collision. The cops showed up and I told them I was driving the speed limit so it wasn't my fault. But guess what? They gave me another ticket. Why? They said I was driving the wrong way down a one-way street.

So now I was confident that I knew enough to avoid any more accidents. I would drive the speed limit and I would drive the correct way down the streets. But the very next week, as I was driving through town, some guy rammed right into the side of my car! This time I was fuming mad! When the cops showed up, I told them that I was going the speed limit and was driving down the street in the right direction. But once again, *I* got blamed for the accident. Apparently, those red lights above the intersections aren't just for decoration. According to the police, I am supposed to stop when the red light is on. That probably explains why everyone honked at me when I drove through red lights. I had thought everyone was just being friendly.

I could go on and tell you about the time I drove drunk, the time I drove with a revoked license, the time I tried driving backward, the time I drove with my eyes shut, the time I drove with no hands, the time I drove while sitting in the backseat, and the time I drove while sitting in the passenger seat like my mailman does. But every single time, I was the one who got the ticket. Every single time I also learned a new rule about driving. But even though I think I've finally learned all the rules about driving, it's too late. They took away my license and won't let me ever drive again.

I only wish someone had given me rules for driving before I ever got into a car.

This is obviously a fictional story. In real life, I've only been in two fender benders, and neither one was my fault. Seriously! I am a good driver, and I doubt that anyone in the history of driving is as bad as the driver in the story I just presented. And yet, if there were no rules for driving, or if drivers were not expected to learn driving rules before getting behind a wheel, the sorts of accidents I just described would be quite common.

Have you ever thought about the act of driving? If I invented a carnival ride that strapped people into little metal boxes before sending them shooting down a concrete path at 65 mph with thousands of other people on the same path in similar boxes, and everybody is steering their own little metal box wherever they want, you likely would not be too eager to try this carnival ride. And yet, that is pretty much exactly what we do every single day when we drive to work, go shopping, or head to the mountains for the weekend.

The only reason we don't all get killed on the roads is because there are certain rules to driving that everybody tries to follow. As long as people follow these rules for driving, what should be a deadly and terrifying activity is actually quite safe and enjoyable. Accidents still happen, but for the most part, driving is a central and important aspect of life for every person on earth because most people know and follow the rules for driving.[1]

RULES FOR STUDYING SCRIPTURE

Just as rules must exist and must be obeyed for everyone to drive safely, so also rules must exist and be followed for Christians to understand the Bible correctly. But the sad reality is that most Christians study their Bibles the way I drove a car in the fictional illustration above. Many Christians don't know the rules for studying Scripture, or that there even *are* rules, and so when they read and study the Bible, they fall into every possible mistake and error, and end up believing and teaching a lot of terrible ideas. Then, when they encounter someone who is driving down the theological road in a different direction, they think it is the *other* person who is at fault. When this happens, both Christians get into an argument, and start

---

[1] I wasn't aware of this when I wrote the story above, but after I had finished writing this book and was performing further reading and research in other, related books, I came across a similar illustration in Roy B. Zuck, *Basic Bible Interpretation* (Wheaton: Victor, 1991), 27.

calling each other a heretic, until eventually the police show up to settle the matter.

But if all Christians learned and followed certain rules of Bible study, there would be far fewer disagreements in the church and much less confusion in Christianity today. If we all learned to follow the proper Bible study rules, there wouldn't be so many church splits and denominational splinters. We would all be more unified. We would be "one," just as Jesus prayed that we would be (John 17:21-23).

Yet sadly, just like with driving, most Christians don't know the rules of Bible study, and many are not even aware that there *are* rules. And so everybody drives down the doctrinal roadways however the wind blows (Eph 4:14), thereby creating confusion, chaos, disagreement, and disunity in the church of God.

Of course, even if all Christians did know the basic rules to Bible study and all sought to follow them, there will still be some disagreements, just as there are still some driving accidents. But just as driving rules help us drive more safely, so also the rules of Bible study help us understand and teach the Bible more correctly. If we know and follow the rules, there will still be some doctrinal disagreements, but there will be far, far fewer than there are today.

And thankfully, just as there are no secret driving rules, there are no secret Bible study rules. You don't need access to some special club to unfold the glorious truths of Scripture. Like the rules of driving, the rules of Bible study are easily learned and easily followed. However, also like the rules of driving, you need to practice applying the rules of Bible study. Though the rules of Bible study are not difficult or hidden, learning to follow them takes some discipline and practice, just like learning to drive.

This book provides the basic rules for Bible study, while also presenting some tips and suggestions that will make your Bible study efforts more fruitful and effective. I have been following these principles for decades and find that they rarely lead me astray. As you follow these rules in your own Bible study, you also will be able to navigate the difficult portions of Scripture with ease and uncover some of the greatest truths revealed by God in the Bible.

ONE RULE TO GUIDE THEM

When it comes right down to it, there is really only one rule to studying Scripture, and it is this:

Read and study the Bible
as you would any other book.

For some reason, many Christians read the Bible in a way that is completely different from how they read other books. The reason for this mistake is easily understood.

In the minds of most Christians, the Bible is "THE BIBLE!" Most Christians don't think the Bible is like any other book. It is often printed with a fine leather cover and gold lettering. Many Bibles include the adjective "holy" on the front, as in "The *Holy* Bible." These factors lead some people to think there are special rules for reading and studying the Bible. But there are not any special rules for Bible study. If you know how to read and study other books, you can also read and study the Bible.

There are two main aspects of reading the Bible the way we would read any other book. First, you must understand the various *genres* of the books in the Bible, and second, you must understand the authorial intent of these books. I will discuss these further in later chapters of this book, but let me briefly introduce them here.

First, when you read a normal book, you first understand its *genre*. A *genre* is a type of literature. If the book is a novel, you understand it will tell you a story. If it is history, you read it to learn about historical events and facts. If it is a book of poetry, you look for the rhythm, imagery, and word play that is often found in poems. If you have a cookbook, you don't read the book from cover to cover, but find the recipe you want to use, and then follow the instructions of that recipe. In the same way, when you approach the Bible, you need to understand its *genre,* and then read it the way you would also read other books of the same *genre.* We will discuss this more in a later chapter.

Second, when you read a book, you must give priority to *authorial intent.* That is, you must make sure that what the author of the book intended to say is the most important thing. We all assume that when an author writes a book, they are trying to relay some information to the reader through what is written on the page. As the reader, our job is to understand the information the author intended to convey. If you are reading a history book, you try to understand what the author is saying about the historical events they wrote about. If you are reading a science book, you try to understand what the author is saying about the area of science they wrote about.

When you seek to understand what the author of a book is saying, this does not automatically mean you will agree with that author. You may end up disagreeing with the author. But whether you agree or disagree, your first task is to understand what the author is saying. After all, you can't really agree or disagree with an author until you have first understood what the author wrote.

Now, when it comes to Scripture, we do not plan on disagreeing with what is written. We want to agree with everything that is written. But how can we agree with what is written if we don't understand what the original author meant when they wrote the text? So, when we read the Bible, we must primarily seek to understand the ideas that the original author intended to convey. We must not come to Scripture with our own ideas about what we want it to say. This would not be honest to the biblical text, nor would it be respectful to the author who wrote it.

Let us say, for example, that you decided to leave a review of this book on Amazon.com. Let us say that although this book is about Bible study, you decided to read it as a book about politics. And since this is a terrible book about politics, you left a 1-star review on Amazon because it says nothing about the subject. If I saw this 1-star review, I would scratch my head and wonder if you were sane. This book has nothing whatsoever to do with politics, and other than this paragraph right here, I will not mention politics anywhere else. It would be silly for you to read this book about Bible study, but then review it as a book about politics. But this is exactly the sort of thing that some people do with the Bible. They come to Scripture with their own selfish agendas and goals, thinking that what they want to get from Scripture is more important than what the original author wanted to convey. Such an approach is wrong for any book, including the Bible.

In Christianity today, there are numerous ways this selfish approach to the Bible occurs. For example, some Christians approach the Bible as if it were a guide to daily living. They view the Bible as a self-help book that provides answers to all your questions about life. Some even say the Bible is "Basic Instructions Before Leaving Earth" (B-I-B-L-E). But the Bible is *not* a self-help guide. The Bible is not your life coach. To read the Bible as if it were a self-help guide is to read the Bible in a way that none of its authors wanted or intended.

Nor is the Bible a mysterious document filled with secret, hidden, prophetic codes. One method these people use is called "Equidistant Lettering." Those who selfishly approach Scripture this way teach that there are hidden Bible prophecies in the Hebrew and Greek which only advanced computer programs can find. The Greek and Hebrew texts are fed into a computer, and then the computer is programmed to search for sentences or phrases in the text by pulling out individual letters in various patterns. So, for example, the computer program might read every seventh letter backwards, or will arrange the letters in a grid and then read the letters diagonally across a page. When this is done, the computer program finds "prophecies" in the biblical text about historical events. This is then used to show the divine nature and origin of Scripture.

However, this is just another selfish way of reading the Bible that has nothing whatsoever to do with the message that the original authors of Scripture intended. Sure, you will sell a lot of books to gullible Christians if you discover these secret hidden codes, but you will also end up disrespecting the Bible.

Now, I do admit that some of what they find this way is quite fantastic. I have a news article in which a computer was programmed to look for these secret codes. The computer found alleged prophecies about the assassinations of Abraham Lincoln, Gandhi, Martin Luther King Jr., and John F. Kennedy. The prophecy about Lincoln, says, "Abe Lincoln cut down. Bang. Killed." Regarding the death of Martin Luther King, Jr., the text says "ML King prepared for death. To be killed. Gun. In Tenn. US Agent." The statement about JFK says this: "Kennedy. In car. Rifle. Shot. Head. Coffin." I must hasten to add, however, that the text used for these specific examples was not the Bible but was Herman Melville's *Moby Dick*. And Mormons have done something similar with *The Book of Mormon*. If equidistant lettering were proof that the Bible is divinely inspired and contains the secret signature of God, then *Moby Dick* and *The Book of Mormon* are also divinely inspired, for they too contain this so-called "signature of God."

But equidistant lettering is not proof of anything except that some people have too much time on their hands and that some Christians will buy books on anything. No book in human history should be approached this way, as no author ever had such things in mind when they wrote their books. The same thing is true with the Bible. Using equidistant lettering to find hidden Bible codes does not take the Bible seriously or naturally. You wouldn't read any other book this way, and you shouldn't read the Bible this way either.

One final example of how people read the Bible selfishly rather than as the original author intended is when some Christians try to find deep, spiritual truths in every little detail of the text. Yes, the entire Bible is inspired. We will talk about that later. But this doesn't mean that every little detail of the text has some deep spiritual meaning.

For example, Genesis 14:14 says that Abraham had 318 servants. This is an interesting historical fact, but it is not very "spiritual." So in an attempt to make this number more spiritual, some people engage in hermeneutical gymnastics to make this number more meaningful. One Bible teacher pointed out that if you assign numerical values to the Hebrew consonants of Abraham's name and then add these numbers together, the total value is 318. To make this "spiritually" significant, the teacher then converted the number 318 to Greek letters. The Greek letter *tau* stands for 300, the *iota* for 10, and the *epsilon* for 8. He then went on to teach that since the *tau* looks like the cross, and the *iota* and *epsilon* are the first two letters of Jesus' name, the number 318 in Genesis 14:14 is a prophecy about the crucifixion of Jesus. In the book where I read this, the author went on to say this: "God knows that I never taught to anyone a more certain truth."

Is this truly a "certain truth?" It is definitely true that Abraham had 318 servants. It is also definitely true that Jesus died on the cross. But the number of Abraham's servants is in no way a prophecy about Jesus Christ. It is simply telling the reader about Abraham's wealth and how God blessed him. To seek some greater spiritual meaning to the number is to read ideas into Scripture that are not there. We would not treat any other book this way, and so we must not treat the Bible this way either. To approach Scripture in such a manner is to disrespect the Word of God. We must take the Bible seriously and naturally. When the plain sense makes sense, seek no other sense.

So the first and primary rule of Bible study is that when you read and study Scripture, make sure you approach it as you would any other book. Proper Bible study does not use a special set of rules. When you read and study Scripture, you can read and study it as you would any other book. Seek to understand the intent of the original author, and how the original audience would have understood their words. This is how you would read any other book, and should also be how you read the Bible.

Having said this, let me clarify that while we can read and study the Bible like any other book, this does not mean that the Bible itself is *just like* any other book. It isn't. There are three central characteristics of Scripture which sets it apart from all other books in human history. These three characteristics are foundational to proper Bible study, and while they do not change the fact that we can read Scripture like any other book, they do guide us in our reading and studying of Scripture. The next chapter explores these three foundational truths about Scripture.

DISCUSSION QUESTIONS

1. How are the rules for driving cars similar to the rules for studying and teaching Scripture? Why is it important to learn both?

2. This chapter suggested one reason for there being so much disagreement and disunity in Christianity today. What was this reason and do you agree or disagree? Why?

3. There is one basic rule that guides all Bible study. What is it?

4. In what ways is the Bible just like any other book? In what ways is it different? Do you agree that we should read the Bible as we read any other book? Why or why not?

5. Have you ever written a letter, email, or text message which was misunderstood by others? If so, how did it make you feel, and what did you do to correct the misunderstanding? What does this teach us about working to properly understand the message of the Bible?

CHAPTER 2

THREE FOUNDATIONAL TRUTHS FOR STUDYING SCRIPTURE

In my book, *God's Blueprints for Church Growth,* I tell a story about the time when Ravi Zacharias toured the world's first "deconstructionist building." Ravi described the building as follows:

> Its white scaffolding, red brick turrets, and Colorado grass pods evoke a double take. But puzzlement only intensifies when you enter the building, for inside you encounter stairways that go nowhere, pillars that hang from the ceiling without purpose, and angled surfaces configured to create a sense of vertigo.

> The architect, we are duly informed, designed this building to reflect life itself—senseless and incoherent—and the 'capriciousness of the rules that organize the built world.' When the rationale was explained to me, I had just one question: 'Did he do the same with the foundation?'[1]

---

[1] Ravi Zacharias, *Can Man Live Without God* (Dallas: Word, 1994), 21.

As Ravi correctly points out, all buildings need good foundations, regardless of what the building looks like or how it is built. If the building is going to stand, certain rules must be followed when laying the foundation. If this is true in architecture, it is also true in theology and Bible study. A solid foundation for understanding Scripture is essential for proper interpretation and explanation.

One of the reasons there is so much disagreement in Christian circles today about what the Bible teaches is because many Christians misunderstand (or outright reject) the three foundational principles of Scripture: the inspiration, inerrancy, and authority of the Bible. All three concepts will be defined and clarified below, with some surprising insights.

Let me note that if inspiration, inerrancy, and the authority of Scripture are set aside, the uniqueness of Christianity is abandoned. After all, if we do not have special revelation from God and if the Bible cannot be trusted, then the Bible is no different than the Qur'an for Muslims, the Vedas for Hindus, or even the daily news for the average person. Without inspiration and inerrancy, the Bible is little more than another manmade religious text containing nothing but human opinions on various topics. So the rest of this chapter will briefly consider the three foundational truths of the Bible, namely, inspiration, inerrancy, and authority.

At the outset, I want to make clear that I believe in all

three doctrines with a few minor refinements which make them more helpful in our study of Scripture. The reason these minor modifications are necessary is because the traditional doctrines of inspiration, inerrancy, and authority have sometimes been used to turn the Bible into a battering ram or a book of magic words. Some people who hold to the inspiration, inerrancy, and authority of Scripture think that these doctrines allow them to use the Bible to beat people over the head with Bible verses or lay claim to promises in Scripture simply because the verses are "inspired, inerrant, and authoritative."

Such an approach to Scripture has never been helpful to Christianity, which is why some authors, scholars, and pastors have rejected these doctrines. But rather than throw the baby out with the bathwater, it's better to just make sure the baby gets properly washed and rinsed. My explanation of these three doctrines seeks to do just that. After briefly presenting these doctrines as traditionally taught, I will suggest slight adjustments to each which allows the doctrine to be retained as a helpful foundation to our ongoing investigation into the teachings of Scripture.

THE INSPIRATION OF SCRIPTURE

Traditionally, the doctrine of the inspiration of Scripture teaches that God guided human authors to write

Scripture so that they penned what He wanted to say. The authors were not passive instruments in this process, mechanically recording what God dictated, but the Holy Spirit worked with their human personalities and individuality to record God's written revelation to humankind (cf. John 14:26; 1 Cor 2:12-13; 2 Tim 3:16; 2 Pet 1:21).

While I am a strong proponent of the inspiration of Scripture, the doctrine carries a lot of theological baggage and controversy. For example, people wonder about the extent of inspiration. Does it apply only to the *ideas* of Scripture or to the very words themselves? To put it another way, did God give the authors a *general sense* of what to write while letting them choose the specific words to express these ideas, or did He guide them in their *selection of the very words* that they were to write?

Also, does the doctrine of inspiration apply to the original manuscripts only (which no longer exist), or to the copies of these manuscripts as well? If it also applies to the copies, then how do we explain the copyist errors that have crept into these manuscripts over the centuries? What about Bible translations? If only the original Greek and Hebrew manuscripts were inspired, then how does that help people today who want to study Scripture in English, Mandarin, or Russian? Since the original manuscripts no longer exist, in what sense can we speak of the inspired text of Scripture today?

Then there are questions about the word "inspired" itself. When we talk about the "inspiration" of Scripture, what separates the inspired Bible from other human works of literature, music, or art that some describe as "inspired"? How can other works be "inspired" while the Bible holds a unique role as divinely inspired? Is it somehow "extra-inspired"?

For these reasons (and many more), rather than teach and write about the "inspiration" of Scripture, I prefer to talk about the divine "empowering" of Scripture. I also occasionally use the terms "inbreathing" and "enlivening." I find these terms more helpful than "inspiration" because they not only explain some of the texts that talk about the origin and nature of Scripture, but they also carry parallels or allusions to the empowering, inbreathing, or enlivening work of God in creation as described in Genesis 1. It is helpful to remember that nature is God's first Bible and is available to all people in all languages throughout all time (Rom 1:20). Thus, the written revelation of God, the Bible, contains similar revelatory powers as those seen in nature. So when we look at the creation account of Genesis 1, we see God speaking creation into existence, giving life and light through the power of His word. When it came to humanity, God breathed into Adam the breath of life, and this life is passed down from Adam to all humans who came from him. God empowered, inbreathed, and enlivened His creation in Genesis 1.

Paul alludes to these exact same concepts in 2 Timothy 3:16. This passage is the most widely referenced text on the "inspiration" of Scripture. The key Greek term in the verse, *theopneustos*, often gets translated as "inspired," but this may not be the best translation. The Greek word literally means "God-breathed." But even if we go with this as a translation, what does it mean? Is Scripture the breath of God? Does it mean that Scripture was verbally spoken by God? Some note that the root of *pneustos* is *pneuma*, which is the word for wind, breath, or spirit. Based on this, some think of *theopneustos* as having something to do with God's Spirit. Thus, Scripture could be understood as "God-Spirited." But again, what does this mean?

Part of the problem with understanding the meaning of Paul's word *theopneustos* is that it is a rare word in Greek literature and is not used anywhere else in the Bible. Thankfully, Paul seems to have anticipated that his use of this word might cause confusion, and so Paul provided some help on how to understand this rare Greek word. In Greek, 2 Timothy 3:16 could be laid out in outline form as follows:

> *pasa graphē*
> > *theopneustos*
> > *kai ōphelimos*

pros didaskalian
pros elegmon
pros epanorthōsin
pros paideian tēn en dikaiosunē

In English, it looks like this:

All Scripture
    is God-breathed
    and profitable
        for teaching
        for reproof
        for correction
        for training in righteousness

When the text is laid out this way, note that it contains three pairs of phrases. The first pair, "God-breathed" and "profitable," is followed by four other words which further describe *how* Scripture is profitable. The four descriptive words also form two pairs. The first descriptive term, "teaching," is paired with the last term, "training," and both speak of the positive instruction (what to do) that comes from Scripture. The second and third terms, "reproof" and "correction," refer to negative instruction (what not to do). These two sets of words are parallel, meaning that each is a synonym of the other, or explains the other. Teaching and training explain each other, and reproof and correction also explain each other.

The parallel nature of these four descriptive terms indicates that the first pair of words, "God-breathed" and "profitable," are also parallel terms. Since "teaching" and "training" are synonymous, and "reproof" and "correction" are synonymous, this means that "profitable" can be understood as synonymous with "God-breathed." Since Paul knew that he was using a word his readers might misunderstand, he provided a second word, "profitable," to define and explain the first word, *theopneustos*, "God-breathed."

This means that the word *theopneustos* does not primarily refer to the *origin* of Scripture (where it came from and how we got it) but rather to its purpose. God inspired Scripture to be useful and profitable. The terms "God-breathed" and "profitable" are parallel to each other and refer to the purpose and usefulness of Scripture, specifically in the ways described by the four terms that follow.

When the word *theopneustos* was used in other Greek literature of the time, it described poets and philosophers who seemed to speak with a certain passion and urgency that made people *not only listen to what they were saying, but obey them as well.* Yet this was only true when the poet or philosopher was *speaking.* If someone recorded their words and passed the written record on to others, the written record of what had been spoken was *never* described as *theopneustos*.[2] Inspiring words, once written down, lost their inspiring power.

But not so with the written Word of God! Paul is pointing out that the *written* Word of God, unlike any other writings, retains its profitability and inspiring power. When we read Scripture, it is as if God is speaking it to us all over again, fresh, for our own ears. It is not simply a "divinely inspired record of what God said in history" but is the actual voice of God, speaking directly into our lives. It is so real, you can almost feel His breath whispering His revelation into your ears.

Paul's point seems to be that while the original prophetic message spoken by the prophets and apostles had the power and authority of God, this message did not lose its power and authority when it was written down. It retained this power and authority. So when we read the Bible, we can be inspired by what it says so that we step out to both listen and obey. Thus, Scripture retains its "Godness," its divine power and origin, even in written form. Scripture is not God, but is rather the voice of God, the breath of God, the whisper of God into our ears telling us what to know and how to live (cf. 1 Kings 19:12; Matt 10:27; Luke 12:3). Paul is saying in 2 Timothy 3:16 that Scripture is the breath or whisper of God into our lives in a way that makes it profitable even for us today. Though

---

[2] Gerhard Kittel, ed. *Theological Dictionary of the New Testament*, 10 vols. (Grand Rapids: Eerdmans), VI:454.

written, it retains its "inspiring" power to make us more like Jesus.

The alert reader will also recognize the parallels in Paul's concept of Scripture with the original creation story of Genesis 1. Just as God made creation through the power of His spoken word before creating man from the dust of the ground, and then "breathing in" to his nostrils the breath of life so that man became a living being, so also, Paul's use of *theopneustos* to describe Scripture indicates that God has done something similar for the Bible. Just as the in-breathing of God empowered Adam to live and do what God wanted done in this world, so also, the in-breathing of God on Scripture empowers it to teach, correct, and instruct us on how God wants us to live in this world.

Furthermore, just as the empowerment of Adam did not end with him, but was carried forward to all human generations that came from him, so also, it seems that the empowerment of Scripture did not stop with the original manuscripts penned by the original authors. Scripture is still powerful and effective for accomplishing what God wants in His people. This is even true for the copies of the original manuscripts, as well as for the translations that come from them, whether they are English, Mandarin, Russian, or any other language. The inspiration and profitability of Scripture applies to all of these forms of the Bible, not just to the original manuscripts.

Let me provide one caveat. I am not saying that the Bible *itself* is the voice or breath of God. This would be akin to making the Bible part of God Himself, which borders on bibliolatry, making the Bible an idol. We do not worship the Bible, nor are we people of a book. We are people of God. So the Bible itself is not so much the voice of God as it is a *record* of the voice of God. The Bible is not God's spoken voice; it is God's written Word. If I write a book, it is my word, but it is not my voice. A written account is nothing more than a record of my past thoughts. It shows the reader the way I think and the kinds of things I would say if I were speaking to them in person. This is how we can view the written record of God's voice in Scripture. By reading and studying the biblical record, we learn to hear and recognize the voice of God in our lives today. In this way, the Bible continues to be inspiring and profitable.

Many people claim that we should go to Scripture to "hear from God." I used to be one of these. Earlier in my teaching and writing ministry, I used to pray and ask God to speak to me through Scripture, to let me hear His voice in the written Word of God. At the time, I believed I frequently heard the voice of God in this manner. Looking back now, however, while I do believe I "heard God's voice" during these times, I was not hearing His voice in the way I thought. I thought that when God spoke to me through Scripture, I was hearing His voice through the ink and paper of the Bible. Today, this way of thinking about Scripture seems terribly idolatrous and magical. I viewed Scripture in the same way witchdoctors view bird intestines, or the way psychics look at tea leaves. I was seeking divine guidance through something physical.

Instead, what actually happened (and still happens today) is that the written Word of God taught me to recognize the whispered Word of God to my spirit through the Holy Spirit. By prayerfully and humbly reading and studying Scripture, I placed myself in a position to better hear God's still, small voice spoken directly to me.

Yes, God has spoken, and He has done so through Scripture. Yes, Scripture is God's written Word, and it does contain what God has said. The problem, however, is that what He has spoken in the past was not spoken to us, but to those who were in the past. The scholarly fields of "Bible Study Methods and Hermeneutics" have arisen to help us take the words that God spoke to those in the past and bring them forward into our own time, like a divine time-traveling machine, so that we can hear the voice of God speaking to us today in our own time. Today, God does not speak to us through the Bible. However, by reading and studying the Bible, we learn to hear God's voice spoken to us today.

When viewed this way, Scripture is not so much "God's Word to us" but is instead a record of "God's word to them" so that we can learn to recognize and hear

God's Word to us. Scripture helps us recognize the voice of God so that we can hear what God is saying to our generation today. As His sheep, Scripture helps us learn to hear and recognize His voice (John 10:1-5).

None of this means that God is inspiring authors to write more books of the Bible today. The canon of Scripture is closed, and what God has provided in Scripture is sufficient to teach us how to recognize the whispered words of God today. This is why reading and studying Scripture is so important for those who would hear the voice of God today. The written Word of God gives us the divine trajectory of history, the plan, goal, direction, and characteristics of God's movements and voice today. Scripture gives us an idea of what God is shaping in history.[3] Scripture provides a record of what God has said so that we can be trained to hear what God is saying.

Reading and studying Scripture pulls us into the whirlpool of divine direction, so that when we think, act, speak, and pray, we are doing so within the flow of the Spirit. We are not looking for new revelation, but new directions and actions, based on existing revelation. We are looking for "fresh covenant tasks"[4] of redemption, reconciliation, and resurrection. "As we let the Bible be the Bible, God works through us—and it—to do what

---

[3] N. T. Wright, "How Can the Bible Be Authoritative? ," *Vox Evangelica* 21: 9.

[4] Ibid., 12.

He intends to do in and for the church and the world."[5] This is how to understand the significance of the inspiration of Scripture, and why such a concept is essential for properly approaching the Bible.

This view on "inspiration" teaches that although Scripture was originally *spoken* into existence by God through the prophets and apostles, God also then guided the recording of *written* Scripture so that it retained the power and authority of God to accomplish His will in our lives. God continues to superintend and empower the translation and teaching of Scripture today so that we can learn to live for God in our day.

So rather than talk about the "inspiration" of Scripture, it might be better to talk about the divine "empowering" or "enlivening" of Scripture. God "enlivened" Scripture so that it was not just powerful and effective in the original manuscripts, but is also powerful and effective for us today as we seek to learn from what was done in the past so we can do similar things in our own lives.

With this in mind, let us turn then to the second foundational truth for studying Scripture: the doctrine of inerrancy.

THE INERRANCY OF SCRIPTURE

The traditional doctrine of inerrancy teaches that there

[5] Ibid., 14.

are no errors of any kind in the Bible. Inerrancy applies to both the words and ideas of Scripture, and only to the original documents that were penned by the authors of Scripture. I believe in this understanding of inerrancy. However, I also agree that due to the transmission of the texts through human copyists, errors have crept into Scripture over the centuries. There are also numerous translation errors in the various versions of the Bible. But due to the understanding of inspiration as outlined above, such transmission and translation errors have not negatively affected the authority or ability of Scripture to teach us how to hear the voice of God today.

Although copyist errors and translation issues exist in every biblical text today, this has not limited or restricted God's ability to speak through Scripture, guide His people, or teach and train us how to live profitable and effective lives for Him in this world. To see how this is so, it is helpful to think once again about the inbreathing of God in the Garden of Eden to give life to Adam. God breathed life into Adam, and yet Adam later rebelled against God and fell into sin, and all humanity with Him. But this has not stopped God's ability to work with, in, and among humanity. Even though Adam was created by God without sin or error (just like the original manuscripts of Scripture), sin has crept into the world so that all humans are now sinners (as errors have crept into all copies and translations of Scripture). But humans today are still filled with the breath of life and are empowered by God to accomplish His will in this world. So also with Scripture. Though there may be problems with the biblical text, the creative sovereignty of God is not hindered or blocked from speaking through the text to accomplish His purpose and will in our lives and in this world. Therefore, when we take into account the *purpose* of inspired Scripture, it is not wrong to say that the Bible *was* inerrant and still *is* inerrant, for it continues to perfectly declare the voice of God and accomplish the purpose for which God gave the Scriptures.

So what about the copyist and translation errors that have crept into Scripture? Upon careful consideration, these issues are not as serious as some claim. Four clarifications about the doctrine of inerrancy help make this clear.

Four Clarifications about Inerrancy

First, even when people teach that there are errors in the Bible, there are really not as many as most people assume. The vast majority of the so-called "errors" in the Bible are actually just copyist errors where some scribe who was copying the Bible by hand misspelled a word, left out or added a word, or transcribed two words (switched their order). Almost none of these affect the meaning of the verses in which they appear. When it comes right down to it, there really are only twenty-four verses in the Bible that most people point to as actual "errors" in the text that cause significant problems, and of these, only about twelve are serious. Here are four examples:

Genesis 1:11-12 says that the land produced vegetation, but in Genesis 2:5-7, it says that no shrub had yet sprung up from the land.[6] Many people like to ask, "Where did Cain get his wife?" because Genesis 4:17 says that he had a wife, but up to this point in the text, the only people on earth were Adam, Eve, and Cain (Abel was born, but murdered).[7] Numbers 25:9 says that 24,000 died in a plague, but in talking about the same plague, 1 Corinthians 10:8 says that 23,000 died.[8] In 2 Samuel 24:1, we read that God incited David to take a census of Israel, but 1 Chronicles 21:1 says that it was Satan who incited David.[9]

Do you see? None of these are really all that serious. They do not affect any major doctrines, beliefs, or practices of Christianity. They are not so much errors as

[6] Genesis 1:11-12 refers to the Garden of Eden only, while Genesis 2:5-7 refers to the rest of the earth. Humans were to take the plants and trees from the Garden to cultivate the rest of the earth.

[7] Cain married his sister, or maybe a niece. Genetic lines were pure at this time, and there was no prohibition yet on marrying a relative.

[8] These are round numbers. The actual number was probably somewhere between the two, so that Moses rounded up and Paul rounded down.

[9] In Scripture, God is often described as doing something that He only actually "allowed." Such may be the case here. This discrepancy is also helped by recognizing that "satan" is not an actual being, but is instead the "spirit of accusation" that lies at the root of all violent tendencies.

apparent contradictions. And apparent contradictions can all be solved with further research and understanding. Nevertheless, even though a few such difficulties do exist, most people who claim that there are errors in the Bible cannot point out a single one. People like to say "The Bible is full of errors"—even though they don't know of one—because this attitude allows them to disregard all of Scripture as authoritative and instructive in their lives.

Second, some people forget the cardinal rule of Bible study and fail to read the Bible like any other book. When they do this, they end up finding errors all over the place. They might forget to read biblical poetry as poetry, and so think that Psalm 18:2 is saying that God is literally a rock, a fortress, a shield, and a horn. Or they think the Bible cannot round numbers like other books, so that although 1 Kings 7:23 says that the large bowl of cast bronze in the temple was 10 cubits across and 30 cubits around, it really should be 31.4 cubits around (10 cubits across times Pi equals 31.4). Or they have problems reconciling Genesis 1 with science because they fail to see that Genesis 1 is not a scientific explanation about how the world began, but a theological treatise about the power and nonviolence of God (See my "Redeeming God Podcast" studies on Genesis 1 for an explanation of this). So again, most of the supposed "errors" of the Bible disappear when we remember to read the Bible like any other book.

Third, we must recognize that there is a vast difference

between what the Bible says and what we *think* the Bible says. The Bible can be correct in something it teaches even though people are wrong in what they claim the Bible teaches. It is distressing how few people understand this distinction. Often, when people teach Scripture, they claim they're "just teaching the Bible." But they really aren't. Instead, they are teaching what they *think* the Bible teaches. Even though a person's teachings about the Bible can be full of errors, this does not mean the Bible itself is full of errors.

For example, throughout church history, many believed and taught that the earth was flat. Indeed, some fringe-group Christians continue to believe this today and quote many Bible verses in defense of this view (cf. Dan 4:11; Matt 4:8; Rev 7:1). In searching the internet for some of these texts, I found one website that claimed there were over 100 verses in Scripture that support the flat-earth theory. But is this what the Bible teaches? Is the earth flat? No, of course not. Does this mean, then, that those 100 verses are in error? No. Quite to the contrary, when we allow for figures of speech and cultural idiomatic language (as we allow in any other book), all these passages make perfect sense. Though people are in error about what these passages mean, the passages themselves are not in error.

Whenever you disagree with somebody over what the Bible teaches, don't make the mistake of thinking that you "just believe the Bible" while they don't. This is *never* true in theological debate. No one "just believes the Bible." Instead, you believe the Bible teaches one thing, and they believe the Bible teaches something else. The goal in such situations is to properly understand the view of the other person, and then engage in careful Bible study with them in an attempt to determine the truth of Scripture. Be open to the possibility that they might be right and you might be wrong (or maybe both of you are wrong!).

The fourth and final clarification to remember about inerrancy is that the Bible can be inerrant while still containing false statements. This truth is vitally important to grasp, yet sadly, it is the one that most people do not understand. The Bible can contain lies and falsehoods and even untrue statements about God while still being inerrant. This sounds illogical and contradictory until you see some examples.

Some of the obvious examples are the times when Scripture records the words of lying prophets (1 Kings 13:18) or the words of Satan during the temptation of Jesus in the wilderness (Luke 4:1-13). Are these words in Scripture lies? Yes. But are they true and inerrant? Yes. They are inerrant records of false statements. But this is not the only way that the Bible can inerrantly record false statements. Often, the Bible records false ideas of humans so that we can learn what *not* to believe. While much of Scripture contains positive examples we *are* to follow, other sections of Scripture contain negative examples we are *not* to follow.

The book of Job is a perfect example. In this story, Job is a righteous man who has lost his house, possessions, family, and health. His friends show up to comfort him, and for chapter after chapter after chapter in the book of Job, they attempt to teach Job about the nature and character of God, and why God punishes people for their sin. They claim Job's difficulties were due to hidden sin, and if Job would just confess his sin, and repent before God, then all would be well with him.

Now this is actually a very popular way of thinking about God, sin, and the bad things that happen to humans in life. When you have something bad happen to you in life, it is quite likely that you will have some well-meaning friends come around to say that God must be punishing you for some sin. You might even be tempted to think this as well. It's not an exaggeration to say that most religions, including some forms of Christianity, are built around this concept. God hates sin, so God punishes people who sin. If bad things are happening to you, then it must be because you sinned and God is punishing you for your sin. You have undoubtedly heard something like this from sermons and books.

But at the end of the book, God appears to Job and says that this whole way of thinking about Him is wrong. God reveals that He was not punishing Job, nor did He send the bad events upon Job. Instead, Job's friends were wrong in nearly everything they said. They were teaching false theology. They were speaking errors about God.

Yet these errors are found within the pages of Scripture. Nearly everything Job's friends said about God is wrong, and yet nearly the entire book of Job contains the false teachings of Job's friends. Thus, the book of Job contains an inerrant account of the false ideas Job's friends held about God (and which many people still believe today). In this way, Scripture contains an accurate representation about the errors and false ideas that Job's friends had about God. The book of Job is a historical record about popular theological errors regarding God. When we read what Job's friends believe, we are not to say, "Well, the Bible says it; I believe it; that settles it." If we did that, we would end up believing false ideas about God. Instead, we are to recognize that one way the Bible exposes errors in human thinking and behavior is through providing accurate historical accounts of the wrong things that some people believed and did. These things are not written in Scripture so that we can believe what they believed and do what they did, but so that we can learn from their errors and turn from them.[10]

There are many of these sorts of errors in the Bible. More than most people imagine. The entire Pentateuch,

---

[10] I write about this concept in great detail in my book *The Bible Mirror* (Forthcoming). See Appendix III.

for example, was written around one such error. Moses was aware of the error, but the people of Israel were not, and so Moses wrote the Pentateuch in an attempt to point out this error to them. When you view the five books of Moses as a whole, from Genesis 1 to Deuteronomy 34, you see this particular error pop up over and over, as Moses seeks to expose it to the minds of his audience. Unfortunately, most people miss Moses' message, assuming he meant the opposite.

And what is the message of the Pentateuch? What error did Moses want to expose? The error is the idea that people can approach God through the law, through a list of Do's and Don'ts. In Genesis 1–2, we see that God created humanity to live in relationship with Him, completely apart from a long list of laws. The rest of the Pentateuch shows how humans rejected a relationship with God and sought after law and religious obligation instead. The Pentateuch shows over and over how this way of approaching God is a complete failure. Near the end of Deuteronomy, Moses tells the people that they are going to continue to fail at living with God in a relationship based on law until they finally realize that it cannot be done. At this point, they will return to God and will learn to live with God in a relationship based on love, just as God always wanted and desired (Deut 30:6, 11-20).

When people do not recognize this meaning and message of the Pentateuch, that it was written to expose a harmful way of approaching God, they end up doing the exact opposite of what Moses intended for the Pentateuch. Many assume Moses wrote the Pentateuch to prescribe laws and commands for us to follow. But this is the exact opposite of why the Pentateuch was written. Moses, under the inspiration of God, wrote the Pentateuch to help us see that we can never live in a relationship with God (or anyone else) when that relationship is based on law. Relationships function best when based on love. Moses wanted his readers to get back to the relationship that Adam had with God in the Garden of Eden where they both walked side by side as friends in the cool of the day.

So do you see? The Bible contains many wrong ideas and bad teachings about God, but it records these ideas, not so we *believe* them, but to *expose* them for what they are. When these false statements and theological errors are recorded in Scripture, they are written down for the purpose of reproving and correcting (2 Tim 3:16), so that we can turn from such errors in our own life. The primary difficulty, then, is learning to recognize when these errors are being exposed. It can be challenging to discern whether Scripture presents a positive example to follow or a negative one to avoid. But aside from looking at the immediate context of the passages, the greatest key to developing this discernment is to read Scripture through the lens of Jesus Christ. He provides us with an interpretive perspective for the true meaning of Scripture. We will learn more about this in the next chapter.

A few modern examples might also help illustrate how this works. A while ago, I read a news account of a mother who drowned her children in a bathtub. When investigators asked why she did it, she claimed God told her to drown her children. We read such a story in the news and recognize that the woman was quite confused and maybe a little insane. But what if you read such a story in the Bible? Would you then assume she was right? That God did, *in fact,* tell her to drown her children? I would hope not! I would hope that you would still recognize this story as an inspired and inerrant historical account of what one woman *thought* God was telling her to do, even though she was terribly, horribly wrong. God does not tell mothers to drown their children.

And in fact, we have this exact sort of account in Matthew 15:4 and Mark 7:10. The law contains a statement that parents should stone their disobedient children. But does God really want this? How is it that the same God who says "Let the little children come to me ... for of such is the kingdom of heaven" (Matt 19:14) can then turn around and instruct parents to stone their children when they curse their parents (Exod 21:17)?

In the context of Matthew 15 and Mark 7, Jesus uses this terrible law to show how the religious leaders were missing the entire point of the law. Jesus basically says, "Good job! You recognized that this command was bad.

Well done; we shouldn't stone children. But then you created an equally bad command that allows children not to take care of their parents. The original intent of the bad law was for children to respect their parents, but you are allowing them to disrespect their parents. Then, to top it all off, you claim you are following and obeying the law in its entirety. But you aren't! You are now disobeying both the spirit *and* the letter of the law! So just be honest and give it up!" It's a masterful argument from Jesus. No matter which way the religious leaders go, they are stuck by their own wrong interpretation of the text.

However, none of this means that Exodus 21:17 was never actually part of the law. It was. It's right there in the text. Just as we would say God never told the woman to drown her children, we can also say God never told the Israelites to stone their children to death when they mouth off. Yes, we have a historical record of Israelite people who *thought* God told this to them, but later revelation from God in Jesus Christ reveals that God never wanted such a thing, nor did He command it. The revelation of God in Jesus reveals the truth about the heart of God for children. God never commands parents to kill their children, either by stoning or by drowning.

So the Bible can be an inspired and inerrant account of what actually happened, even though many of the statements and commands in Scripture might not actually be what is *really* is God's heart, or what God *really* wanted to happen. In such cases, the Bible is a completely accurate historical account of what people thought about God. We are to learn from their example by *not* following in their patterns of thinking or behavior. In this way, the Bible remains true and without error, even though some texts and passages contain bad ideas about God and false instructions about how to live in this world.

When I was at Dallas Theological Seminary, one of my seminary professors said this about inerrancy:

> The Bible is a record of things as they actually were, and a true account of those things about which it speaks.

I completely agree with this statement. The Bible is a completely accurate historical record of things as they were, but it is not necessarily an endorsement of these things. This is quite different than being a completely accurate listing of how things should be and what we should do. When we read the Bible as a "To Do" list, it is then that we begin to use the Bible to justify genocide, slavery, the mistreatment of women, and a whole host of terrible sins that are spoken of in the Bible.

The Bible is an accurate and inerrant historical record of what people believed and how they behaved. It is not primarily a scientific explanation of how things work, or a theological treatise on what to believe and how to behave. While it contains statements about what to believe and how to behave, it is not primarily a book about such things. While the Bible accurately records the thoughts, actions, and ideas of the various biblical authors and characters, these thoughts, actions, and ideas may not actually be the thoughts, actions, and ideas that God endorses, nor the thoughts, ideas, and actions that we are to copy. They might instead be written to expose and reveal our own hearts to us, so that we can turn away from such behaviors and beliefs, and turn toward the living God as revealed in Jesus Christ.

Let us close out this section on inerrancy with the three reasons that inerrancy is so important.

Three Reasons Inerrancy is Important

First, it is important to have a reliable and trustworthy account of what God is doing in the world. As indicated previously in the section on Inspiration, without an inspired and inerrant Bible, we would not have a reliable standard by which to determine truth. If the Bible is full of errors, then we have no way of knowing for sure if there is a God, or what happens after death, or how humanity came into being. We would also know nothing certain about the person and work of Jesus Christ. And since Jesus is central to all the teachings and claims of Christianity, there would be no firm foundation for anything that Christianity holds dear. Without an inspired and inerrant text, we are set adrift on a sea of uncertainty about all things.

Indeed, we see that those who abandon inerrancy

quickly abandon many other key elements of Christianity as well. This is the second reason inerrancy is so important. Maintaining an inerrant view of Scripture allows us to know what sorts of beliefs and behaviors God thinks are important. Those who deny inerrancy allow their own desires and whims to become the guide by which they determine correct beliefs and proper behavior. Those who reject inerrancy quickly succumb to every cultural wind of immorality and subjectivity. Many see nothing wrong in taking human life in war or in the womb. Some turn to various forms of sexual immorality and call it "love."

Without the inerrancy of Scripture, every person is allowed to do whatever they see fit in their own eyes, which only creates confusion and chaos. The Christian church and Christian theology need a reliable guide to help us understand what is correct to teach, know, and do in this world. Without inerrant Scripture, the foundation of truth is reduced to individual subjectivity.

Finally, a belief in inerrancy allows us to mine the Scriptures for the greatest and deepest truths of God. Without a belief in inerrancy, we will miss out on the greatest truths of Scripture. When it comes to mining for gold and jewels in the earth, it is often true that the richest nuggets and the biggest diamonds lie hidden in the deepest depths. The same is true with Scripture. When we get out our hermeneutical pickaxe and shovel, praying for the illumination of the Holy Spirit, and dig into the words and ideas of the Bible, it is amazing what gems we uncover. But only those who hold to inerrancy tend to take the time and trouble to dig for these precious jewels. Those who believe the Bible is full of errors quickly throw up their hands in frustration, call the cave of inquiry "empty," and head back to the comfortable daylight above. But if they had persisted in their studies, asking God, "Why did you inspire this text to be recorded in Scripture, and how does it fit with the other texts in the Bible that seem to contradict it?" they would have dug a little deeper and found some of the greatest truths ever revealed to humankind.

I speak from personal experience. I cannot tell you how often I have been on the verge of giving up my studies on a particular text because the problems are too numerous and the difficulties too hard, only to have a breakthrough within the next day or two that changed the entire trajectory of my life and theology. The only reason I kept digging was because I refused to consign that particular section of Scripture to the theological garbage heap known as "errors in the text." Those who stop digging when they hit bedrock miss out on discovering the most startling and beautiful facets of Scripture.

Inerrancy is a foundational requirement for properly studying Scripture. Without inerrancy, students of Scripture will not feel the need or desire to dig deep into the hard texts of the Bible, but will instead look to their own inner feelings or the winds of cultural change as a guide to determine which texts are authoritative and which are not. But with the twin pillars of inspiration and inerrancy in place, we are then able to turn to Scripture as *the* authority in all aspects of Christian life and theology. The authority of Scripture is the third and final foundational truth for Bible study.

THE AUTHORITY OF SCRIPTURE

One of the rallying cries of the Reformation was *sola Scriptura,* Scripture alone. Opponents of the Reformation were trying to undermine the ideas and arguments of the Reformers and often used arguments from church tradition and extra-biblical teachings to do so. In response, the Reformers taught that Scripture alone was their primary authority. In recent centuries, the concept of *sola Scriptura* has been modified and refined, but within the broad tent of modern evangelical Christianity, most people still seek to follow this principle. We all seek to know what Scripture says so that we can follow its teachings and instructions.

This is the concept known as the authority of Scripture. The authority of Scripture is the idea that the Bible is an authoritative guide for all of Christian life, beliefs, and practice. However, while nearly all Christians hold to a concept of the authority of Scripture, there is not a lot of consensus about *how* the Bible is authoritative. Even though some claim, "The Bible Says It; I Believe It; That Settles It," nobody completely practices such a statement. Even those who claim to believe and follow every word of the Bible don't actually do this in practice. For example, as previously considered, nobody follows the clear biblical instruction to stone children when they mouth off to their parents (Exod 21:17). Also, few people worry about mixing fabrics in their clothes (Lev 19:19; Deut 22:11) or cooking meat and dairy together (Exod 23:19) in a fondue, a cream-based soup, or on a cheeseburger. In addition, no Christian will force a woman to drink muddy water to see if she has committed adultery (Num 5:11-31).

So once again, when it comes to the authority of Scripture, the issue is not, "What does the Bible say?" but rather, "What does the Bible *mean*?" Or more specifically, "How does the Bible guide our beliefs and behaviors today?" This last question is the question of authority. In what way does the Bible guide my life? Recognizing the authority of Scripture over all of life and practice is an essential element to properly reading, studying, and obeying Scripture. But the question is not "Is the Bible authoritative?" (for all Christians say it is), but rather, "*How* is the Bible authoritative?"

Three insights about the authority of Scripture help

us understand how the Bible is authoritative for Christians today.

The Bible is a Story

The first insight that helps us understand how the Bible is authoritative is that the Bible is a story. Although not every part of the Bible can be considered "narrative," even the non-narrative sections (such as the prophetic, poetic, and epistolary books) have a story behind them that fits into the overall narrative of Scripture.

Many Christians struggle with reading and applying the Bible because they fail to recognize this important point. Many Christians come to the Bible as if it were a recipe book for how to live the Christian life, or as a list of do's and don'ts which provide a guideline for godly living. Some teach that the Bible is a roadmap to life. I have even heard that the Bible can function as an acrostic for "Basic Instructions Before Leaving Earth."

But this is the wrong way to approach Scripture. Although we think it would be helpful to have a book that gives us instructions on how to live and lists of things to do and believe, this is not the sort of book that God provided. God did not give us the Bible we want; He gave us the Bible we need.

When we begin to think of the Bible as a story, this mindset affects how we approach Scripture. People read a novel by Charles Dickens quite differently from how they read an instruction manual on building a picnic table. A novel inspires and entertains while subtly shaping how you think about people and situations. An instruction manual or recipe just provides a list of things to do in order to accomplish a task. There is very little inspiration or change that results from reading a manual or a recipe.

Just consider what it would be like if God had provided a book full of instructions on how to live. It would contain almost nothing but a list of do's and don'ts for one group of people in one culture during one era of human history. And while this sounds great for them, this list would not apply to another group of people in another culture at another time in history. Again, just consider the difficulties we have today to understand and apply the instructions God provided to the Hebrew people in the books of Exodus and Leviticus. These laws were helpful for them, but they don't transfer well to other people in other places at other times. So this is why God didn't give us a helpful list of things to do and believe. Instead, He gave us a grand story of what other people did and believed, and yes, even some of what He commanded them to do and believe.

Typically, today, pastors and Bible teachers understand that the Bible, as it is written, is not all that helpful for what they want it to do. They want a helpful list of things to do and believe, but the Bible is not organized or presented this way. But since this is what pastors and teachers want, they go through the Bible, pulling out bits of advice from one section, pairing it with a wise command from some other section, and then adding in a command or inspiring verse from some third section. These ideas are then arranged in an orderly and coherent fashion for the purpose of presenting a nice three-point sermon. When the Bible is treated this way, it becomes nothing more than a jumbled collection of beliefs and ethics that must be organized and categorized into neat and tidy doctrinal statements and codes of conduct.

Pastors and church leaders read and study the Bible to find individual verses and passages that seem to bear significance for our lives today, and then systematize these passages into lists of what people must believe and how people must behave if they are going to belong to their church or group. Thus, the Bible is seen as helpful only after being sifted, sorted, and reorganized into the kind of book we want and which we think we need.

But what if God never intended or wanted for the Bible to be reorganized and rearranged in such a fashion? What if the book we need is exactly the book God provided? What if the Bible is exactly as God wants it, and does not need to be rearranged, sorted, categorized, and systematized into neat bullet points and numbered lists in order to act as a guide for following Jesus? Could it be that God knows better than we do what kind of book we need, and we have tried to change it into something more "helpful"? If the answer is "Yes" to these questions (and it is), then rather than try to reorganize the Bible into what we want it to be, we should instead approach the Bible for what it is, and then try to understand why God gave the Bible to us in this way.[11]

And what sort of book did God give us? He gave us a story. It is a long, complex story, with some odd pieces of poetry and personal letters thrown in. But all the parts, when taken together, fit into a grand, sweeping narrative of what God is doing in the world. And we must accept the Bible in this way. We must accept the Bible the way God gave it to us, trusting that the kind of book we need is the kind of book God gave. If we want something different than what God gave, that is our problem, not His.

Since God gave us a story, the task of the student of Scripture is not to rearrange and reorganize the story by cutting it up into pieces to make it more "helpful." Rather, the task of the student of Scripture is to figure out *why* God chose to give us such a book.

The answer to this question is that God gave us a story because God knows that a story is more powerful than a list, a recipe, or a manual. A story has more transformative power than a doctrinal statement or an ethical code of conduct. A story transcends time and culture, while lists and instruction manuals do not. When the Bible is

---

[11] N. T. Wright argues similarly. See N. T. Wright, *The Last Word* (New York: HarperOne, 2006), 27.

taken as a story, it becomes far more powerful and effective in changing lives and transforming society than any book of doctrine or code of ethics ever could.

Indeed, we see that this is exactly what has happened in human history. It is evident that significant advances in medicine, science, equality, health, art, music, prosperity, longevity, and other positive traits have flourished most where the Bible is taught and followed faithfully. When cultures that have the Scriptures begin to abandon them (as is happening in Western culture), that society begins to degenerate once again toward lawlessness and sub-human depravity.

When we watch a movie, read a book, look at art, or listen to a song, we are being changed, whether we recognize it or not. Our mind is expanding to see things in a new way, understand people from a new perspective, or think creatively about a new idea. Stories, novels, plays, music, and art fundamentally transform people in ways that ethical codes and moral guidelines can never accomplish.

Sociologists and Psychologists have been doing studies on this for years. People who watch lots of movies about people sleeping around often end up sleeping around. People who watch lots of movies about murder and violence often become more violent. They may not commit murder, but they become desensitized to it and may also treat other people with less dignity and respect.

The change is slow, but not imperceptible.

Yet while movies, novels, and songs often lead people astray into false directions of fulfilling their selfish longings and desires, the story of Scripture serves as a better guide. It leads us into the way of Jesus, helping us become and accomplish what God is seeking to do in this world.

The story of Scripture is a story of humanity's quest for God, and God's quest to reveal Himself to humanity. As a story, the Bible does not tell us what to do or how to live. It tells us what people have done and how they have lived, and what the consequences were of their decisions. The Bible does not tell us what to believe and do, but shows us what people believed and what they did. As we read the Bible as a story, we learn how God worked in generations past, what sorts of endeavors the people of God embarked upon, and how these endeavors turned out. Some were successful; but others were complete failures.

Thus, Scripture describes what was done in the past, not what we must do today. As we try to follow God in spreading His message, His rule, and His reign, we can learn from the past, not to duplicate past actions, but to learn from the successes and failures of the past as a way of informing our Spirit-guided and Scripture-guided decisions on how to act similarly or differently today. Though men and women throughout history have had various ideas about who God is and what God is like,

Jesus settled all the disputes and showed us who God truly is. "We are forever getting confused into thinking that scripture is mainly about what we are supposed to do rather than a picture of who God is."[12]

This leads to the second insight about how the Bible is authoritative. If the Bible is a story, then it is changing us and inviting us to take part. The Bible is an invitation to have a starring role in a play.

The Bible is an Invitation to Star in a Play

Since the Bible is a story, it does not tell us how to live, but tells us instead how people have lived. But this does not mean that the Bible contains no guidelines or instructions on we ourselves should live.

In his two books, *The Last Word* and *Scripture and the Authority of God*, N. T. Wright uses a helpful illustration about how God's story functions and where we fit into the plot.[13] Wright portrays history as a play with five Acts. The five Acts of the play are:

I.   Creation
II.   Fall
III.   Israel
IV.   Jesus
V.   The Church

[12] Stanley Hauerwas and William H. Willimon, *Resident Aliens* (Nashville: Abingdon), 85.

[13] See Wright, *The Last Word*, 121-127.

N. T. Wright explains that Act V is unfinished, and so we are to pick up where the play drops off and finish the story. We don't do this without guidance, however, but must play our part based on how the story has progressed up to this point. There is no script or memorized lines for the rest of Act V, and we don't simply repeat the first part of Act V over and over again. Instead, we are to follow the trajectory and storyline that has been presented up to this point, and allow the direction of the Holy Spirit (the Director) to whisper our lines and stage positions to us as needed.[14]

This is a beautiful way of viewing Scripture and our role within the unfolding story of God's purposes for this world. However, I would prefer to tweak the image slightly and say that God has also included a few clues and hints about what to expect in Act VI. While we may be living in Act V, God has provided in Scripture some foreshadowing about where the story is headed. We can read some of this in various prophetic books of the Bible, including the book of Revelation and what it says about the new heavens and new earth. Knowing where the story is going will help us make better decisions about how to act and what to say in Act V of this divine play.

So really, the story outline of Scripture could be presented this way:

[14] See ibid., 56.

I.   Creation
II.   Fall
III.   Israel
IV.   Jesus
V.   Part A: The First 100 Years of the Church
        Part B: Our Part in the Play
VI.   New Heavens & New Earth

This helps clarify how we are to read and follow the Bible today, and how we are not. The way the Bible is often taught today, we are encouraged to simply see what people said and did in the past, and then do those things today as well. It is not uncommon to hear pastors and Bible teachers say, "Well, God's law is timeless, and this is what He inspired Moses to write, and so we must do these things today as well." Or "If Jesus commanded His disciples to do these things, we must do them also since we are His disciples." A similar idea is taught by the popular phrase, "What did Jesus do?" Apparently, we are supposed to see what Jesus did, and then do it too.

But this is not how we are to read, study, or follow Scripture. God does not want us to simply copy what has been done in the past, but rather to learn from what has been said and done so that we can learn our *own part* in the play as it unfolds today.

Furthermore, Moses, Jesus, Paul, and every biblical person is not living in our day, in our culture, and with our questions and issues. It makes about as much sense to copy and imitate their words and actions today as it would be to copy and imitate the medical practices of 2000 or 4000 years ago. We study the words, teachings, and actions of Moses, Jesus, Paul, and other biblical characters, because their stories form the foundation for the story we find ourselves in today. We have a part to play in an ongoing story, and the question is this: "What part will you play?"

Walt Whitman hit on a similar idea in his poem "O me! O life!" as he struggled with the meaning of life and what we intend to do with our life. Here is what he wrote:

> *Oh me! Oh life! of the questions of these recurring,*
>
> *Of the endless trains of the faithless, of cities fill'd with the foolish,*
>
> *Of myself forever reproaching myself, (for who more foolish than I, and who more faithless?)*
>
> *Of eyes that vainly crave the light, of the objects mean, of the struggle ever renew'd,*
>
> *Of the poor results of all, of the plodding and sordid crowds I see around me,*
>
> *Of the empty and useless years of the rest, with the rest me intertwined,*
>
> *The question, O me! so sad, recurring—What good amid these, O me, O life?*

Answer:

That you are here—that life exists and identity,

That the powerful play goes on, and you may contribute a verse.

Yes. "The powerful play goes on, and you may contribute a verse." We are in the middle of a play, and there is no script for this part of the play, but we are playing an important role in this play, and so we must figure out what we are to say and do. But it would be foolish (and boring!) to simply repeat the words and actions from Act IV, or the first part of Act V. No, we must learn to improvise based on the progression of the story up to this point and where we know the story is headed in the future. Nor do we sit around twiddling our thumbs waiting for Act VI to begin. We are not in the intermission! We are living in the climax of the story. The spotlight is on you. You must contribute a verse! What will you say? What will you do? The Bible is the greatest "Choose Your Own Adventure" story of all time, and at the end, you are invited in to play your part, make your decisions, and keep the story moving forward.

> The notion of improvising is important, but sometimes misunderstood. As all musicians know, improvisation does not at all mean a free-for-all where "anything goes," but

precisely a disciplined and careful listening to the themes, rhythms, and harmonies of the complete performance so far, the performance which we are now called to continue. At the same time, of course, it invites us, while being fully obedient to the music so far, and fully attentive to the voices around us, to explore fresh expressions, provided they will eventually lead to that ultimate resolution which appears in the New Testament as the goal, the full and complete new creation which was gloriously anticipated in Jesus's resurrection.[15]

Writing about how to live life and understand the world, neuroscientist Iain McGilchrist writes similarly:

It is a process of creative collaboration, of co-creation. What if the music is ... something more like sublime jazz, or an Indian *raga* or Portuguese *fado*? Something we improvise—within bounds. Whatever it is will emerge from a balance of freedom and constraint. It won't exist until it is being performed: no-one can know exactly what it will be like. But it will not be random: it will emerge from the players' continuous interaction, and from the music's own 'history' as it unfolds; what comes next will be anticipated by what has gone before. It will also be molded by the imagination, skill and training we bring, our past experience of playing (together and apart), the conventions of certain traditions, and shared expectations, quite apart from the fundamental laws of acoustics. Our co-creation of the music does not occur *ex nihilo*, and is not just a projection of

[15] Ibid., 127.

ourselves. Yet we, and you, partake of its making, even if we are only listeners.[16]

This is why we read and study Scripture. It is not about repeating what was done in the past, but about knowing what to do today. The story of the Bible calls us to live and act in a way that is faithful to what has happened in the past, so that the story moves forward to where it is going in the future. In this way, the Bible serves as a guideline for the sorts of things that can be said and done in the part we are playing in Act V. Such a way of viewing Scriptures allows us to live in a way today that is "consistent with, though not necessarily envisaged by, Scripture's explicit statements."[17] The Bible does not provide instructions for what we should do, but rather describes what was done in the past. This concept introduces the third and final insight about how the Bible is authoritative for Christians today.

The Bible is Descriptive, Not Prescriptive

The first two insights about the authority of Scripture logically lead to the third, that the Bible is descriptive, not prescriptive. In other words, the Bible describes what has been said and done; it does not tell us what we must say and do. Since the Bible is a story of what was said and

---

[16] Iain McGilchrist, *The Matter with Things: Our Brains, Our Delusions, and the Unmasking of the World* (London: Perspectiva, 2023), 1:13.

[17] Wright, *The Last Word*, 80.

done in the past, this means it is not a book that tells us what to do and think today. Through Scripture, God does not tell us *what* to think; He simply tells us *to think*.

This is a challenging concept for some Christians to accept. We are so accustomed to going to the Bible for instructions on what to believe and how to behave, it is difficult to view the Bible as anything else.

But once we recognize that there is not a single book, letter, or word in the Bible that was primarily written to us today, but that all of the books and letters of the Bible were written to other people at other times in other cultures, it is then that we begin to see that the Bible does not tell *us today* what to do. Yes, it may have told others what to do in their time and culture, but that is not the same as telling us what we should do. And yes, some of what they were told to believe and do might be identical to what we should believe and do, but this does not mean that the Bible was written to us today.

Every book of the Bible was written to someone else (whether an individual person or a group of people), and when we read the Bible, we are reading their mail, so to speak. If we think Moses wrote the Pentateuch to us, to tell us how to live in modern Western civilization, we will end up with a distorted view of Scripture and what God wants for us here and now. If we read Paul's letters to the Corinthians, the Philippians, or to Timothy, and think that he was writing these letters to us today, we will end up believing and doing some very odd things in the church.

The main reason modern Christians think the Bible was written for us today is our egocentric view of life. We tend to think everything is about us, and we approach the Bible as if God wrote it as a "love letter" just to you and to me. We assume the Bible offers daily guidance for decisions about jobs, finances, and parenting. But such a way of viewing Scripture has led to most of the abusive behavior by the church throughout the history of Western Christianity.

But we cannot just take what the Bible says and apply it directly to our lives, because the Bible was not written to us. The various books of the Bible were written to the people to whom they were written. These people lived at different times, in different cultures, in different places, and spoke different languages, had different beliefs and values, and faced different issues and challenges. The books of the Bible were written to them, not to us.

For example, when a king (in England or France or Spain in the Middle Ages) thinks the Bible was written to him, to guide and instruct him, he takes some of the commands and instructions in the Bible that God gave to other kings as things that he and his nation should be doing. When people think that the books of Exodus and Leviticus were written to them, they become legalistic and judgmental in trying to force people to obey the

Mosaic Law. Church leaders will sometimes use God's biblical instructions for the temple as justification for constructing massive and expensive church buildings. We use prophetic condemnations of other groups to justify our wars and our own hatred of people who are not like us. When we think the entire Bible was written to us, we use a random verse or two from Leviticus to condemn gays and lesbians and a verse or two from Paul to silence women in the church.

For thousands of years, Christians have struggled with how to make sense of the passages in the book of Joshua where God tells the Israelites to go kill all the men, women, children, and even animals of various tribes and nations that were living in Canaan when Israel arrived there after wandering for 40 years in the desert. Some Christians have used Joshua as a way to justify similar behavior today toward those they think are the enemies of God.

But Joshua was not written to us. The book of Joshua is an inspired and inerrant account of what Joshua and the other leaders of Israel thought God was telling them to do. Based on this, they made their decisions and acted as they thought best. So when Joshua wrote the book of Joshua, he accurately recorded his thoughts and ideas about how God was working in his life and in the people of Israel, to bring them into the "Promised Land" of Canaan. The later history of Israel shows what happened as a result of these decisions. Today, in light of the supreme revelation of God in Jesus Christ, we can make better decisions than Joshua about how to treat other people.

The Ten Commandments are another example. Despite what many think and say, the Ten Commandments were not written to you or to me. We were not there when the Ten Commandments were written. We were not even alive. Instead, the Ten Commandments were written down for the people of Israel who had just come out of slavery in Egypt and were headed for Canaan. They were not written to us today. They are lines that are found in Act III of this play. They were said in a different setting, at a different time, to a different people, of a different culture. To think that they were said to us is to take lines from Act III and bring them into the second half of Act V, where they do not belong and do not fit in the overall story.

When hearing this, some point to the teachings of Jesus in Matthew 5:21-30 where He amplified two of the Ten Commandments. These people say, "Jesus thought the Ten Commandments were still in effect for His day, and in fact, even raised the bar on how to keep them." I do not dispute this. But let me state the idea once again: None of us were there in the crowd that day when Jesus said these words in Matthew 5. The words we read in Matthew 5 describe what Jesus taught to the people gathered there on that day; they do not prescribe what we must do today.

I know this sounds like dangerous teaching. But note something very important about this way of reading Scripture. Although the Bible is descriptive rather than prescriptive, this does not mean that we disregard, neglect, avoid, or ignore the teachings and behaviors that are described in the Bible. Quite to the contrary! The *reason* these teachings and behaviors are described in the Bible is *so that* we can know how to live and what to believe today. We have an important role in this ongoing play.

> The purpose of Scripture is not just to issue a series of reports about God's past action which we can accept by hearsay. It is to invite and excite the reader to look with their own eyes and listen with their own ears to the One two whom the Bible with all its images, stories, and metaphors unerringly points.[18]

In this way, the Bible becomes *more* authoritative, not less. If we cannot blindly repeat the lines and follow the behaviors of people from the past, then we are forced to diligently study and learn from what was said and done in the past so we can play the best part possible today. And as we study and learn, we will discover that the part God wants us to play today requires us to refrain from murdering, lusting, and stealing, and follow many of the other teachings and instructions we find in Scripture.

[18] Wayne G. Rollins, *Jung and the Bible* (Eugene: Wipf & Stock, 1983), 115.

They were not written *to us*, but they do *guide us* in our own part of this play.

So the entire Bible is descriptive, but not prescriptive. It describes what people did and thought and said, but does not tell us what to do, think, or say. In this way, the Bible is inerrant, true, and accurate, but is not a book of mandated beliefs and behaviors. As N. T. Wright comments,

> All Scripture is "culturally conditioned." It is naïve to pretend that some parts are not, and can therefore be treated as in some sense "primary" or "universal," while other parts are, and can therefore be safely set aside.[19]

Certainly, we will believe and do many of the same things that we read about in Scripture (for the Bible does contain many timeless truths and teachings), but we will do so, not because "It's in the Bible, and so we have to do it," but because the overall trajectory of Scripture and supreme revelation in Jesus Christ shows us how to live and act today.

Someone might object by quoting Romans 15:4 (cf. also 1 Cor 10:11) that everything which was written in the past was written to teach us today. I do not disagree with Paul's statement at all. To the contrary, I have been arguing the same thing. The things that are written and recorded in Scripture were guided by God to teach us

---

[19] Wright, *The Last Word*, 128.

what has been done in the past, so that we can learn from others about how we are to believe and behave today. We do not copy what is in the Bible simply because it is in the Bible, but rather, we learn from the behaviors and beliefs that we read about in the Bible, so that we can learn how to live today.

So is the Bible a guide for living? Yes, it is. But not as many Christians use it. It is not an instruction manual. It is a story that shows how people lived and thought, what they did, what God thought of such beliefs and behaviors, and also what the consequences were of these beliefs and behaviors. As we read and study this story, we learn how to live in our own time and culture today as well.

Though we are living in a different time and culture, we can assume that many of the similar behaviors and beliefs will lead to similar consequences, but such is not always the case. So instead, we learn from the lives of those who went before us, and then, with our minds filled with Scripture, and with an understanding of our times and culture, and not neglecting the gentle leading of the Holy Spirit, we try to do our best to live our lives within the "stream," "flow," or "trajectory" of biblical revelation. The Bible helps us learn what the will of God was for people in the past. But this does not necessarily mean that the will of God for us today is identical, for we are different people, living in difficult places, with different cultures, at a different time.

God has a different will for you and me in our time and culture than He had for a Jewish person living in the Babylonian captivity 2500 years ago. And that's a good thing. I work with a lot of different religions, and I see all of them (Christians included) trying to follow commands and ideas that made a lot of sense 2000 years ago, or 1000 years ago, or even 100 years ago, but which today are pure insanity. There will be some overlap between how God wanted people to live thousands of years ago and how He wants us to live today (for example, murder, adultery, and stealing are always wrong), but there will also be many new directions that God wants us to follow today that are not found anywhere in Scripture. The direction of the Holy Spirit, as guided by the story of Scripture, helps us discern what these new directions might be.

God gave us Scripture, and He gave us brains, and He has given us the Holy Spirit. He wants us to use all three to determine His will for our lives today.

CONCLUSION

The inspiration, inerrancy, and authority of Scripture are the three foundational pillars upon which proper Bible study is based. When we neglect one or more of these pillars, our study of Scripture becomes unstable, resulting in shaky theology and dubious ideas about the character of God and how we are to live our lives today.

To properly study the Bible, approach it with the knowledge that it contains the exact words and ideas that God wants you to know, and is accurate in everything it says and teaches (even in a negative way), so that we can learn from the mistakes and successes of the past to better follow the way of Jesus in our time and culture today. When approached this way, the Bible truly does become a guide for daily living, but in a way that inspires and directs, rather than commands and restricts. When properly studied and understood, the Bible liberates us to follow Jesus in freedom and creativity, rather than with fear and trepidation.

So with these three foundational truths undergirding our Scripture study, we are now ready to learn the five critical contexts to consider when studying God's written Word. Having laid the foundation, these five contextual areas of research provide the bricks and mortar of all proper Bible study.

DISCUSSION QUESTIONS

1. What does the traditional doctrine of inspiration teach?

2. What modification to the doctrine of inspiration was suggested in this chapter? What do you think of this proposed change?

3. What does the traditional doctrine of inerrancy teach?

4. What is your reaction to the fourth clarification about the doctrine of inerrancy?

5. What does the traditional doctrine of the authority of Scripture teach?

6. How does it help to think of history as a 5-act play, of which Scripture records the first four? How does this help you understand how to read the Bible and use it as a guide for your life now?

7. Here are six guidelines to help you solve Bible difficulties:

   A. Recognize that the existence of tensions and apparent contradictions is not something new in the study of Scripture.

   B. The admission of certain textual problems is an honest and open response that invites study and positive evaluation.

   C. Be clear about the distinction between actual and apparent errors.

   D. Realize that the resolution of these

problems must take place within an interpretive framework that takes account of the Bible as a whole.

E. Remember that the doctrine of inerrancy teaches that solutions to problems in Scripture do exist, but the doctrine itself does not guarantee a ready solution.

F. Recognize that there are currently unexplained difficulties, but this does not mean that they will always be unexplained. Further research in linguistics, archaeology, science, and Scripture may uncover a solution in the future.

CHAPTER 3

FIVE CONTEXTS TO CONSIDER IN BIBLE STUDY

The following story illustrates an essential component of proper Bible study. The story is titled "Agassiz and the Fish."[1]

It was more than fifteen years ago that I entered the laboratory of Professor Agassiz, and told him I had enrolled my name in the scientific school as a student of natural history. He asked me a few questions about my object in coming, my antecedents generally, the mode in which I afterwards proposed to use the knowledge I might acquire, and finally, whether I wished to study any special branch. To the latter I replied that while I wished to be well grounded in all departments of zoology, I purposed to devote myself especially to insects.

"When do you wish to begin?" he asked.

"Now," I replied.

---

[1] Samuel H. Scudder, *American Poems*, 3rd ed., (Boston: Houghton, 1879).

This seemed to please him, and with an energetic "Very well," he reached from a shelf a huge jar of specimens in yellow alcohol. "Take this fish," he said, "and look at it; we call it a Haemulon; by and by I will ask what you have seen."

With that he left me. … I was conscious of a passing feeling of disappointment, for gazing at a fish did not commend itself to an ardent entomologist.

In ten minutes I had seen all that could be seen in that fish, and started in search of the professor, who had, however, left the museum; and when I returned, after lingering over some of the odd animals stored in the upper apartment, my specimen was dry all over. I dashed the fluid over the fish as if to resuscitate it from a fainting-fit, and looked with anxiety for a return of a normal, sloppy appearance. This little excitement over, nothing was to be done but return to a steadfast gaze at my mute companion. Half an hour passed, an hour, another hour; the fish began to look loathsome. I turned it over and around; looked it in the face—ghastly; from behind, beneath, above, sideways, at a three-quarters view—just as ghastly. I was in despair; at an early hour, I concluded that lunch was necessary; so with infinite relief, the fish was carefully replaced in the jar, and for an hour I was free.

On my return, I learned that Professor Agassiz had been at the museum, but had gone and would not return for several hours. My fellow students were too busy to be disturbed by continued conversation. Slowly I drew forth that hideous fish, and with a feeling of desperation again looked at it. I might not use a magnifying glass; instruments of all kinds were interdicted. My two hands, my two eyes, and the fish; it seemed a most limited field. I pushed my fingers down its throat to see how sharp its teeth were. I began to count the scales in the different rows until I was convinced that that was nonsense. At last a happy thought struck me—I would draw the fish; and now with surprise I began to discover new features in the creature. Just then the professor returned.

"That is right," said he. "A pencil is one of the best eyes. I am glad to notice, too, that you keep your specimen wet and your bottle corked." With these encouraging words he added, "Well, what is it like?"

He listened attentively to my brief rehearsal of the structure of parts whose names were still unknown to me; the fringed gill-arches and movable operculum; the pores of the head, fleshly lips, and lidless eyes; the lateral line, the spinous fin, and forked tail; the compressed and arched body. When I had finished, he waited as if expecting more, and then, with an air of disappointment: "You have not looked very carefully; why," he continued, more earnestly, "you haven't seen one of the most conspicuous features of the animal, which is as plainly before your eyes as the fish itself. Look again; look again!" And he left me to my misery.

I was piqued; I was mortified. Still more of that wretched fish? But now I set myself to the task with a will, and discovered one new thing after another, until I saw how just the professor's criticism had been. The afternoon passed quickly, and when, towards its close, the professor inquired, "Do you see it yet?"

"No," I replied. "I am certain I do not, but I see how little I saw before."

"That is next best," said he earnestly. "But I won't hear you now; put away your fish and go home; perhaps you will be ready with a better answer in the morning. I will examine you before you look at the fish."

This was disconcerting; not only must I think of my fish all night, studying, without the object before me, what this unknown but most visible feature might be, but also, without reviewing my new discoveries, I must give an exact account of them the next day. I had a bad memory; so I walked home by Charles River in a distracted state, with my two perplexities.

The cordial greeting from the professor the next morning was reassuring; here was a man who seemed to be quite as anxious as I that I should see for myself what he saw.

"Do you perhaps mean," I asked, "that the fish has symmetrical sides with paired organs?"

His thoroughly pleased, "Of course! Of course!" repaid the wakeful hours of the previous night. After he had discoursed most happily and enthusiastically—as he always did—upon the importance of this point, I ventured to ask what I should do next.

"Oh, look at your fish!" he said, and left me again to my own devices. In a little more than an hour he returned and heard my new catalogue.

"That is good! That is good!" he repeated. "But that is not all; go on." And so for three long days, he placed that fish before my eyes, forbidding me to look at anything else, or to use any artificial aid. "Look, look, look," was his repeated injunction.

This was the best entomological lesson I ever had—a lesson whose influence was extended to the details of every subsequent study; a legacy the professor has left to me, as he left it to many others, of inestimable value, which we could not buy, with which we cannot part.

The fourth day a second fish of the same group was placed beside the first, and I was bidden to point out the resemblances and differences between the two; another and another followed, until the entire family lay before me, and a whole legion of jars covered the table and surrounding shelves; the odor had become a pleasant perfume; and even now, the sight of an old six-inch worm-eaten cork brings fragrant memories!

The whole group of Haemulons was thus brought into review; and whether engaged upon the dissection of the internal organs, preparation and examination of the bony framework, or the description of the various parts, Agassiz's training in the method of observing facts in their orderly arrangement, was ever accompanied by the urgent exhortation not to be content with them.

"Facts are stupid things," he would say, "until brought into connection with some general law."

At the end of eight months, it was almost with reluctance that I left these friends and turned to insects; but what I gained by this outside experience has been of greater value than years of later investigation in my favorite groups.

I first heard this story from Dr. Howard Hendricks while attending Dallas Theological Seminary.[2] He told us that the first and most important element of Bible study was observation. To properly understand a text, we must first observe it until we think there is nothing left to observe, and then we must observe some more, just like this student and the fish.

"And so," Dr. Hendricks told us, "I am going to give you your fish." He turned and wrote "Acts 1:8" on the whiteboard and said that as an assignment for the next class, we were to write down 25 observations about Acts 1:8. So this is what we did. And we all came to the next class with our 25 observations neatly typed on a piece of

[2] Most of the content of Dr. Hendricks' course on hermeneutics can be found in his book, *Living by the Book* (Chicago: Moody, 1991).

paper, ready to turn in. However, Dr. Hendricks told us to keep the paper and return to the next class with an *additional* 25 observations. He allowed us to submit the assignment after 50 observations on Acts 1:8, but informed us that even with 50 observations, none of us had even scratched the surface of what could be observed from this single verse. He said that an industrious student had once compiled all the papers into a single master list, resulting in over 400 observations on Acts 1:8.

I am including my list of 50 observations below. Before you read through them, I encourage you to take ten minutes to see how many observations on Acts 1:8 you can come up with on your own. Below is the list of 50 observations I turned in to Dr. Howard Hendricks. (I am not saying these observations are *good*; they're just the ones I turned in. And yes, some observations are drawn from outside verse 8 to help explain it.) I include them here as examples of the types of observations that can be drawn from Scripture.

1. The verse begins with the adversative or contrastive conjunction, "But."
2. It is part of a dialogue.
3. Jesus is the one speaking (vv 1-6).
4. Jesus is speaking to the group of disciples (*You* refers back to *them* in v 7).
5. It speaks of an event that will happen in the future.
6. It speaks of something that will be given and

received, not taken.

7. Power is the item that will be given.
8. This power is the causal result of another event.
9. The power comes with the Holy Spirit, not by some other means.
10. They didn't have the power yet, as it is being promised for the future.
11. The article in "the Holy Spirit" indicates there is only one.
12. The word "Spirit" indicates a non-material being.
13. The Holy Spirit will come "upon" rather than "to" or "in."
14. The Holy Spirit will come upon the same "you" that is being spoken to by Jesus.
15. The second part of verse 8 is introduced with another coordinating conjunction indicating a response.
16. This response is also future—further into the future than the first future event.
17. The word "witnesses" is plural, indicating more than one witness.
18. They are to witness about the one speaking to them.
19. "In" is a preposition indicating the location where they will be witnesses.
20. Their witnessing will begin in Jerusalem.
21. They will also witness in Judea.
22. Judea is the area surrounding Jerusalem.
23. They will also witness in Samaria.
24. Samaria is the geographical region north of Jerusalem.
25. They will also witness to the end of the earth.

26. The three coordinating conjunctions indicate sequence. They will begin to witness in Jerusalem and expand outward into all the earth.
27. The nouns of the verse are: Spirit, witnesses, Jerusalem, Judea, Samaria, and earth.
28. "Will" is the main verb.
29. The pronouns are you and Me.
30. Verse 8 concludes the final words of Jesus on earth.
31. They had wanted to know about the kingdom being set up on earth (v 6), but He is telling them that it will not yet happen.
32. The word "Holy" is an adjective of Spirit.
33. Jesus is talking to them in (or near) Jerusalem.
34. The Holy Spirit will come by the baptism of the Holy Spirit.
35. Jesus is telling them these things so that they can carry on His mission even though He will not physically be with them any longer.
36. Though Jesus will not be with them, the Holy Spirit will be.
37. The power they will receive is the same power Jesus used in His ministry.
38. The power will come upon the in a similar way it came upon him early in His ministry.
39. It is not by their own power that they will be His witnesses.
40. Only those who have the Holy Spirit will have this power.
41. Verse 8 is a promise.
42. The "to me" is sometimes translated "my."
43. Their task of witnessing begins where they are at, not somewhere else.

44. "End" of the earth is singular, rather than the plural "ends."
45. Only those who have received the Spirit can be a witness.
46. It is the Spirit's job to witness to Jesus through those who have received Him.
47. The job is not done until the message has spread to the end of the earth.
48. Jerusalem and Judea contain Jews.
49. Samaria includes those who were only partly Jews.
50. The end of the earth includes Gentiles.

This exercise shows that numerous sermons and Bible studies could be drawn from these fifty observations alone. Thus, making observations of the text is the *single greatest key* to correct Bible study. Before any sermon or study can be drawn from a text, you need as much data about the text as possible. The list of fifty items shows that when we engage in Bible study, we can observe key terms, people, places, and events. We can bombard the text with the six central questions: Who? What? Where? When? Why? And How? We can note grammatical structure such as verbs, nouns, adjectives, pronouns, conjunctions, and prepositions, and along with them, the plural and singular nouns, the tenses of verbs, and how all these words fit together to form clauses, sentences, and paragraphs. We can observe literary form, noting if the text is legal, historical, poetic, narrative, wisdom, prophetic, or personal letter. We can note which things are emphasized, repeated, related, alike, or unlike.

All such observations can be summarized under one word: context. When we make observations about the text, we are seeking to understand the context. An old joke states that the five rules of Bible study are:

1. Context
2. Context
3. Context
4. Context
5. Context

I didn't say it was a *funny* joke (this is about as funny as jokes get in theology). Yet even though the joke isn't very funny, it is definitely true. Making observations about the various contexts of a particular bible passage is the key to understanding any particular verse or passage.

Of course, context is key not just for Bible reading, but for every type of reading. Politicians are often quoted out of context in political ads by their opponents, which rightly upsets them. It is also essential to know the context of a statement you might read in the newspaper. If you read the news headline, "Farmer Bill Dies in House," what would you assume the story was about? It could be about a man named Bill who was a farmer, and how he died in his house. Alternately, it could be about a farming law that the government was trying to pass but lacked the necessary votes to pass out of the House of Representatives. Without knowing the context of this headline, you cannot be sure which story it refers to. If you knew a few more details about the newspaper, you might be able to make an educated guess. For example, if it were the New York Times, then it would almost certainly be a story about a law in Congress. But if it were a story in a small local newspaper of a tiny farming community, then you could probably guess that the story was about a well-known and beloved farmer named Bill who died in his farmhouse. Until you knew the context of the headline, it would be foolish to go around quoting it, for you might be spreading misinformation.

The same thing must be done with Scripture. Context is required for the study of every and any text. Without proper contextual analysis, the Bible can be made to say or teach almost anything. I once had a seminary professor say that without proper Bible study methods, somebody could use the Bible to support the idea that Jesus was an intergalactic space taco. His statement was an exaggeration, but was still valid. Throughout history, the Bible has been used to support and defend some of the most outlandish ideas, doctrines, and behaviors. To put it in a more scholarly fashion, "A text without a context is a proof text for a pretext." In other words, if you are quoting verses out of their context, you are likely just cherry-picking Bible passages to prove some pet doctrine or human teaching, rather than seeking to learn what the Bible really says. So we must observe what the text says, and we do this by observing the context.

When it comes to the context of a verse or passage, five main types of contexts are critical to observe. All five are explained below.

HISTORICAL-CULTURAL CONTEXT

The first type of context to consider when studying Scripture is the historical-cultural context. While history and culture are technically two distinct subjects, they are so closely intertwined and connected that it is hard to talk about one without the other. Historical events often cause and result from cultural shifts, which in turn lead to further historical events. So both will be considered together.

When seeking to discover historical background information about a biblical text, you ask questions about the historical events that were taking place in the time and region during which the author wrote the book. It might be helpful to consider the heritage, education, occupation, and religious experiences of the author. When it comes to the historical situation of the audience, you should seek to understand their race, religion, location, perspective, values, questions, and socio-economic situation. All of these factors influence how the author communicates with his audience.

Regarding culture, you would ask similar questions about the author of the book and the audience to whom the book was written. You seek to discover the identity and values of both the author and audience, as well as the sorts of questions and issues that were important to them at the time. While the historical context seeks to discover what happened at a particular time in a specific place, the cultural context seeks to learn what people thought, did, said, made, and valued in that time and at that place.

In seeking to discover this contextual information, it is helpful to consider the writings, plays, music, clothing styles, architecture, diet, and art of that time. But don't stop there. Culture is also seen in the political and military realms, the beliefs and practices of other religions, and what is happening agriculturally and economically. Of course, family structure and traditions are also fruitful areas for cultural investigation.[3]

A lack of proper cultural understanding can lead to grave errors in judgment when interacting with people from other cultures, whether these people are encountered on the pages of Scripture or in real-life situations. Several years ago, I spent six weeks in India. Before going, our team sat through several days of classes in which we learned about the Indian people and culture. We were told, among other things, that we should take our shoes

[3] Cf. Zuck, *Basic Bible Interpretation*, 80-90.

off at the door before going into someone's home, that it would not be strange to see men walking around holding hands, and that we should never, ever, under any circumstances, touch any person or any food with our left hand. The reason for this last prohibition was that in India, people use little containers of water to splash themselves clean after using the restroom, and they use their left hand for this practice. Therefore, the left hand was considered unclean.

Imagine if this practice were also common in biblical times, and we modern Westerners were unaware of it. We would be stumped by a passage in which a man killed someone after being touched by this person's left hand. We would be puzzled by a prophetic passage in which God complained that His people were using their left hands to bring Him sacrifices and offerings. These examples don't actually exist in the Bible. They are only provided as examples of how a cultural understanding can help the student of Scripture understand what is happening in a certain story or what is being taught in a particular text.

This sort of mistake happened quite frequently in the Middle Ages. There is much European religious art from the Middle Ages that shows scenes from the Bible. In these paintings, the biblical characters are often depicted as wearing the same clothing, robes, weapons, armor, and hairstyles that were common in Medieval Europe. But did Jesus and the apostles, or King David and King Solomon, dress and act like Medieval Europeans? Of course not! But people in Medieval Europe didn't know much about other cultures, especially not biblical culture, and so they just assumed that everyone had always dressed and looked like themselves.

Another example is cultural values. In our modern Western culture, one of our primary values is materialism. We value money, wealth, and possessions. In our culture, we assume that everyone works to get a nicer house, a nicer car, and better clothes. So when we read the Bible, we assume that is what they valued as well. But it wasn't. Ancient biblical culture was not materialistic. They valued honor. Everything they did was to earn honor for themselves and for their family and to avoid shame. If we do not understand the differences in these two value systems, we will often misunderstand and misapply passages of Scripture that deal with money or honor. We will consider several examples of this later, but the point for now is that any Bible student who lacks an understanding of ancient Middle Eastern history and culture will be severely handicapped in their attempts to read and study Scripture. Historical and cultural studies are critically important for understanding the Bible.

It can also be helpful to learn about the geographical location of the author and audience, as this often helps narrow down the range of study. After all, if both the author and audience lived in Israel, it doesn't really matter what was happening at that time in China. Similarly, it is helpful to know the time period in which the book was written, for again, if somebody wrote in the 10th century B. C., it doesn't matter what was happening 500 years later.

It is important to note, however, that biblical authors often wrote about historical events that were several hundred (or thousand) years in the past. For example, when Moses wrote Genesis (as I believe he did), he was most likely writing around 1450 B. C. (I hold to an early date of the Exodus). But much of what he wrote (all of Genesis, for example) took place hundreds of years before, or even thousands, when you consider the events of Genesis 1–11. In this case, the student of Scripture would need to discover the historical-cultural background of the time when the events actually took place, *and also* the historical-cultural background of the time when Moses wrote Genesis for the Israelites. In other words, to understand the stories of Abraham, Isaac, Jacob, and Joseph, you need to not only understand the historical-cultural background of the days in which these forefathers lived, but also the historical-cultural background of Moses' day when he wrote the stories for the Israelites.

As you can see, the historical-cultural context is vast and complex. It attempts to understand the worldview, questions, issues, concerns, values, goals, popular beliefs, stories, myths, and other religions of the surrounding culture. Of the various contexts, this one is simultaneously the most difficult and the most important. It is the most difficult because there is so much to learn and consider, but it is the most important because one overlooked historical or cultural fact can drastically change the meaning or significance of a single text. "An ignorance of certain cultural customs may lead to faulty interpretations."[4]

Take Jeremiah 10:1-5 as an example. I have read a couple of books and heard a few sermons in which this passage is used to condemn the use of Christmas trees during the Christmas holiday. After all, it mentions cutting down a tree in the forest, propping it up with nails, and decorating it with gold and silver. But are modern Christmas trees really what Jeremiah had in mind when he wrote this text? No. Christmas trees first began to be used less than 500 years ago. So Jeremiah obviously cannot be talking about Christmas trees.

To the contrary, when these five verses are carefully considered in their historical and cultural contexts, we see that Jeremiah is not talking about Christmas trees at all, but about the making, carving, crafting, decorating, and worshipping of idols. Jeremiah is mocking the practice of cutting down a tree, carving it into the shape of an idol, covering it with gold and silver, fastening it down with nails so that it doesn't topple, and then praying to this

---

[4] Ibid., 64.

human-created object as a deity. Jeremiah 10:1-5 is indeed a warning about idolatry, and as such, it might have something to say to people today who idolize material possessions, but this passage has nothing whatsoever to say about the use of Christmas trees to help celebrate the birth of Jesus.

The Parable of the Talents in Matthew 25:14-30 and Luke 19:11-27 is another example. In our modern, western, materialistic, capitalistic culture, the Parable of the Talents is a perfect text for encouraging Christians to take what they have and invest it in the future, so that they can end up with more than what they started with. The standard explanation today makes the first servant the hero, for he takes his five talents and turns them into ten and is further rewarded at the end of the story by getting the one talent from the servant who buried it (Matt 25:20-21, 28).

Yet in their *Social-Science Commentary on the Synoptic Gospels*, Bruce J. Malina and Richard L. Rohrbaugh point out that people in the Mediterranean world at the time of Jesus and the early church had a "zero-sum" view of economics. This meant that if one person gained more wealth, land, and possessions, it was only because they took it from someone else. Therefore, a man like Zacchaeus was despised and hated because he enriched himself on the backs of his fellow Israelites (Luke 19:1-10. Note that this passage precedes the Parable of the Minas in Luke 19:11-27). Thus, Malina and Rohrbaugh argue that the true hero is the servant who hid his talent and did nothing with it. He didn't even deposit the money in the bank to collect interest, because he knew that this would violate the Mosaic laws against usury. The master gets mad at this third servant and tries to shame him by taking away (read "stealing") his possessions and giving it to the one who is already rich. This again is shameful behavior on the part of the master, but it explains why two servants behaved in such shameful ways—they have a shameful master.

Obviously, in this alternate way of reading the Parable of the Talents, since the master behaves shamefully and teaches his servants to do the same, the master cannot represent Jesus. So who does the master represent? The master represents the god of this age, the one who teaches models and the morally reprehensible behavior of stealing from the poor to make themselves rich. Jesus is teaching that this is the kind of behavior Christians can expect from the world when we try to live according to His new code of honor ethics. Jesus tells the Parable to show His disciples what this world thinks is important, and then contrasts this in the following Parable with what He thinks is important (Matt 25:31-46 praises those who serve the poor and needy, thereby giving back to them rather than stealing from them).[5]

Do you see how much one cultural insight can radically change the meaning and point of a single passage? And nearly every passage in Scripture can be imbued with greater meaning and significance when understood in its historical and cultural contexts. As further examples, check out my studies on Genesis 1–4, the book of Esther, and the book of Jonah. Key cultural and historical insights allow you to view these sections of Scripture in a completely different light.

It is critical to note that when we study the historical and cultural contexts of a passage, what we are actually doing is seeking to get inside the mind of the author and audience. We are seeking to understand them. We want to know what the author had in mind when he wrote the text, and what the audience would have thought when they read (or heard) the text. Of these two mindsets, authorial intent is of primary importance. As mentioned earlier, if a student of Scripture does not seek to understand what the author meant when they wrote the text, the Bible can be made to say almost anything, including the outlandish idea that Jesus was an intergalactic space taco.

[5] Yes, I know this short explanation raises more questions than it answers. But now you have something to study! You can start here: https://redeeminggod.com/the-parable-of-the-talents-revisited/. I also write about this Parable in my forthcoming book, *The Gospel Dictionary*.

If you wrote a book or letter, would you want someone who read that book or letter to try to understand what you were saying, or to simply invent whatever they wanted you to say, even if it was the furthest thing from your mind or flatly contradicted what you wrote? No. Of course not! When you write something, you write to make a point and to be understood. It is the height of arrogance and ignorance to twist an author's words so that they say the opposite of what the author intended. And yet it happens all the time with Scripture. It even happens in other areas of literature as well.

I think it was C. S. Lewis who once remarked how humorous it was for him to read the way some literature critics analyzed his books to make them say things that he himself never intended or meant to say. He went on to say that if this is what book reviewers and critics do with the books of authors who still live, imagine how wrong we must be in many of our attempts to analyze the stories and writings of authors from previous generations and other cultures. Though it takes a lot of work, if we want to properly understand the Bible, we must begin by seeking to understand what the biblical authors had in mind when they wrote Scripture.

On this note, a word should be said about the JEDP theory, which argues that the Pentateuch was not written by Moses, but was compiled and redacted by some scribe or editor who likely lived in the days of King Josiah. The standard argument is that King Josiah wanted some religious and political reforms made during his rule, and so had one of the court prophets or scribes compile (and possibly invent) the various sections of the Pentateuch as a way to create an authoritative source for these reforms. The claim is that the document which Josiah "found" during the reconstruction of the Jerusalem temple (cf. 2 Kings 22–23) is the Pentateuch as we have it today, and that prior to King Josiah inventing and then finding this document, it did not exist. The JEDP theory further states that other portions of the Pentateuch may have been added in the 4th century, possibly by Ezra.

Based on this theory, modern scholars then analyze the Pentateuch in an attempt to discern where the various parts and pieces came from. They have discovered four main "sources" for this compilation of documents. Some sections emphasize Yahweh as the name for God, and are labelled as "J" (for Jehovah, which is one way of pronouncing Yahweh). Other sections emphasize Elohim as the name for God, and make up the "E" portions. Most of Deuteronomy is thought to have been written by a third author, and so is labeled "D." Finally, many of the priestly law codes would have been added by an author who considered such things to be important. These sections are labeled "P."

As you can imagine, this four-source hypothesis and the times in which the various sections are assumed to have been written, lead people who study and teach the Pentateuch to quite different conclusions about the text than those who believe Moses wrote most of it himself in the mid-15th century as he was leading Israel out of bondage in Egypt and toward the Promised Land. I believe that Moses wrote most of the Pentateuch, though some of the stories and accounts certainly predate him, and were probably passed down as oral tradition before Moses recorded them in the Pentateuch. As a result, my view of the Pentateuch is quite different from that of the liberal scholar who has a late date for the first five books of the Bible.

The ironic thing about the JEDP theory is that something similar could be proven for almost any author. It could certainly be proven about my own writings. When I read today some of what I wrote twenty years ago, I am amazed at how the central themes and terms I used two decades ago are completely absent from the themes and words I focus on today. How I refer to Jesus is one example. Twenty years ago, I almost always referred to Him as "Christ." I would teach and write about "following Christ" and "believing in Christ." Today, however, since I am better attuned to the fact that "Christ" is more of a title than a name, I prefer to speak about our Savior using His name, Jesus. (Yes, this is the English translation of His name, but that's not the point.)

Similarly, most of my writings and teachings from 20

years ago emphasized the importance of attending church, listening to sermons, and engaging in daily Bible study. Almost every sermon I preached contains an exhortation along these lines of some sort. Today, since my views on church, preaching, and Bible study have changed, I don't talk about such things as much, and instead focus on loving and serving others in tangible ways as we go about our day-to-day lives.

In this way, it would be easy for someone who lives a thousand years from now to analyze my various sets of writings and note the different names used in my writings and the different things emphasized from one set of sermons to another, and claim that though all these writings bear the name "Jeremy Myers," they clearly came from four different authors, represented by the letters CJBL (Christ, Jesus, Bible Study, Love). But such an argument would be completely wrong. I wrote all of these documents that bear my name, though they were written twenty years apart. During that time, my thinking and terminology evolved.

Who can say that over the course of 40 years shepherding in the Sinai Peninsula and then another 40 years wandering in the wilderness, the same thing couldn't have happened to Moses? If similar changes can occur with one author today, why couldn't they have occurred then? The answer is that Moses probably did change in his thinking and theology somewhat over eighty years, and some of his writings reflect this development. Furthermore, if he did use some sources for writing the Pentateuch (as he clearly did), then these sources would also be reflected in the themes and language of his writings. The point, however, is that when we read and study the Pentateuch, we can do so with Moses and the Israelites in mind, asking ourselves what they had just experienced, what they were facing in Canaan, how the 40 years of wilderness wandering changed them, and what sorts of questions they were asking during this time. These sorts of historical-cultural questions help us understand authorial intent, and therefore, the meaning of the Pentateuch as well.

So the historical-cultural context of a passage helps us learn the meaning of that passage, and authorial intent is of paramount importance within this area of study. Since this is a huge area of study, there are many hundreds of resources that will help you discover some of this information. Here is a brief list of some of the tools I have found helpful over the years:

- *The Moody Bible Atlas* (for the Geography)
- *The New Daily Study Bible* Commentary series by William Barclay
- The *For Everyone* Commentary series by N. T. Wright
- *The IVP Bible Background Commentaries* by John Walton and Craig Keener

-*The Social-Science Commentary* series by Malina, Pilch, Rohrbagh, and others
-*The Socio-Rhetorical Commentary* series by Witherington III, Keener, deSilva, and others
-*The IVP Bible Dictionary* series
-*The International Standard Bible Encyclopedia*
-Books by Kenneth Bailey, Jerome Neyrey, Bruce Malina, Craig Keener, John Walton

Let me make one final observation about authorial intent. You will sometimes hear people criticize the rules of exegesis and hermeneutics by saying that the original authors never intended their letters and writings to undergo the critical and detailed study that is required by the rules of proper Bible study. After all, when you and I write a letter or a book, we intend our audience to simply understand what we say without the need for cultural-historical background studies, word studies, and all the other tools of the hermeneutical trade. So if authorial intent is really a primary concern in exegesis, then exegesis is not a valid pursuit, because the authors never intended their writings to need exegesis. Therefore, it is claimed, we should just read the Bible and not try to study it.

However, although the authors wrote with the intent of being clearly understood by their reading audience, we are not their reading audience any longer. We are a different audience, separated by numerous barriers, including time, culture, language, geography, and worldview. Therefore, it is impossible today to properly understand the original message of the Bible without engaging in the practice of good hermeneutics and exegesis. It is somewhat ironic, but to honor authorial intent, we must somewhat violate authorial intent. To properly understand what they were actually saying in their writings, and to enable us to "just read" the text, we must do something that the original authors would never have imagined their original audience doing. Namely, we must engage in a detailed study of the text from numerous different angles.

In this way, exegesis creates a time machine so that we can attempt to go back and *become* the original audience, so that we can hear the words of the biblical author in the way they originally intended. If we perform this task properly, we take ourselves back in time to enter the minds, culture, and history of the original audience. This is why we have the rules and methods of Bible study, so that we *can* "just read" the text.

LITERARY CONTEXT

The second context to consider when studying Scripture is the literary context. The Bible is a book that contains numerous types of literature, or genres, with each genre having its own unique characteristics of composition and rules for interpretation.

> As literature, the Bible records human experiences. It speaks of people's emotions and conflicts, victories and defeats, joys and heartaches, imperfections and sins, spiritual losses and gains. Intrigue, suspense, excitement, foibles, disappointment, reversals—these and many other experiences of mankind are seen in the Bible.[6]

Since this is so, the person who studies Scripture needs to be aware of what types of literature the Bible contains and how to read and understand them. Here is a list of several of the major genres of biblical literature, and the books that go with each (this is not an exhaustive list of the genres of literature one might find in the Bible):

Historical Narrative (Genesis-Esther, Matthew-Acts)
Law (Exodus-Deuteronomy)
Poetic (Job and Psalms)
Wisdom (Proverbs)
Philosophical (Ecclesiastes)
Romance (Ruth, Song of Solomon)
Prophetic (Isaiah-Malachi)
Gospel (Matthew-John)
Epistles, or Letters (Romans-Jude)
Apocalyptic (Revelation)

---

[6] Zuck, *Basic Bible Interpretation*, 125.

While each of the 66 books of the Bible fit within one genre, nearly every book contains shorter sections within them from different genres. For example, many of the "Prophetic" books also contain narrative sections. Some books, like the books of Exodus and Numbers, are "cross genre," in that they could fit in more than one category. In this case, Exodus and Numbers could be narrative, but they could also be law. And then there are some books that do not fit neatly into any genre. The book of Job is a narrative that is written in poetic form and contains an extended philosophical discussion about the character of God and the nature of life. So is it narrative, poetic, wisdom, or philosophical? The answer is "Yes."

When reading each book or section of a book within its literary genre, the basic rule of all Bible study applies once again: Read the Bible as you would any other book. The average person knows that reading a book of history is quite different than reading a book of poetry and both are different than a book of philosophy. So when you approach a book of the Bible, keep in mind which genre you are reading, and then apply the appropriate framework.

So, for example, when you read one of the narrative books, seek to know the characters and how the plot develops. Look for the protagonist and antagonist and how the conflicts between them develop. Keep an eye out for the climax and resolution to the story. Seek to be moved by what happens (or does not happen) in the story, and by the surprises and plot twists the story contains. But don't do any of these things when reading poetry. Poetry generally has no plot structure or character development. Instead, when reading one of the poetic books, look for repeated themes and ideas, imagery, and symbolism. Look for how questions are asked and answered, and how all of these things relate to the big issues and emotions of human life. Seek to be moved by the rhythm, wordplay, and artistry of the book.

I am not going to provide suggestions for what to look for in all of the biblical genres. This is because you don't really need to be told what these rules are. If you are familiar with the various genres in regular literature, then you can simply apply these rules to biblical literature as well. If, however, you do want a summary of the sorts of things to watch out for when reading and studying biblical literature, get and read some of the recommended resources at the end of this section. However, there are several literary devices and figures of speech that can be looked for when studying a passage of Scripture. Here is a short list of some of the more prominent types.

Literary Devices

- Exposition: Explaining a text, topic, or idea (1 Cor 15:35-49)

- Description: Describing what one sees (Rev 1:12-16)

- Dialogue: Conversation between two or more people (Num 22:32-35)

- Series: A list of at least three similar things (1 Cor 13:13)

- Parallelism: Items that are stated in parallel to explain each other (Prov 20:13)

- Comparison: Two or more things described that are like each other (Matt 13:24)

- Contrast: Two or more things described that are different from one another (Prov 10:1)

- Command: Use of imperative to give a direct order (1 Thess 5:16-22)

- Exhortation: Encouragement to perform a certain action (Heb 4:16)

- Climax: Progression from least to greatest through several steps (Rom 8:35-39)

- Quotation: Repeating words that are used in another text (Matt 2:18; cf. Jer 31:15)

- Autobiographical Note: A reference to a historical event in the life of the author (1 Thess 2:10-12)

- Summary: A restatement in a few words of longer explanation that either precedes or follows the summary (Heb 8:1-2 summarizes Hebrews 7)

- Generalization: Move from general to particular, or particular to general (1 Corinthians 8 and 13)

- Chiasm: Organizing the text around a central idea so that the points work in toward the central idea, and then back out again, such as in an ABCBA pattern (Joel 3:17-21)

- Acrostic: Using the first letter of a word, phrase, or alphabet to arrange a text (Psalm 119)[7]

Figures of Speech

- Simile: Using "like" or "as" to describe something (Luke 10:3; 1 Pet 1:24)
- Metaphor: Comparison of two or more items (Isa 40:6; Luke 8:21)
- Metonymy: Substituting one name for another (Isa 22:22; Luke 16:29)
- Synecdoche: Substituting one idea for another (Psa 87:2; Luke 2:1)
- Personification: Giving personal attributes to an object (Psalm 114; Isa 55:12)
- Apostrophe: Addressing a thing as if it were a person (Zech 13:7)
- Anthropomorphism: Ascribing human characteristics to God (Psa 19:1; Isa 59:1)
- Anthropopathism: Ascribing human emotions to God (Jer 4:8; Mal 1:2-3)
- Ellipses: Omission of a word or phrase (Acts 18:6)
- Hyperbole: Exaggeration for effect (Deut 1:28; John 21:25)
- Litotes: Understatement for effect (Acts 1:5; 1 Thess 2:14-15; Rev 3:5)

---

[7] Paul D. Neven, Th.D. *Elements of Bible Study* (Chicago: Moody, 1988), 37.

- Irony: Using language opposite in meaning of what is intended, such as with sarcasm, ridicule, or satire (1 Kings 18:27; Job 12:2)
- Polemic: Arguing forcefully and passionately against a particular belief or action, often using the words and ideas of others against them (Genesis 1)
- Paradox: A seeming contradiction (Matt 8:35; 13:12)
- Euphemism: Substituting a less offensive word for a more graphic one (Judg 3:24; 5:26-27)
- Rhetorical Question: Asking a question that does not require an answer (Psa 94:9-10; Jer 32:27; Rom 8:31-34)

Let me provide a few examples of how the literary context can open up new vistas of insight and understanding to the student of Scripture. Ever since Charles Darwin wrote *On the Origin of Species,* the debate has raged about how to understand Genesis 1. Creationists argue that God created the world in seven days, just as Genesis 1 states. Evolutionists, however, deny the scientific value of Genesis 1, and point to science as proof that the universe came into existence billions of years ago and life has evolved through chance and natural selection into what it is today.

The entire debate is resolved by recognizing that Genesis 1 is not a scientific document, but is a theological polemic against the religious beliefs of Egypt, Babylon, and Canaan. After the Israelites were freed from Egypt and headed toward Canaan, they wanted to know what their God was like, and how He compared to the gods of Egypt, Babylon, and Canaan. So Moses took the creation myths of Egypt, Babylon, and Canaan, and rewrote them to show that the God of Israel was more loving, caring, involved, and relational than any of the other gods of the surrounding cultures.

As long as we try to read Genesis 1 as a scientific account of the creation of the world, we will miss the message and significance of this opening chapter of the Bible. But a proper understanding of the genre of Genesis 1 helps us better understand what Moses intended to say, how the Israelites understood this text, and also how Genesis 1 does not contradict any scientific theory about the origin of the universe. If you want to learn more about this, listen to the first twenty-five episodes of my podcast, "The Redeeming God Podcast."

The four Gospels of Matthew, Mark, Luke, and John provide a second example. Many people do not realize that "Gospel" narratives were a common genre in the days of Jesus and the early church. Historians have discovered "Caesar Gospels" which were written and distributed around the Roman Empire at the inauguration of each new Caesar. These Caesar Gospels often contains stories about the miraculous birth of the Caesar, and how he had performed various miracles and military victories on his way to the throne. The Caesar Gospels were intended to tell Romans Citizens about their new ruler, and how he had been blessed by the gods to usher in an age of peace and prosperity upon all who declared that "Caesar is Lord."

The four Gospel accounts about Jesus bear many striking similarities to the Caesar Gospels. By comparing and contrasting these similarities, we can better understand what Matthew, Mark, Luke, and John were intending to teach about Jesus, and also why their Gospel accounts were viewed as treasonous to the Roman Empire. We should not, of course, think that since the four Gospels are patterned after the fictitious Caesar Gospels, this means that the Jesus Gospels are also fictitious. They aren't. But we can learn more about the history of Jesus, and the central message and meaning of the Gospels by comparing the Caesar Gospel genre with what we have in Matthew, Mark, Luke, and John.

One final example is the book of Acts. It is widely considered to be one of the best and most accurate ancient historical records ever written. One way we see this is in how Luke introduces and organizes the material. It contains a beautiful and logical literary structure. In the introduction, Luke records the final instructions of Jesus. Jesus tells His disciples to carry the news about Him to Jerusalem, Judea, Samaria, and to the ends of the earth. This not only serves as a record of what Jesus said, but also an introductory outline for the rest of this historical book. Luke shows how the apostles took the good news about Jesus to Jerusalem (Acts 1–7), Judea and Samaria (Acts 8–12), and the ends of the earth (Acts 13–28).[8]

So much like the historical-cultural context, the literary context is vast and varied, and the student of Scripture will always find that there is more to learn about this context so that the Bible can be better understood and taught. Yet it is worth considering, for a single insight into the literary theme or structure of a text can help uncover spiritual gems of inestimable worth. To help learn more about the literary context of Scripture, here are a few suggested resources:

-*How to Read the Bible as Literature* by Leland Ryken
-*Words of Delight: A Literary Introduction to the Bible* by Leland Ryken
-*The Dictionary of Biblical Imagery* edited by Ryken and Wilhoit
-*Basic Bible Interpretation* by Roy B. Zuck
-*Figures of Speech Used in the Bible* by E. W. Bullinger

GRAMMATICAL CONTEXT

Many of us in the "older" generations remember taking grammar in grade school, and most of us remember

[8] See Zuck, *Basic Bible Interpretation*, 123-168.

hating it. Sadly, schools don't really teach grammar any longer in the United States. It is shocking to discover how few high-school graduates and college-age students don't know the basic parts of speech. But if you are going to study Scripture, you will absolutely need to know some basic grammar. The meaning of any sentence or paragraph in the Bible depends entirely on the meaning of those words and how they are organized and structured together. Yes, grammar is dull and boring, but without a basic knowledge of grammar, any attempt to study and understand Scripture is doomed from the start. It is possible to read, study, and understand the Bible with limited knowledge of the other four types of contexts, but if you have little to no knowledge of grammar, you will not be able to understand even the most basic concepts. The grammatical context of Scripture is critically important.

While it would be ideal to know Greek and Hebrew grammar, a working knowledge of English grammar works just fine for the study of most passages in Scripture. Though some Bible teachers claim that knowledge of Greek and Hebrew is absolutely essential for the proper study of Scripture, this is only true if you plan on being an actual Bible *scholar* who plans to teach in a seminary or write academic books. Generally, any good "literal" Bible translation in your native language will work just fine. For English, the three translations I recommend most are the New American Standard, the New King James, and the New Revised Standard.

When it comes to grammar, you will need to be able to recognize the difference between the various parts of speech. You must not only know the difference between a noun and a verb, but also the different types of nouns (subject, direct object, indirect object, etc.) and verbs (their tenses, voices, moods, etc.), and the ways that gender (masculine, feminine, neuter), number (singular and plural), and person (first, second, and third) affect both. Beyond this, you will need to recognize adverbs, adjectives, articles, conjunctions, prepositions, and participles.

Once you have learned to recognize the various parts of speech, you will need to understand how they all fit together to form clauses, sentences, and paragraphs. And of course, it is essential to know the definition or meaning of the words that are used, and something about their etymology (the origin and roots of words) and morphology (how words are formed and put together).

Clearly, becoming adept at the grammatical context of Scripture requires a lot of learning about how languages work. But the bare bones, introductory approach to grammar can simply be to consider the following questions:

- What words are used?
- What do the words mean?
- How are the words used in relation to other words to form sentences?

- How are the sentences organized to form paragraphs?
- How do the paragraphs form chapters and books and advance the argument, ideas, or story of the book?

If you answer these sorts of questions from the text, you will be well on your way toward understanding the grammatical context of the book or passage you are studying.

Matthew 28:19-20 is one of the more famous examples of how grammar helps us understand Scripture. Depending on the Bible translation, there appear to be four verbs in Matthew 28:19-20, namely "go, make disciples, baptizing, and teaching." Preachers often point out during sermons at mission's conferences and discipleship seminars that the verb "make disciples" (it is one word in the Greek) is the main verb of this sentence. It is a command, or an imperative. The other three verbs are actually participles, which means they explain more about "how" the main verb should occur. In this case, the church is to make disciples through going, baptizing, and teaching.[9]

Ephesians 4:11 is another example. The question is

---

[9] Incidentally, as I point out in my book *Dying to Religion and Empire* and also in my online course "The Gospel Dictionary" (under "Baptism") the word "baptizing" in this verse doesn't refer to dunking someone under water (or sprinkling them with water). It instead refers to *immersing* someone in the teachings and truths of Jesus so that they can become a disciple.

whether there are four or five spiritual gifts mentioned in Ephesians 4:11. Some think Paul is referring to five gifts, the "apostles, prophets, evangelists, pastors, and teachers," while others think it is only four, the "apostles, prophets, evangelists, and pastor-teachers." The reason for this difference is that the two words "and some" (Gk., *tous de*) appear only four times in the text; there is only the coordinating conjunction "and" (Gk., *kai*) between "pastor" and "teacher." It seems that the parallelism of the phrase "and some" indicates that Paul is thinking about four spiritual roles, while the fourth one, the "pastors" receives a little extra clarification. Paul wants to emphasize that pastors are to be teaching. In this case, the Greek word *kai* could be translated as "that is." The grammar reveals that, from Paul's perspective, a pastor is primarily a teacher. The pastor (or shepherd) feeds his flock by giving them plenty of green grass to eat and clean water to drink.

As important as the various parts of speech are, the smallest parts of grammar must not be overlooked. I'm referring to punctuation. Punctuation is critically important for understanding any text, including Scripture. In her excellent book on punctuation, Lynn Truss points out that the phrase "Eats shoots and leaves" means something quite different than "Eats, shoots and leaves." In the first instance, we envision an animal (likely a panda) eating bamboo shoots and leaves. There is one verb (eats) followed by two nouns (shoots and leaves). In the second case, however, we imagine a person eating a meal, shooting a gun, and then walking away. In this case, there are three verbs in a row. The addition of the comma in the second form of this sentence changed two words from nouns to verbs, and as a result, drastically changed the meaning of the sentence as well. (Personally, since I am a strong advocate for the Oxford comma, I would have written this phrase as "Eats, shoots, and leaves" since it is three distinct actions.) This shows the importance of punctuation.

Ephesians 4:12 is one text where a single comma makes a huge difference. Previously, we saw that there are either four or five spiritual gifts mentioned in Ephesians 4:11. Ephesians 4:12 indicates what the people with these gifts are supposed to do with them in the church. And the question here is whether Paul lists two or three tasks. Does God want the spiritual leaders of Ephesians 4:11 to (1) equip the saints, (2) do the work of the ministry, and (3) edify the Body of Christ, or are they to (1) equip the saints to do the work of the ministry, and (2) edify the Body of Christ? In the first instance, those with the spiritual gifts of Ephesians 4:11 do *all the work* of the ministry themselves. But in the second instance, those with the spiritual gifts *train other people* in the church to do the work of the ministry.

How can we decide which is true? The context helps

here as well. In Ephesians 4:16, Paul uses the imagery of a body to talk about each part and joint of the body, providing for the health and growth of the whole body. Since Paul imagines every single part of the body having a role to play for the overall well-being of the body, this indicates that Paul thinks each person should be doing something within the church to encourage and edify the other parts. Therefore, the task of the four spiritual gifts listed in Ephesians 4:11 is *not* to do the work of the ministry themselves, but rather to teach and train *everybody else* to do the work of the ministry.[10] So the first comma in Ephesians 4:12 should not be included. The spiritual leaders are to equip the saints, and the saints are to do the work of ministry. As this happens, the whole body will be edified. The absence of a comma enables this verse to teach Christians how to have a healthy and productive church body.

Quotation marks are also critically important. For example, the meaning of James 2:18-20 is significantly altered by where the quotation ends. Though the beginning of the quote is obvious, where it ends is much less obvious. While some translations consider the quote to be only "You have faith, and I have works," other translations end the quote at the end of verse 18, while a few (such as *The Weymouth New Testament*) end the quote at

---

[10] I write about this entire concept in my book *God's Blueprints for Church Growth* (Dallas, OR: Redeeming Press, 2019).

the end of verse 19. Quote marks can also radically change how the entire book of Romans is read and understood.[11]

So how the text is punctuated can have significant ramifications for the meaning of the text. However, it is important to point out that the original Greek and Hebrew texts did not have punctuation. Punctuation has been added by our translators to make the text more understandable for modern readers. As a result, it is not uncommon to see different Bible translations use different punctuation for the same verse. This means that we cannot be dogmatic about any conclusions drawn from the text based on punctuation. But as seen from Ephesians 4:11-12, other contextual clues can help verify the accuracy of the punctuation.

Along with basic grammar and punctuation, word emphasis is also a helpful thing to consider in the study of any biblical text. To understand the importance of emphasis, consider the following sentence: "I didn't say bring me that book." The sentence has seven words, but it can mean seven different things depending on which word is emphasized. If you emphasize the word "I," then the sentence means that while *someone else* might have said, "Bring me that book," *I* am not the one who said it. Whereas, if you emphasize the second word, "didn't,"

[11] See my article "Epistolary Diatribe in the Letters of Paul (No, really! It's Interesting. I promise!)". https://redeeminggod.com/epistolary-diatribe-letters-of-paul/

then the sentence means that while I *did* say something, I *didn't* say, "Bring me that book." Emphasizing the other five words shows the five other potential meanings as well.

The challenge with emphasis is that it is often difficult to discern in written text. The Greek language can help with this a little bit, in that if the writer wants to emphasize a word or phrase in the text, they will often place it first. Though this tends to sound strange in English, putting a word or phrase in the "emphatic position" is completely normal and natural in Greek. For example, in 1 Corinthians 7:17, Paul puts the words "to each one" first. In English, it could be translated as "To each one God has distributed ..." Paul writes this to a group of believers where some were trying to get praise and glory for their own spiritual gifts. By emphasizing that each person has a gift, Paul seeks to correct the spiritual gift hierarchy that existed in Corinth.

It is also difficult to discern tone of voice in written text, but when we seek to read different texts with different tones of voice, entirely different meanings can emerge. For example, when the prophet Nathan confronts David about David's adultery with Bathsheba (2 Sam 12:7), Nathan's words can be read with either angry or mournful undertones. Since Nathan is conveying God's message to David, the tone in which you read the text gives you an impression about how God feels toward people who sin. If you think Nathan's words are full of anger, rage, and frustration, then this passage can be used to teach that God hates sinners and is out to destroy and punish them. But if Nathan's words are read with sorrow and compassion, then this passage reveals that God mourns for the bad things that will come upon David as a result of his disobedience. Though the exact same words are used, different tones give completely different meanings to the text.

Many of the parables of Jesus are similar. If you read some of the parables of Jesus imagining that His tone was stern and serious, you will derive a completely different message from the text than if you imagine that Jesus told the parables with a smile on His lips and a twinkle in His eye because of the humorous ideas He was presenting through these scandalous stories.

As with emphasis, however, it is nearly impossible to know with certainty what tone was intended with the text. In fact, the tone you use in these sorts of texts might tell you more about your own view of God than anything else. If you read 2 Samuel 12:7 with an angry voice, then this doesn't mean that God is angry, but that you think God is angry toward sinners. Whereas, if you read the text with a loving, compassionate, sorrowful voice, then this also tells you what you think about God's attitude toward sinners. So tone is more of a litmus test on your own heart toward the character of God, than it is on the true nature and character of God. Therefore, trying different tones on various passages can open up new possibilities within the text.

The last element of grammatical context to consider is that of word studies. Along with grammar, punctuation, emphasis, and tone, it is also important to know the meaning of words. When I teach people how to study the Bible, at one point in the lessons, I often write the word "trunk" on a whiteboard and then tell the students to draw a picture of what this word means. Once they are done, I invite them to share their picture with the rest of the class. Invariably, we are shown a variety of pictures. Some students draw a picture of a tree trunk. Others draw a picture of an elephant's trunk. There are usually some pictures of a storage trunk or a car trunk. Occasionally, we also get a picture of swimming trunks.[12] This exercise shows that by itself, words can have a variety of meanings and so it is critical to know what a word means if we are going to understand the sentence in which it is used.

Even the smallest words in Scripture can have great significance. D. Martin Lloyd-Jones once preached an entire sermon on the word "But" in Ephesians 2:4. And for good reason. In the context of Ephesians 2, this is a *big* "but." Or take *The New World Translation* of the Jehovah Witnesses where they add the word "a" to John 1:1

[12] Again, as I mentioned in the introduction, it appears that I learned this illustration from Roy Zuck, but forgot about it until after I finished writing this book. See Zuck, *Basic Bible Interpretation*, 65.

so that it reads "In the beginning was the Word, and the Word was with God, and the Word was *a* god." Inserting the little word "a" at the end of the verse radically changes the meaning of the verse. Jehovah Witnesses teach that we can all become gods just like Jesus, and that Jesus was the first god among many, and they use their translation of this verse to support that view. But when the word "a" is not added to the verse, then John 1:1 teaches that Jesus is eternally divine, is equal with God, and is the only God (within the Trinitarian relationship).

Many people remember the impeachment hearings during the Bill Clinton and Monica Lewinsky hearings. When Bill Clinton was asked, "What is your relationship with Monica Lewinsky?" Bill Clinton replied, "It depends on what the meaning of 'is' is." Frankly, he was probably using this answer as an attempt to squirm his way out of a tricky situation, but he was nevertheless correct. If the word "is" is in the present tense, meaning "What is your relationship with Monica *right now?*" then Bill Clinton could truly say, "I do not have a relationship with Monica Lewinsky," because he had ended it. But if "is" is in the past tense, which should then have been phrased "was," then Bill would have to answer truthfully about the relationship he had shared with Monica Lewinsky in the past. I am in no way trying to defend Bill Clinton. I am, however, attempting to show the importance of using the right words and properly defining our words.

To see that the word "is" is important in Scripture, consider Matthew 26:26. During the Last Supper in the Upper Room with His disciples, Jesus held up the bread and the wine and said, "This is my body ... this is my blood." What did Jesus mean? Well, it all depends on what the meaning of "is" is. Catholics say that Jesus meant that the bread and the wine are literally the blood and body of Jesus Christ. Catholics believe in something called "Transubstantiation," which means that when the priest blesses the bread and wine, it transforms and becomes the actual body and blood of Jesus Christ. They use Matthew 26:26 as a proof text for this idea. Jesus says, "This is my body ... this is my blood," so it must be His actual body and blood.

Lutherans, however, take a different view. They understand the word "is" to mean "like." So they hold to a view called "Consubstantiation," which means that the bread and wine are like the body and blood of Jesus. The bread and wine do not materially change, but rather gain the spiritual essence of the body and blood of Jesus. They say that the spiritual body and blood of Jesus coexist with the physical bread and wine.

The third view, which is the view of most evangelical Christians, is that Jesus was using the word "is" metaphorically. This view holds that the bread and wine are symbolic. The elements do not change physically or spiritually, but only represent the body and blood of Jesus. They are a symbolic picture or reminder of what Jesus accomplished through His death, burial, and resurrection.

So word meanings and usage are critically important for proper Bible study. But how does one go about performing a word study? People often try to perform word studies all by themselves with nothing but an English Bible and a Concordance. While a basic word study can be done this way, the vast majority of Christians simply don't have the linguistic skill or knowledge to arrive at proper conclusions about the meaning of a word if this is the only method they use. Instead, when it comes to word studies, it is best and wisest to depend on the scholarship of other more knowledgeable Christians who have done most of the heavy lifting for us.

The very first—and most important—step in performing a word study is to clear your mind of what you think the word you are studying means. I cannot stress this step enough. There are hundreds of words in the Bible that are critical for proper Christian theology, but which have gained giant piles of incorrect theological baggage around them.[13] If you are unable to clear away

[13] This is why I am writing a series of volumes titled *The Gospel Dictionary*. These volumes look at 52 key words of the gospel, seeking to define and explain these words so that we can better understand, share, and live the gospel in our lives. There is also an online course at RedeemingGod.com that goes along with the volumes.

these obstacles, you will never properly understand the word you are seeking to study.

The word "salvation" is a perfect example. When most Christians think of the word "salvation" (and the other words in the word family, such as "saved, saving, Savior"), they think the word refers to "being forgiven of our sins so we can escape the clutches of hell and go to heaven when we die." If you were to ask the average Christian to define the word "salvation," they would likely give you something along these lines. Yet, remarkably, the word "salvation" is never used this way in the entire Bible. But since people think that salvation means "going to heaven when you die," they read this definition into a myriad of texts that teach nothing of the sort, and as a result, end up with terrible theology from these passages. So before studying the word "salvation," or any biblical word, the very first step is to completely forget everything you think you know about the word.

The second step is to discover the range of possible definitions for the word you are studying. A word will usually have more than one possible meaning, depending on how it is used in a sentence of a paragraph. So you need to create a list or a short explanation of all the possible meanings of the word. This includes not only how the word is variously used in Scripture, but also how the word is used in ancient literature that is not Scripture. Here is where word study tools and dictionaries are invaluable. To find the range of possible definitions for a word, you should consult several Bible dictionaries, Greek and Hebrew dictionaries, and theological dictionaries. Since the Bible was not written in English, English dictionaries are of limited value and can safely be ignored.

When studying the possible range of meanings, it is helpful to remember that word meanings often change over time. As you collect the various definitions of a word, it is helpful to take note of the time periods associated with each definition. For example, the meaning of the word "gay" has drastically changed over the past century, and it would be necessary for anyone seeking to define the word to note that what the word meant in 1900 is entirely different than what the word meant in 2000.

Once the range of possible meanings is determined, the third step is to discern which meaning is most likely in the verse being considered. This is done first by comparing the word itself with its immediate context. In modern American culture, the English term "Big Mac" can have three possible meanings. It can refer to a sandwich sold by McDonald's, a burly man named Mac, or a large Mac truck. But which meaning is best can usually be easily determined by how the term is used in its immediate context. Even if I said, "Big Mac drove his big Mac to McDonald's to eat a Big Mac," you would immediately be able to determine which of the three meanings fits best with each of the three uses. The same thing can usually also be done with biblical texts.

Let me illustrate with the word "save" again. The basic meaning of the word "save" is "to deliver," and it usually refers to being delivered from some sort of temporal calamity, such as enemies, sickness, premature physical death. However, it can also refer to being delivered from temptation, delivered from shame at the Judgment Seat of Christ, delivered from a life of insignificance here on earth, and a variety of other forms of deliverance. But if I am reading Matthew 8:25 where the disciples cry out to Jesus, "Lord, save us!" the immediate context of the passage reveals that they were asking Jesus to deliver them from drowning in the stormy sea. The immediate context clearly indicates which meaning of the word "save" is best.

But if the meaning of the word cannot be clearly determined in this way, then the fourth and final step is to consider the concentric contexts of the verse or passage. This means that you start considering broader and broader contexts of the verse, starting with the closest context. If you think of a verse or passage as the center of a bullseye, and the widening contexts as the surrounding rings, then your first goal is to see if the word in question was used in the smallest ring, which is the few verses on either side of the passage in question. Following this, you will want to consider the chapter in which the verse is found, and then the specific book of the Bible. Following this, the next concentric ring is other books of the Bible written by the same author. Further out are other books of the Bible written in a similar time and geographical location.

When examining the concentric contexts in this manner, you can often see that even though the meaning of a word may be unclear in the text you are studying, the same word is often used within a few verses or paragraphs, where the meaning becomes much clearer. Most often, if a biblical author uses a word in one way in one passage, he will continue to use the word in that same way in the surrounding paragraphs, and usually even throughout the entire book.

The word "salvation" once again provides the perfect example. Someone might be confused when reading Romans 10:9-10 that "salvation" apparently requires us to confess with our mouth that Jesus is Lord. Isn't this some sort of good work? If so, how then can "salvation" be by faith alone in Jesus Christ alone? The dilemma is solved, first of all, by recognizing that the words "saved" and "salvation" do not refer to gaining eternal life or going to heaven when we die. Second, by performing a word study on how the word "saved" and "salvation" is used in the book of Romans, we discover that when Paul writes about "salvation" in this book, he is referring to being delivered, or saved, from wrath (cf. Rom 1:16–3:31). Since "wrath" in Romans is not a reference to hell, but is instead a reference to the deadly and destructive consequences of sin *here and now in this life* (another word study is required to reveal this), then salvation in Romans refers to being delivered from the destructive consequences of sin in our lives now.

With this understanding, it becomes clear what Paul is teaching in Romans 10:9-10. One way to help avoid the devastating and destructive consequences of sin in our lives now is to make a public confession before others that Jesus is your Lord and Master. This makes you accountable to them for how you live and act, and your public confession of a commitment to Jesus will help keep you from sin, and therefore, the devastation to your life that sin can cause. One does not need to confess that Jesus is Lord in order to receive the free gift of eternal life, for the righteousness of God is given to anyone who believes in Jesus for it (cf. Rom 4:1-5). But if we want to move toward sanctification and holiness, a public confession that we are followers of Jesus will go a long way toward helping us live as Jesus wants.

So this is the basic approach to performing word studies. After learning what a word can possibly mean, determine from context which meaning is best. This practice will allow your grammatical study of Scripture to deliver great rewards as you seek to understand and comprehend the written Word of God.

As with the other forms of contextual study, there are

numerous excellent tools that will aid you in discovering the grammatical context of Scripture. Here are a few suggested resources:

-*The Plain English Handbook* by J. Martyn Walsh

-*Eats, Shoots & Leaves* by Lynn Truss

-*A Greek-English Lexicon of the New Testament* by Bauer and Danker

-*The Brown-Driver-Briggs Hebrew and English Lexicon* by Brown and Driver

-*The Complete Word Study Dictionary: New Testament* by Spiros Zodhiates

-*The Complete Word Study Dictionary: Old Testament* by Spiros Zodhiates

-*The Anchor Bible Dictionary* set edited by David Freedman

-*Vine's Expository Dictionary of Old and New Testament Words*

-*Theological Wordbook of the Old Testament* by Harris and Archer

-*Theological Dictionary of the New Testament* set by Kittel and Friedrich

-*The New International Dictionary of New Testament Theology* by Colin Brown

-*The IVP Bible Dictionary* series

THEOLOGICAL CONTEXT

The fourth type of context that must be considered when studying Scripture is the theological context. This type of context is odd in that, although we turn to Scripture to learn what we are supposed to believe, we also need to know what we should believe to properly understand Scripture. Scripture and theology form a symbiotic relationship in which each supports and informs the other. As we learn more Scripture, it corrects and supports our theology, which in turn, provides clues on how to understand Scripture further.

At the core of the theological context of Scripture is the idea that when all of Scripture is generally understood and synthesized down into general themes or ideas, no individual Scripture will ever contradict the overall message of Scripture. Simply put, Scripture does not contradict Scripture. Though there may be the development of ideas over time (such as with the concept of Satan), any individual Scripture will always be in agreement with what the rest of Scripture teaches.

So the theological context requires that we compare Scripture with Scripture. Scripture is its own best commentary. Of course, when we do study a passage in light of other passages, we must be careful to study these other passages in their historical-cultural, literary, and grammatical contexts. If we have not studied these comparison passages in their contexts, it is dangerous to use them as a guide for shedding light on the primary passage under consideration.

This practice of comparing Scripture with Scripture is sometimes referred to as "The Analogy of Faith." This term was originally a mathematical concept that spoke of proportionality between numbers, but ancient Greek philosophers borrowed the term to refer to the comparison of ideas. Early Christian theologians followed the Greek philosophers in this regard and used the term "Analogy of Faith" as a reference to comparing Scripture passages with one another as a way of discovering the overall teachings of Scripture.

When Scriptures are compared in this way, you will inevitably discover some apparent contradictions. What you think one passage means will appear to contradict with something another passage seems to say. When this occurs, there are only two possibilities: either you are wrong about what one of the passages means, or you are wrong about both of them. In either case, you can use the various types of contextual studies to seek a better understanding of both passages until they come into agreement with each other and with the rest of Scripture.

When seeking to allow Scripture to interpret Scripture in this way, it is critical to hold to the truth that the Bible does not contradict itself. Just as many people miss the most significant truths of Scripture because they are too eager to discard some of the most difficult texts as "errors in Scripture," so also, people miss significant truths of Scripture because they are too willing to allow one passage to contradict another. They might say, "The Scriptures are not univocal. That is, they do not speak with one voice. Instead, they are multi-vocal; they speak with different voices. One biblical author can have one point of view that a later biblical author will disagree with and contradict. The Bible is an unfolding conversation with different perspectives and ideas. They do not all agree."

Such a perspective allows one to avoid grappling with difficult texts of Scripture, from which come the most significant truths. This approach also allows a person to continue in their own wrong thinking about several texts, because rather than seek to understand where they might be wrong in their thinking about one (or both) of the biblical texts, they instead maintain their misunderstanding about what the passages mean and disregard one (or both) of them as a contradiction. It is better to recognize that there are no contradictions in Scripture, and with some careful contextual study, all seeming contradictions can be resolved. Only in this way will we discover our own errors in understanding the text, while also uncovering some of the most important truths in Scripture.

Some examples might help. Let us begin with the infamous "contradiction" between Exodus 20:5 and Ezekiel 18:20. In Exodus 20:5, God states that the sins of the fathers will fall upon the heads of the children to the third and fourth generation. But in Ezekiel 18:20, God says that children will not bear the guilt of the father, nor the father bear the guilt of the children. Many see the apparent contradiction between these passages and believe that Ezekiel is attempting to correct the earlier text written by Moses.

But is Ezekiel attempting to correct Moses by contradicting him? No. Ezekiel is seeking to clarify what Moses wrote in Exodus 20:5. We know this because a careful consideration of both texts reveals that the two do not contradict. We see this in two ways. First of all, it is important to note that when Ezekiel speaks specifically about the relationship between fathers and children and the sins they commit, he clarifies that God does not hold one person *guilty* for the sins of the other (Ezek 18:20). While Ezekiel 18:20 initially seems to be a contradiction of Exodus 20:5, a careful reading of both shows that while Ezekiel 18:20 is about *guilt* not being transferred from the father to the son (or vice versa), Exodus 20:5 is about the actual consequences of sin. The destructive and devastating consequences of sin often have far-reaching results so that children sometimes do suffer for the sins of the parents. An infant might contract AIDS due to the promiscuous living of the mother, or a child might get beaten and abused because her father is a drunk. But Ezekiel clarifies that even though children might suffer in this way, it is not because the guilt of the parents has passed down to the children. No, the children suffer, but they remain innocent of the sins of their parents. Each person is guilty for the sins they themselves commit.

Second, and more importantly, Moses clearly states that the sins of the father will fall on the heads of the children *for those who hate Him*. Moses goes on to write that God shows mercy to those who love and obey Him (Exod 20:6). In other words, it is not that God punishes children for the sins of their parents, but that some children *follow* in the error of their parents rather than change their ways and follow the commands of God. But when a child sees how their parents disobeyed God and suffered as a result, and they turn from these wicked ways to follow the commands of God instead, God will show mercy upon them, and the children will not suffer the consequences of sin as did their parents.

This, incidentally, is exactly what Ezekiel states in great detail in Ezekiel 18. He begins by describing two opposing ways of living that every person is faced with. A person can obey God and do what God has commanded (Ezek 18:5-9) or live in ways that are contrary to God's instructions (Ezek 18:10-13, 18). The son is also faced with the same exact choices (Ezek 18:10-17). In both cases, Ezekiel says, each person is responsible to God for how they themselves lived (Ezek 18:19-32). So both Moses and Ezekiel are in complete agreement. Sin has devastating consequences, which can damage innocent bystanders as well as those who committed the sin. But only the person who commits the sin is guilty for it, and if later generations learn from the mistakes of their fathers, they will be able to avoid the devastating consequences of sin in their own lives and for those around them.

A second example is found in the accounts of the four Gospels. Many compare the various accounts about Jesus in Matthew, Mark, Luke, and John, and see numerous discrepancies and apparent contradictions. For example, the two genealogies of Jesus in Matthew 1:1-17 and Luke 3:23-38 are not identical. Similarly, the two records of the Sermon on the Mount in Matthew 5–7 and Luke 6:20-49 vary greatly in length, content, and wording. Various parables, miracles, and teachings also contain different events and wording from one Gospel to another. Even the resurrection accounts have numerous differences, such as how many times Peter denied Jesus, who Jesus appeared to first after He rose from the dead, and how the women reacted to Jesus when they saw the empty tomb (cf. Matt 28:6-8; Mark 16:8; Luke 24:9-12; John 20:1-2).

However, a basic understanding of how history unfolds, how ministry occurs, and how historical records are documented can provide answers to most of the "discrepancies" in the Gospels. First of all, Jesus, just like any pastor or teacher in human history, likely taught similar truths at different times during His ministry. I doubt, for example, that the Sermon on the Mount in Matthew 5–7 was the only time Jesus spoke of these sorts of things. I am convinced that the account in Luke 6:20-49 took place at a different time and a different location. The same applies to many of Jesus' parables and perhaps some of His miracles. Most of the supposed "errors" in the Gospels can be cleared up with this realization.

During an election year, whenever you listen to a politician giving a speech to an audience, you know (and have likely heard) that this politician has said similar things to different audiences at different times. If you were given transcripts of two of these speeches, you would not think for a second that one of the transcripts was in error because it was shorter than the other, or because one of them contained different stories, or different illustrations than the other. You would know that the transcripts were records of two different (but similar) speeches. It is the same with many of the recorded teachings of Jesus in the Gospels.

Furthermore, as historians, the four Gospel authors emphasize different aspects of Jesus' teaching and ministry to bring out different points or reveal different truths. If four people observed the same sporting event, all four would emphasize and remember different plays and different aspects of the game. But these differences are not errors. They are simply details that represent four different points of view. When all are taken together, they do not contradict each other, but corroborate the overall story of what actually took place. This is how to view the four Gospels. And with some creative thinking and a dedication to contextual study, all of the "discrepancies" of the Gospels can be cleared away.

Again, to return to the illustration of the politician giving speeches on the campaign trail, if you were to read different newspaper accounts of the same speech, you would likely see that the news stories emphasize different elements of the speech. This is not because they heard wrong or recorded wrong, but because the author wanted to make a different point to the reading audience. Maybe one newspaper is more conservative or liberal than the other. Maybe the politician said something that spoke to a specific concern in the community. But you would never assume that the reporters were wrong in what they wrote (Well, in the era of fake news, you might assume this …). This is how to read the different Gospel accounts about Jesus. The differences are there for a reason, and the differences help show us what the author wanted his audience to hear from Jesus.

A third example is found in 1 Corinthians. In 1 Corinthians 11:1-12, Paul provides instructions about how women can pray and prophecy. These instructions are challenging in themselves, but we will leave that aside for now. The point is that Paul expects women to speak in various capacities. But a few chapters later, in 1 Corinthians 14:34-35, Paul writes that women should remain silent in church, and if they have a question, they should ask their husbands at home.

This is odd, isn't it? Can it be imagined that Paul would blatantly contradict himself within a few short paragraphs? How can women pray and prophesy while remaining silent in church? The simple solution is to recognize that when Paul writes about women praying and prophesying in 1 Corinthians 11, this does not take place during the gathering of believers, but rather at home. Later, when he is giving instructions about the order of the church meeting, he instructs women to remain silent in this setting. So in Paul's mind, women can pray and prophecy at home, but not during the gathering of the church.

Of course, the follow-up question to such instructions is why Paul gave such instructions in the first place, and whether or not such practices are to be applied to marriages and church meetings today. My own conviction is that numerous historical and cultural considerations led to Paul making these sorts of statements to the Corinthian church. As a result, the instructions of Paul to the women in the Corinthian church cannot be applied to women or churches today. Or maybe it is better to say that they *can* be applied to some women today, but only if the same exact principles are applied to some men for the same reasons.

So what was happening in Corinth that caused Paul to write these words? Some women were causing disruptions in the Corinthian church, and Paul wanted these disruptions to cease until the women learned proper Christian behavior and beliefs. The same principles can be applied to any man or woman today who causes problems in the church due to spiritual immaturity, or who seeks positions of leadership in the church before they are ready.

One final example of apparent contradictions comes from 1 John 1:8 and 3:9. I was first made aware of this apparent contradiction when I was a student at Moody Bible Institute, and I overheard a debate in the library between Dr. John Hart and one of my fellow students. Here is a verbatim account of their discussion:

> **Student:** Whoever has been born of God does not sin.

> **Dr. Hart:** If we say that we have no sin, we deceive ourselves, and the truth is not in us.

> **Student:** Whoever has been born of God does not sin.

> **Dr. Hart:** If we say that we have no sin, we deceive ourselves, and the truth is not in us.

> **Student:** Whoever has been born of God does not sin.

Dr. Hart: If we say that we have no sin, we deceive ourselves, and the truth is not in us.

Since I sat through Dr. Hart's class on the General Epistles, I knew what this debate was about. Dr. Hart taught that true Christians can indeed sin, and sin egregiously. There are numerous examples of such behavior in the Bible, from King David's adultery and murder to Peter's denial of Jesus. The student apparently disagreed. He thought, as many do, that if a person was truly a Christian, they would stop sinning, or would at least start to sin less. And the student had a verse to prove his position in 1 John 3:9. But Dr. Hart rightly pointed out that if anyone claims to be without sin, then they're lying. This doesn't mean that a person can say that they used to sin, but no longer do. No, it means that anyone who says they have reached a point of sinlessness is a liar.

So how can 1 John 1:8 and 3:9 be reconciled? The solution is to recognize that every person is a sinner (as numerous biblical authors attest. See Rom 3:23; Jas 2:10). And as long as we are alive, we keep on sinning. There will never come a day when any single person is able to live without sinning. Even many of our righteous acts are filthy rags in the sight of God (Isa 64:6). But when we sin, we must never think that our sinful behavior came about as a result of God's presence within us. When we sin, it is because we are still walking according to darkness and lawlessness (1 John 2:9-11; 3:4). When a person sins, they are, in that sinful action, following the devil instead of Jesus (1 John 3:5-8). But the part of us that is born of God will never, ever sin (1 John 3:8).[14] The reason this was an essential point for the Apostle John to make is because there were some people in that day who were arguing that certain sins were good and godly, coming from the divine side of our being, rather than from the sinful flesh (cf. 1 John 2:18-27; 3:12; 4:1-6; etc.). So even here, there is no contradiction. The historical-cultural, grammatical, and theological contexts reveal the truth of what John is teaching.

In the end, the theological context of Scripture is somewhat like the Excel spreadsheet of faith that I write about in my book *What is Faith?* You do not have to understand everything in Scripture, or even believe everything in Scripture to study and learn what Scripture says. But as you learn some of the basic truths of the Bible, you are then able to build upon these foundational ideas and learn more advanced truths. And each new doctrine discovered has a cascading or rippling effect through numerous other doctrines on the spreadsheet.

This interconnectivity of biblical doctrines and ideas forms the theological context of Scripture. What we learn from one passage helps us understand other passages, and

---

[14] Cf. Zuck, *Basic Bible Interpretation*, 66. For more on this way of reading 1 John, see Zane C. Hodges, *The Epistles of John: Walking in the Light of God's love: A Verse by Verse Commentary* (Irving, TX: Grace Evangelical Society, 1999).

all ultimately agree in a coherent whole. Such an approach requires us to read the Bible, not just theologically, but *logically* as well. We must use reason to figure out what the Bible means, and how various texts can both be true, even though they may seem to contradict.

If you don't know where to begin, start with the basics. Drink milk before trying to eat meat (1 Pet 2:2). When a Christian tries to eat meat when they should be drinking milk, they end up with a poor understanding of Scripture, terrible theology, and rude, haughty, judgmental behavior toward others. Bad beliefs and behaviors come from trying to jump too quickly into some of the weightier matters of Scripture. Topics such as election and predestination, end-times prophecy, and issues related to angels and demons might be exciting to study, but an overemphasis on these peripheral issues rarely leads to Christian unity or Christian maturity. Christians who spend a lot of time and energy studying and debating these secondary topics without a solid foundation in the central topics will rarely grow in their knowledge of Scripture or Christlike living.

If you are looking for an example of some milk doctrines to begin studying, I recommend the list proposed by the author of Hebrews in 6:1-2. The author says that we should not move on to other things until we first know what the Scriptures teach about repentance from dead works, faith toward God, the doctrine of baptisms, the laying on of hands, the resurrection of the dead, and of eternal judgment. If that list doesn't humble you, then nothing in Scripture will. These are considered the "Kindergarten" doctrines, yet most Christians barely understand the first thing about any of them. This list is where I started over three decades ago, and I have not moved past these doctrines to this very day.[15]

To help you in your own study of building a solid theological foundation, here are some good resources to get you moving in the right direction.

-See my list of recommendations of best Christian books at RedeemingGod.com/best-christian-books/
-*Final Destiny* by Joseph Dillow
-*Hard Sayings of the Bible* by Walter Kaiser, Jr.
-*When Critics Ask* by Norman Geisler
-*When Skeptics Ask* by Norman Geisler

CHRISTOLOGICAL CONTEXT

The final context to keep in mind when studying Scripture is the Christological context. The Christological context is the truth that Jesus is the guiding and interpretive lens through which all Scripture is read and studied. Jesus is the trump card of all aspects of Bible study. Jesus

---

[15] Eventually, I plan to write a book on what I have learned about these doctrines *so far*.

said that He is not only the One of Whom all Scripture speaks (John 5:39-40), but is also the One who reveals the Father to us (John 1:16-18; 10:30; 12:45; 14:7-9; cf. 2 Cor 4:4-6; Col 1:15-17; Heb 1:3). So Jesus interprets Scripture for us. He is the Word incarnate, God in the flesh. As C. S. Lewis wrote, "It is Christ Himself, not the Bible, who is the true Word of God."[16] If we want to understand the meaning of Scripture, we need only look at Jesus, look to Jesus, and look for Jesus.

In this way, Jesus is the first hermeneutical rule of Bible study. He is "the purpose, center, and interpretive key to Scripture."[17] He is the guiding light, the prime interpretive hermeneutic, the keystone to all good Bible study. This means that if we interpret a passage of Scripture, and the results of our study provide us with a teaching that does not look like Jesus or lead us to think and act like Jesus in the Gospels, we can assume that we have wrongly understood that Scripture.

> If believers want to rightly understand Scripture, every narrative, every prayer, every proverb, every law, every Epistle needs ... to be read and understood always and only in the light of Jesus Christ and God reconciling the

---

[16] C. S. Lewis, quoted in Christian Smith, *The Bible Made Impossible: Why Biblicism Is Not a Truly Evangelical Reading of Scripture* (Grand Rapids: Brazos, 2012), 117.

[17] Ibid., 97.

world to himself through him.[18]

Since a basic rule of hermeneutics is that the simpler and clearer texts should guide our understanding of the more difficult and troubling texts, and if Jesus Christ is the clearest revelation of all that God wants us to know and believe, then Jesus is the single greatest clarifying "text" of Scripture. Therefore, when a troubling text seems to teach a truth that is contrary to the clear revelation in Jesus, we must always side with Jesus. While we always consider the whole counsel of God, we must recognize that Jesus is the primary lens and grid through which the whole counsel of God is understood. The revelation we have in Jesus explains the revelation we have in Scripture.

Although the Bible is indeed the Word of God in written form, Jesus is the Word of God in human form.[19] The Bible is the Word of God in black and white; Jesus is the Word of God in flesh and blood. And both are needed for different purposes. Without the written, black and white Word of God, we would know nothing for certain about Jesus. Yet since Jesus is the living, flesh and blood Word of God, He shows us how to read and understand the written Word of God. To put it another

---

[18] Ibid., 99.

[19] Peter Enns, *Inspiration and Incarnation: Evangelicals and the Problem of the Old Testament* (Grand Rapids: Baker Academic, 2005), 110.

way, since Jesus is the culmination and climax of all biblical revelation, we can only understand every other element of biblical revelation by viewing it through the lens of Jesus Christ. Jesus is the rule by which we understand and interpret the rest of Scripture. Jesus is the Canon of the canon of Scripture.

And since one primary purpose of the Word of God is to teach us how to live as humans, Jesus as the human Word of God trumps Scripture as the written Word of God. No matter which biblical text we consider, the basic questions are these: Does it look like Jesus? If not, how can we understand this text in light of Jesus? Or, how can we explain and apply this text in a way that looks more like Jesus? And ultimately, how can we apply this text so that it inspires us to love and live like Jesus?

Of course, Jesus is not just the trump card of *Scripture*; He is also the trump card of God, humanity, and human history. As I explained in my two books, *Nothing but the Blood of Jesus* and *The Atonement of God,* Jesus not only perfectly reveals God to us, He also perfectly reveals humanity to us. Through His life, Jesus showed us how God wanted humanity to live, and through His crucifixion, He showed how humanity actually lives in instead. Once we see the twin revelations of God and humanity in Jesus, we are better situated to understand the truth of Scripture. To know what God is like, simply look at Jesus. If you want to know what humanity is supposed to be like, all you have to do is look at Jesus. And if you want to know how humanity has strayed from God's plan and goal for us, once again, all you have to do is look at Jesus (and specifically, the crucifixion of Jesus).

Indeed, it is this revelation in Jesus that helps us see with certainty that the Bible is inspired and inerrant. The Scriptures reveal truths that could not have originally come from any human source, and as such, are not found in any human document, text, or teaching that predates their revelation in Scripture. When read in the light of Jesus Christ, Scripture reveals truths about ourselves, about God, and about human culture that no human could ever imagine or invent, but which, when they are investigated, turn out to be true. These truths were hidden since the foundation of the world, but were fully revealed in Jesus Christ.[20]

The biblical revelation (when properly understood through Jesus) about the nature and extent of sin, the character of God, and the horrors of religion are not found in any other religious text in human history, or in any other piece of literature. What Scripture teaches about these sorts of ideas is unique to the Bible, and therefore, unique to Christianity. Without such inspired and revelatory truths in Scripture, we humans would continue to dwell in darkness and ignorance about our true

---

[20] See René Girard, *Things Hidden Since the Foundation of the World* (Stanford, CA: Stanford, 1987).

condition and what God has done to rescue us from it. And Jesus helps us see all of this. Yet when the interpretation of Scripture ignores Jesus as the trump card of Bible study, it ends up with a distorted view of things about which the Scriptures teach.

So in Jesus, the entire Bible is reframed. He is the lens that provides the true interpretation of Scripture. "Jesus is the norm—the standard, the lens—through which Christians are to understand the Bible."[21] We must read Scripture through a Christological or Christotelic lens.[22] More specifically, it is not just that we must read the Bible through the lens of Jesus, but through the lens of Jesus

---

[21] Marcus J. Borg, *Convictions: How I Learned What Matters Most* (New York: HarperOne, 2014), 81.

[22] C. S. Cowles, *Who is God? His Character Revealed in the Christ* (Kansas City, MO: Beacon Hill, 2005), 116; Enns, *Inspiration and Incarnation*, 154. Some theologians refer to a *Christocentric* or *Christonormative* perspective. See the quote from Thomas A. Noble in Stanley N. Gundry, ed. *Show Them No Mercy: 4 Views on God and Canaanite Genocide*, Counterpoints (Grand Rapids: Zondervan, 2003), 23. See also Eric A. Seibert, *Disturbing Divine Behavior: Troubling Old Testament Images of God* (Minneapolis: Fortress, 2009), 183ff; Smith, *The Bible Made Impossible*, 93ff. This entire way of reading Scripture through the lens of Jesus is referred to as Cruciform theology, which basically teaches that Jesus did not go to the cross despite being God; He went to the cross because He was God. Therefore, if we want to understand God (and ourselves), we must begin by looking at Jesus, and specifically, Jesus on the cross. It is as Paul wrote, "I determined not to know anything among you except Jesus Christ and Him crucified" (1 Cor 2:2).

on the cross, that is, with a cruciform or *crucivision* lens.[23] Jesus Christ sheds light on Old Testament texts, revealing the substance of what was previously only shadows of things unseen (Col 2:17; Heb 8:5; 10:1).[24] He is the guide who helps us understand difficult passages, the ey which unlocks the puzzle, and He is the end to which all Scripture points. When we seek to understand the violence of God in the Old Testament, we must begin by looking at the end. We must begin by looking at the person and work of Jesus Christ as He is revealed in the Gospels and especially in His crucifixion (1 Cor 2:2).

The clearest example of the Christological context at work is in how we can understand the violence of God in the Old Testament. Any attempt to explain the violence of God in the Old Testament must do so through the filter of Jesus' life and teachings. As we seek to understand the violence of God in the Old Testament, we must never attribute such violence to God if we cannot attribute it to Jesus. If you cannot imagine Jesus doing something, then God did not do it either, and some other explanation of the violent text must be sought.

And Jesus was supremely non-violent. One of the primary characteristics of Jesus in the Gospels is His

[23] J. D. Myers, *The Atonement of God* (Dallas, OR: Redeeming Press, 2016).

[24] J. Todd Billings, *The Word of God for the People of God: An Entryway to the Theological Interpretation of Scripture* (Grand Rapids: Eerdmans, 2010), 19.

complete rejection and repudiation of all violence against humans. He taught that we must love our enemies and pray for those who persecute us (Matt 5:43-48). When given the chance to call ten thousand legions of angels to His defense, He instead chose to go willingly to the cross (Matt 26:53). And while Jesus did teach that following Him in discipleship would bring division to families (Matt 10:34), when one of His disciples actually brought a sword to defend Jesus, Jesus told Him to put it away, and then went on to heal the man whose ear Peter had cut (John 18:10-11). On the cross as He died, in the ultimate revelation of God, rather than call down curses and destruction from heaven, Jesus asked God to forgive those who killed Him (Luke 23:34).

So if Jesus mostly clearly reveals the Father to us, then we cannot say that God does indeed have a side to Him which is full of wrath at sin and a desire to kill those who are evil. If we believe that God engages in violence when Jesus lived and taught the exact opposite, then we must conclude that the Bible is wrong and Jesus did not fully reveal God to us. If God truly does have a bloodlust toward evildoers, then Jesus cannot be said to truly reveal the Father to us, for He never reveals this side of God. Quite to the contrary, Jesus never hurts, never judges, never harms, never condemns. He always loves, always forgives, and always accepts.

But if the Bible is correct, and Jesus truly is the exact

representation of God, then this means that God, like Jesus, is non-violent, and the violent portrayals of God in the Old Testament must be understood differently. The New Testament authors—and Jesus Himself—invite us to read about God in light of Jesus Christ. When we do this, we find a God who is not drunk with the blood of the nations, but is rather covered in His own blood that He shed for the nations.

> *God looks like Jesus.* ... Jesus spent His ministry freeing people from evil and misery. *This is what God seeks to do.* Jesus wars against spiritual forces that oppress people and resist God's good purposes. *This is what God does.* Jesus loved people others rejected—even people who rejected him. *This is how God loves.* Jesus had nothing but compassion for people who were afflicted by sin, disease and tragedy. *This is how God feels.* And Jesus died on the cross of Calvary, suffering in the place of sinful humanity, defeating sin and the devil, because he passionately loves people and wants to reconcile them to God. *This is how God saves.*[25]

It is impossible to emphasize too often the critical truth of the entire New Testament that Jesus reveals God to us. "In Jesus ... we see that God is not a dark deity of death and destruction. ... The God revealed fully and finally in Jesus is not a wanton destroyer, but a life-giving,

---

[25] Gregory A. Boyd, *Is God to Blame?* (Downers Grove: IVP, 2003), 16. Italics his.

life-enhancing, life-redeeming, and life-ennobling Spirit."[26] If you want to understand what God is like, you must begin by looking at Jesus. "To see Jesus is to see God."[27] Jesus wants to reintroduce us to God as well, and in the process, challenge some of our theology.

All of theology and how we understand Scripture and live our lives depends upon our view of God, and our view of God depends upon our view of Jesus. Only when we see Jesus in all His love, mercy, forgiveness, and grace can we begin to grasp the character and nature of God. When all the accounts of Jesus in the Gospels are taken together, we come away with a picture of God and a guiding principle of Scripture and theology which requires us to understand both as being infinitely full of love and mercy, grace and truth, patience and kindness, long-suffering and forgiveness. All of Scripture and theology must be understood in the light of Jesus, as must God Himself.

The question, then, is this: If God is like Jesus, and so God is non-violent like Jesus, then how are we to understand all the violent portraits of God in Scripture? This question is more fully answered in my books *Nothing but the Blood of Jesus* and *The Atonement of God,* as well as in a forthcoming volume, *The Bible Mirror* (see Appendix III). But the short answer is that Jesus shows us that the violent portrayals of God in the Old Testament do not,

---

[26] Cowles, *Who is God?*, 48, cf. 102.

[27] Seibert, *Disturbing Divine Behavior*, 186.

in fact, reveal the actions of God, but instead reveal the heart of humankind. It is not God who engages in violence, but rather we humans who engage in violence, and we do it in God's name. Just as Jesus bore the sins of humanity on His own body on the cross, though He was innocent of all wrongdoing, so also, God has been bearing the sins of humanity on Himself through all human history, though He too is innocent of all wrongdoing (including all violence). Again, I refer you to my books on this subject if you desire a more detailed explanation.

The second example of how Jesus interprets Scripture for us is no less controversial than the first. Just as Jesus explains God to us, Jesus also explains the Mosaic Law to us. There is much controversy in Christian circles about how we are to understand and apply the Mosaic Law today. Even Paul seems to make conflicting statements about the law. In one place, he states that the law is holy, righteous, and good (Rom 7:12). Yet a few verses later, he states that the law cannot accomplish that which the law was intended to accomplish (Rom 8:3). Similar confusing statements are found in Matthew 5:17-18 where Jesus follows His statement that He did not come to abolish the law but to fulfill it with a prophecy about the law passing away as a result of that fulfillment. So did Jesus establish the law or do away with it? There is also John's statement in John 1:17 that while the law was given through Moses, grace and truth came through Jesus

Christ. John sets the law in contrast to grace and truth. Does this mean that the law does not contain grace and truth? The life and ministry of Jesus shows us how to best understand the law. But before we see how Jesus does this, let us first consider how most Christians explain and apply the law today.

When Christians discuss the *law* as it is found in Scripture, it is quite common to hear the various 613 commandments of the Mosaic Law divided up into three categories: the Ceremonial Law, the Judicial/Civil Law, and the Moral Law. The Ceremonial Law is thought to be those laws that concern the Priestly and Levitical responsibilities within the temple. The Judicial/Civil Law consists of those laws that concern the operation of Israel as a nation and the governing of the people. The Moral Law consists of the guidelines and laws that are to be applied to all people everywhere throughout time. This three-fold division helps Christians decide which commands we are to keep, and which ones were specific to the nation of Israel and their worship in the temple.

The main problem with this threefold division is that it is not found in the Bible, and so the division of the various laws into these three categories often seems quite arbitrary and random. As James points out, the entire law stands or falls as a unit (Jas 2:10). This is why you will sometimes hear Christians focus just on the Ten Commandments, all of which are thought to be part of the

Moral Law (with the possible exception of the Sabbath Law, depending on who you ask). Furthermore, the Ten Commandments are conveniently divided into two categories, with the first four laws concerning our relationship with God, and the final six concerning our relationship with humans. (The numbering of these 'differs, depending on who you ask, for there are actually 14 imperatives in the Ten Commandments of Exodus 20.) This two-fold division fits nicely with Jesus' summary of the law in Matthew 22:37-39: "'You shall love the Lord your God with all your heart, with all your soul, and with all your mind.' This is the first and great commandment. And the second is like it: 'You shall love your neighbor as yourself.'"

Yet even though "Love God and love others" is a good summary of the law, it is still law, and Christians are not called to live under to the law (Rom 6:14). Rather than live according to a checklist of responsibilities, Jesus invites us to live in a relationship based on love (John 13:34). While God does want us to love Him and love others, we cannot do this until we know that we are loved unconditionally (1 John 4:19). And we only come to know we are loved unconditionally by God by seeing this love in Jesus. Then once we know God loves us, love for Him and for others flows naturally from Him through us as we live within that love. This makes sense, as no relationship can be built on law. Authentic relationships are always and only built on love.

Imagine if you tried to build your marriage on a checklist of responsibilities. How long would such a marriage last? Let us even assume that the "To do" list was a very good list. It included things like saying "I love you" seven times a day, hugging your spouse three times a day, and having sex once per week. On this list, men were instructed to wash the dishes for their wives on Tuesday nights, and wives were instructed to give their husbands a backrub on Fridays. Imagine that this list had 613 such commandments and you were able to do them all. Would you have a "good" marriage relationship? Well, such a marriage might be better than lots of marriages, but no one would be able to call it a marriage "relationship." It would be a marriage based on a checklist, not a marriage based on love.

This is exactly how to view the law, and in fact, is exactly how the law is presented in Scripture, and is exactly how Jesus invites us to interact with the law. Through His teaching and actions, Jesus shows that the only true way to interact with God and with others is through love. Jesus constantly loved and forgave those who would normally be condemned by the law. But this was because the law was never God's intent or purpose, but was only given as a poor substitute for love.

The law serves as a substitute when a loving relationship is not possible, but no one should ever confuse law keeping with an actual loving relationship. The law can teach people the *sorts of things* one might see in a loving relationship, but even a comprehensive list of 613 items can never substitute for an actual relationship built on love. Jesus shows that when it comes to living with other people, the attitude of the heart leads to the right action (Matt 5:17-48). But where the attitude is wrong, or where the right attitude is absent, law helps guide us on how to treat one another, but only imperfectly. The perfect way to live is with the right attitude, which will then lead to right actions.

So what is the right attitude Jesus wants us to have? It is love. Jesus invites us to love one another, as He has loved us (John 15:12). But where there is no love, we can revert to law, but only as a broken attempt to maintain peace (in reality, law keeping tends to bring more division than peace). Law is a poor substitute for love, but where love does not exist, law keeps us from killing and hurting each other.

So laws are needed where there is no relationship of love. If people reject love, the only alternative is law. Law keeps a peaceful and ordered society in the absence of love. To help with the law, God also provided a priesthood to mediate between Himself and His people, along with instructions about a tabernacle, and basic guidelines on how to get along in community with one another. Law is an inferior and impotent substitute for love. This is the way the law is presented in the Pentateuch by Moses himself. As John Sailhamer points out in *The Meaning of the Pentateuch*, the law is presented as a short-term substitute for the primary goal of a loving relationship between God and His people.

This religion of laws was not His ideal plan for them, but He gave it to them because this is what they wanted. The people of Israel did not initially want an intimate relationship with God where He spoke to them face to face. They wanted to keep their distance from God. And so, just as God later provided a king to the people because they wanted a human king instead of God as their king, He also provided religion because they wanted a human priesthood and physical tabernacle instead of a daily, intimate, direct relationship with God. Though God wanted and offered a relationship based on love, the people rejected this offer and asked for a religion based on laws. So God gave it to them, even though it was not best. The law was good and just, but it could never accomplish what God desired within the midst of a loving relationship with humankind. This relationship with God is what Jesus revealed and modeled for us, so that we also might have fellowship with Him and with one another (cf. 1 John 1:3).

Jesus shows us how to understand the rest of Scripture, and so regardless of which "conclusions" you come to through your study of other biblical passages, these conclusions must always bow before the ruling and reigning Word of God, Jesus Christ. He guides, filters, and controls our understanding and application of every passage of Scripture. If your interpretation of Scripture does not look like Jesus, you have not properly interpreted or understood Scripture. Here are some suggested resources that will help solidify this truth in your mind:

- *The Atonement of God* by J. D. Myers
- *Nothing but the Blood of Jesus* by J. D. Myers
- *A More Christlike God* by Bradley Jersak
- *Sinners in the Hands of a Loving God* by Brian Zahnd
- *Violence Unveiled* by Gil Bailie
- *Saved from Sacrifice* by S. Mark Heim
- *Jesus and the Victory of God* by N. T. Wright
- *How God Became King* by N. T. Wright
- *The Meaning of the Pentateuch* by John Sailhamer
- *Cross Vision* by Greg Boyd

CONCLUSION

Nobody likes to be quoted out of context, so we must make sure that we never quote God's Word out of context either. To avoid this practice, we must engage in serious study of the Bible by making numerous observations from the context of any passage we seek to understand. As we study the Bible in its various contexts, it is then that we will see what God is saying through Scripture, and how we can teach the Bible to others also. Like the student with Professor Agassiz, never stop observing the context of any passage you study, and never think you have discovered all there is to learn. Only when we keep pushing the text to reveal more will we uncover some of the greatest truths and insights from God's written Word.

DISCUSSION QUESTIONS

1. What areas of research do you need to investigate to study the historical-cultural context of any biblical passage?

2. Why is the historical-cultural context the most difficult *and* the most important area of context to study?

3. What types of literature are found in the Bible? What are some of the characteristics of these various types of literature?

4. Describe some literary devices and figures of speech that are found in Scripture, and provide an example of each.

5. Do you need to know Greek and Hebrew to

understand the grammatical context of most Bible passages? Why or why not?

6. List some of the various parts of speech, and how to recognize them in a verse or Bible passage.

7. What does the word "salvation" mean, and how can it best be understood in context?

8. Describe the process of doing a word study using concentric contexts.

9. What is "The Analogy of Faith" and why is it important for studying Scripture?

10. Why is it important to accept the fact that the Bible never contradicts itself? What can happen if a person does not accept this idea?

11. What are some basic, foundational doctrines that Christians should focus on when first starting to study Scripture? Why will learning the basics help them in their future studies?

12. Why can we read the Old Testament through the lens of Jesus Christ even though Jesus lived *after* the events recorded in the Old Testament?

13. How does the revelation of Jesus Christ help us understand the rest of the Bible, including the difficult and tricky portions of the Bible? In other words, how does the living Word of God help us understand the written Word of God?

CHAPTER 4

FIVE STEPS TO BIBLE STUDY

In this chapter, we want to put together everything we have learned about Bible study and show how to *actually* go about studying a passage of Scripture. Before we begin, however, it is essential to note from the start that although the following chapter is presented in a logical and orderly fashion, there are not really "steps" to follow in Bible study, but rather cycles or spirals that carry the student of Scripture around the text numerous times. The goal of each spiraling circuit is to draw closer in to the center of the text, which is what God wanted the reader to understand when He inspired the author to write it.

Since the true, divine meaning of the text is at the center, the student of Scripture is like a swimmer caught in a giant whirlpool or eddy, being pulled closer and closer to the meaning in the middle. As we swim around in the pool of God's revelation, we often study the same passages again and again, seeking new insight and deeper understanding. As we do so, we frequently get swept past many of the same regions we have covered before, but each new detail and insight pulls us closer to the central significance and meaning of the text.

Therefore, the student of Scripture must recognize that Bible study is a lot like sanctification. Just as sanctification is a journey toward holiness that never ends during this life, but is still worth pursuing, so also, the ever-spiraling nature of Bible study will never end in this life, but is also worth traveling. No scholar or student will ever learn all there is to know or understand about any particular text or passage. So we must always remain humble about what we have learned *so far*, and must continually dig deeper into the text as we journey further into what God says in Scripture.

With this never-ending, spiraling nature of Bible study in mind, let us now turn to the various parts of Scripture study which are followed by those who seek to understand God's written Word properly.

SEEK SPIRITUAL GUIDANCE

The first element to remember in all Bible study is that it must be bathed in prayer. The student of Scripture must always seek to rely upon the guiding and illuminating work of the Holy Spirit. This attitude of prayerful, expectant, and studious humility should permeate your entire study. Since the Holy Spirit inspired the writing of the text, the Spirit also aids in providing understanding to those who study it. So listen for the whisper of God as you study Scripture.

Remember that Jesus guides and informs the interpretation of every text. He is the lens through which I determine whether or not a particular understanding of the text is valid. This mindset is further supported by what I know Scripture teaches elsewhere (the Christological and Theological Contexts). Imagine yourself sitting at the feet of Jesus having Him teach the passage to you before you seek to understand it and teach it to others.

There is a danger here, however. Do not think that because you prayed for God to guide your study and sought to rely on the illuminating work of the Holy Spirit, this means that the conclusions of your study are infallible and without error. They are not. The student of Scripture must never arrogantly conclude that what they *feel* God has revealed to them about the text is what He has *actually* revealed. Feelings can be wrong. We can mishear and misunderstand. While the text is inspired and inerrant, our conclusions about the text are not. So even when we feel that the Spirit has guided our study, we must still present the conclusions of our study with humility and grace.

Such an attitude of prayerful study does not stop when you leave your study and go on to other activities in life. Sometimes, the most significant insights into a text arrive when you are not actively studying it. So even after you finish "studying" the text, your mind should often be subconsciously watching and waiting for spiritual insight that brings the text together and gives power to your teaching. As you lie down and get up, eat your meals, take a shower, and brush your teeth, your mind can be thinking through the text and asking God what it means. I often find that my greatest breakthroughs come at 3:00 am or when I am ... "otherwise indisposed." I know, too much information. But when such insights come, jot them down for later. Especially those insights at 3 am. You might think you will be able to remember it in the morning, but you never can. So keep a pen and paper nearby at all times ... even in the bathroom.

Yet there is another grave danger that lurks behind the scenes here as well. While it is important to be prayerfully thinking about the text at all times, even when you are not studying it, you must make sure that you do not ignore or neglect the people who are around you. It is easy to let your mind become consumed by thoughts of the text, thereby ruining your relationships, including your marriage. It is all too easy to have an affair with Scripture while abandoning your spouse and children. Don't let the Bible become your mistress.

Relationships are more important than any insight into Scripture you will ever gain. God does not want your study of Scripture to get in the way of your love for your family. It is important to be able to put aside your ruminations about text so you can focus your attention on those who are in the room. But when you are in the car by yourself, taking a walk alone with the dog, or doing the dishes while your wife tucks the children into bed, this is when you can allow your thoughts to drift toward Scripture and see if there is anything the Spirit wants to teach you from the text. Listening to the Spirit for instruction about Scripture is a helpful practice that all serious students of the Bible must develop.

GET A BIG PICTURE OVERVIEW

When it comes to actually studying a passage of Scripture, it is critically important to first get an overall big picture perspective of the individual passage you will be studying. This eventually involves, of course, gaining some historical and cultural perspective on the book of the Bible you will be studying (the Historical-Cultural Context). But if you are brand new to studying Scripture, it is best to hold off on those contextual studies until later in the process. Do not turn to books at this stage. Instead, restrict yourself to reading the text of Scripture itself without any aids except your own mind and (in line with the previous point) the whisper of the indwelling and illuminating Holy Spirit.

Ideally, regardless of which text of Scripture you are studying, you should have a broad overview understanding of the entire book in which that text is found. You must understand the overall thought flow and argument of the entire book. For example, if you are studying Ephesians 2:8-9, you need to know the overall thought flow, layout, and argument of Ephesians as a whole. You cannot study an individual text or passage without knowing how it fits into the entire book in which it is found.

So before you start studying the verse or text, read the entire book this text is in. And not just once; read the book several times. Maybe even in different translations. Frankly, you should read and reread the entire book as many times as possible, until you are almost weary of it. As you read, read prayerfully, asking the Spirit to help you understand the overall flow, argument, themes, and truths of the text. If possible, use your own initial observations of the text to prepare a rough outline or summary of what the entire book is about. This big picture perspective of the book will guide your understanding of the individual passages within it. Of course, your later study of the individual passages will change and clarify the broader perspective of the book, but you don't need to worry about that too much initially. This refining and clarifying process will happen naturally as you repeatedly cycle through the various steps of Bible study.

When I first became a pastor, the church in which I ministered had gone through some difficult times, and so

I thought it would be good to cheer them up with some sermons about joy. I knew that Philippians was about joy, and so I decided to preach through the text. However, I did not do the best job of getting a big picture overview of Philippians as I should have done. For while Paul does encourage his readers to have joy, it is joy *in the midst of suffering and problems* that is on Paul's mind. So while the book is encouraging, it can also become quite discouraging, for the letter continually reminds the readers of all the problems they face and will continue to face. My understanding of the individual passages modified my overall perspective of the book, which in turn helped change how I taught and applied later texts from Philippians. All of this is part of the studying process, but the better grasp you have from the start about the big picture perspective of the book, the easier it will be for you to study the individual texts.

As you grow more adept at studying Scripture and cycle through the elements outlined in this chapter, it will also be helpful to understand issues related to the authorship, audience, and purpose of the book (the Literary Context). Ideally, you should gain as much of this information as possible by reading other books of the Bible along with the one you will be teaching. For example, if you are teaching a passage from Philippians, you will want to read what the book of Acts says about Paul and his ministry in Philippi. If you are teaching one of the

Psalms of David, then read about David from 2 Samuel and 1 Chronicles.

However, it is sometimes challenging to fully understand authorship, audience, and purpose this way. At this stage of your study, you may need to consult some websites, commentaries, or other study aids that discuss these topics. However, let me issue a warning: Even if you consult resources to understand who wrote the book, why it was written, and to whom, you must discipline yourself to avoid reading specific explanations of the verses or passages you're studying. While you can read background information about the book, do not read any commentary about the verses you will be studying. Do not even look at an outline or summary of the book of the Bible you are studying. You must develop a version of these *on your own*. You can consult outlines, summaries, and explanations later, but it is *critically* important to save these for later. I explain why below.

STUDY THE PASSAGE

After you gain a big picture overview of the entire book, you are now ready to study the individual passages and verses within that book. Ideally, begin with chapter 1, verse 1, and work your way through the book systematically, one verse at a time. Only this process will allow you to verify and refine your big picture overview of the book, which is essential for understanding the meaning of any individual text in the book.

For example, if you are teaching Ephesians, and your overview of the book is wrong, but you skip a detailed study of the first three chapters of the book so that you can focus on a section out of chapter 4, your study of chapter 4 will be based on the faulty foundation of a skewed big picture overview. You can only correct the faulty foundation by carefully studying each section of each chapter in order. As you do this, you will correct the big picture perspective, so that when you arrive at chapter 4, you can properly understand it in the overall context.

I know that the "ideal" approach is not always feasible. So if you are unable to perform this careful, systematic study from 1:1 onward, just remember to add additional humility to your conclusions about the passage you are studying, for your conclusions about the text are more likely to be wrong without the careful study of all the verses that came before it.

Once you are ready to study the passage, begin by reading the text several times. It can be helpful to read the passage in several translations. If you know Greek and Hebrew, you could even write down your own tentative translation of the text. Take note of key phrases, ideas, and words that are repeated or emphasized. Think of how the sentences and paragraphs fit together grammatically, and also notice any figures of speech (the Literary and

Grammatical Contexts). Try to sense the emotional tone of the text as well.

If one is not teaching a narrative text, it is also helpful to prepare a textual outline of the passage you are studying. Such an outline primarily uses the words of the verse or passage, arranging them in an outline format with main points and supporting sub-points. An added benefit of creating an outline directly from the text is that it provides an excellent sermon outline for later use when teaching to others what you have studied.

Here is an example of a textual outline I made for my study of Ephesians 4:11-13:

And He Himself gave:
    Some to be apostles
    Some prophets
    Some evangelists
    Some pastor-teachers
(Why?)
    For the equipping of the saints for the work of the ministry
    For the edifying of the body of Christ
Till we all come (the goal)
    To the unity
        of the faith
        and of the knowledge of the Son of God
    To a perfect man

To the measure of the stature of the fullness of Christ

You can see that some of the connecting words helped form the outline, so that the repeated words "some," "for," and "to" revealed the main sub-points. Furthermore, this way of arranging the text also reveals the main point of the passage. Namely, Paul is saying that God gave gifts to Christians so that we could perform tasks with these gifts. And incidentally, this is a wonderful summary of the book of Ephesians as a whole. The first three chapters of Ephesians are about the riches we have been given in Jesus Christ, and the final three chapters are about the responsibilities we have in using these divine riches. Paul's discussion in Ephesians 4 marks the transition from writing about riches to writing about responsibilities. So this further supports the central idea of this passage, and the overall big picture of Ephesians as a whole.

Once you have discovered the main idea of the passage, as well as the general outline and structure of the argument, it is then time to start digging deeper into the meaning and significance of the individual words of the passage. Word studies will be helpful at this stage, as discussed in the previous chapter under the section on Grammatical Context.

During this step, you should be taking copious

amounts of notes. Since I like the freedom to move things around on a page easily, I prefer to take my notes in a word processor like Microsoft Word. I will type out the textual outline in a Word document, then copy-paste it a second time into the document. This second version becomes the outline for my notes. I work through it one word or phrase at a time, looking up key words in Greek and Hebrew dictionaries, and typing down how the meanings of these words support the overall point of the passage.

As I note the meaning and significance of key words in the text, I also include any historical and cultural background information that I might be aware of. I will not consult books about such matters until later, but you might be aware of several facts from previous passages you have studied.

This stage of studying the text is quite time-consuming. Yet by the time you are done, you have something very close to the skeleton framework of a sermon. You have an outline structure of the passage, an explanation of all the key words in the text, and some historical and cultural background material that will help bring the text to life for the modern person. If you absolutely needed to, these notes could be used to teach or preach the passage. But there are still two steps to go before you should try to teach your text.

READ COMMENTARIES

The final step in studying any passage from Scripture is to read the thoughts and insights of others who have studied the text as well. Nearly every pastor and author uses commentaries and study aids in their research of the biblical text, but there are three common mistakes people make when consulting bible study resources.

The first mistake that some pastors and authors make is the least common. It is typically only found among hyper-fundamentalists and super-Pentecostals. The mistake is not consulting any other books, commentaries, or study resources *at all.* This approach is not widespread, but it is more common than you might think. There are likely at least one or two pastors in every town who consistently advise their congregations that they should never read any spiritual book except for the Bible. The pastor himself will also follow this practice. He will not own any commentaries or Bible dictionaries. He will not read Christian magazines or theological journals. He might say, "The Bible is the only source of divine truth, and so the Bible is the only book we need." Such an approach to Scripture sounds pious, holy, and spiritual, but it is entirely illogical, quite hypocritical, and nearly impossible to practice. I explain why in Appendix I.

The second mistake that some Bible students and teachers make when it comes to reading commentaries about the Bible is that they turn to such resources too quickly. In fact, for many students of Scripture, reading commentaries and Bible study resources is often their first step in understanding a text or passage. They sit down to study a text, and before they even try to understand it on their own or listen to what the Spirit might want to teach them from the text, they open up book after book to listen to what other human authors have to say about the text. Such an approach completely short-circuits their ability to feel the thrill of sitting at the feet of Jesus and having Him teach you directly.

Commentaries and study aids are important and helpful, but they must be used in their proper place, which is at the *end* of your own prayerful study and research of the text. Such an approach gives life and vibrancy to your teaching and writing, because you are primarily sharing what you have learned from the text through direct communication with God, rather than simply regurgitating the ideas and insights of others. A dead and lifeless sermon or book is usually the result of the pastor or author presenting the ideas of others as his own, rather than presenting his own ideas to others. Yes, the commentaries can help affirm and support your ideas from the text, but this is better than having no ideas of your own to begin with.

Of course, along with affirming and supporting your ideas from the text, the commentaries can also correct your ideas. It is difficult when this happens, for it often means that you have to discard everything you have learned and prepared from the text, and start all over with your reading and research of the text. This is the danger of putting commentary reading last, but it is a necessary danger. Commentary reading must be left for last if we are to maintain the life and excitement of our investigation into the text. Besides, if you discover an error or mistake in your personal research, this fuels greater excitement for discovering the truth about the text before passing on errors to others.

I would say that some form of correction happens about 20% of the time. It may be more or less for you. As you turn to commentaries and other Bible study resources after the completion of your own study, you may discover a new grammatical point, literary insight, or historical-cultural key that radically changes what you thought the text was about. If this happens, you must start all over, retracing all the steps and reworking everything you thought you knew about the text in light of this new understanding. It's painful and frustrating, but it is also part of the journey of proper Bible study.

Usually, however, you will discover that the things God taught you from the text are right in line with what He has taught others also, which will be an encouragement to you, that you can study the text with God and discover the meaning that lies within.

This then leads to the third mistake that some scholars

and pastors make when reading commentaries about the biblical text. This third mistake is that most students of Scripture tend to only read commentaries they already agree with. Conservative Christians tend to read only conservative commentaries, avoiding and ignoring those written by liberal scholars. Calvinists read only commentaries from the Calvinistic tradition, ignoring those from Arminian authors. Evangelical Christians ignore Catholic commentaries. Almost all Christian ignore Jewish commentaries. The opposites of all these are also true.

But I have often found that listening to people with whom I disagree has helped me gain new perspectives and insights into the text that I never would have discovered otherwise. Books written by atheists have greatly enriched my understanding. Atheistic authors are refreshing to read, for they have no qualms about being critical of Scripture or asking hard questions from the text. Christians must address the questions and issues raised by atheists to "give an answer to everyone who asks." Besides, they often see things in the text that no Christian will ever see, because we tend to read the Bible with spiritual-colored glasses.

Remember that when it comes to reading commentaries and studies of Scripture, Proverbs 18:17 is your "life verse." It says, "The first one to plead his case seems right, until his neighbor comes and examines him." Your first conclusions about a text might seem right until you allow someone to come and question your views. No human Bible teacher is infallible. When you come to certain conclusions about a text, your conclusions are either correct or incorrect, and the *only* way to know is by allowing your views to be challenged and questioned. But if you only allow the questions to come from people who already agree with you, then you will never be challenged to see the text in a different light, and so you might be missing out on what the text actually teaches.

Reading "contrarian" commentaries will allow you to see the text through new eyes and from different perspectives. Your mind and your ideas will never be stretched unless you allow the insights of others to challenge your thinking and your conclusions about the text. Far too many pastors and teachers only read books and commentaries from authors and scholars who have similar theological positions. While this creates a nice echo chamber for your study, giving you a sense of well-being that you are "on the right track," such an approach will never show you where you might be wrong, and will never allow you to grow in your thinking or theology. So challenge yourself and challenge your theology by reading books and commentaries (with an open mind!) from people on the other side of the theological spectrum.

We are now down with the "study" aspect of Bible study. But, even after you read the commentaries, you are still not done with the biblical text itself. You are *never* done with any particular text of Scripture. Remember, this entire process is a cycle rather than a series of steps. Once you get to the end, you can always circle back around and start over again. I find that it is usually best to let a few years pass in between each cycle. However, as you study other passages of Scripture as outlined above, this will give you further insight and ideas about the meaning and significance of passages you might have studied previously. Also, you might discover some new ideas from various commentaries or journal articles that help reshape your view on a passage you previously studied. So, as you have opportunity, go back and re-study passages you had previously studied so that you can see what new truths God wants to teach you from them. As you do this, your study will draw you ever closer into the center of what God is saying in the text.

But once you are "done" *studying* the text, you are not done with the text. Ideally, you never study a passage merely to learn what it says. God wants us to know Scripture so that we can take what we learn from Him and pass it on to others. Studying the text should always lead to teaching the text. Let us close out this chapter with some suggestions on how to teach the text of Scripture to others.

TEACH THE TEXT

The four elements of Bible study described in this chapter do not provide you with a sermon or teaching that can be presented to others. Instead, following these four steps will only provide a basic structure and some building blocks upon which to build a teaching. You likely have little more than a rough outline of a passage and some biblical data about that passage. To transform this research into something that will be edifying and encouraging to others, you must sort through what you have learned and figure out which aspects and ideas are most interesting, most instructive, and most helpful to other people. Everything you select should support, explain, defend, or apply the single main idea of the passage. In general, you will likely be able to use less than half of what you learned about any one passage.

As you cut unnecessary material from your notes, ensure you remove anything that might make you sound smart or intelligent to your readers. It is not that you want to sound ignorant and uneducated, but pastors often try to include references to Greek and Hebrew words, or quotes from Karl Barth, Rudolf Bultmann, or Jeremy Myers (just kidding!) because such elements make them sound smart to the listening audience. The truth, however, is that you rarely need to use the actual Greek or Hebrew words in your sermon, and even more rarely do you need to read an extended quote from any theologian or biblical scholar. You can often convey the same point by summarizing your findings in your own words.

Once you have cut out all extraneous and unneeded material, you can then arrange what is left in a logical or interesting structure. It is usually best to simply follow the logical flow of the text. Do *not* try to fit what you have learned into the typical "three points and a poem" structure that is popular among so many pastors. Teach the text as it is presented in Scripture, not as preaching books suggest it should be presented. This is *your* sermon, not theirs. And don't worry too much about adding illustrations, stories, and application. Just do what comes naturally and normally to you. If you think of a good story or illustration for a point, add it. If not, don't stress about it.

In fact, when it comes to stories and illustrations, less is more. Modern preachers rely upon them far too heavily. I heard one famous preacher say that at least 50% of any sermon should be illustrations. There are usually two reasons given. First, some claim that people learn best through stories. Second, people often say, "Jesus told stories; and so should we." But both ideas are misleading when it comes to preaching and teaching the Word of God.

First, it is not true that people learn best through stories. Yes, their *attention* is best *held* through stories. Yes, people tend to remember stories more than they remember stated facts. Yes, stories are best suited for involving the emotions of people, which are undoubtedly helpful in the learning process. Yes, stories can be subversive in how they present ideas to people. But this doesn't mean people learn best through stories.

To the contrary, when it comes to directly imparting essential truths and ideas to other people, there is no better method than clearly and directly telling them what they need to know. If you want to teach people how to wash clothes or bake a cake, you do tell them a story; you give them step-by-step instructions, and maybe illustrate the steps by doing them yourself. The same thing applies when teaching others how to live the Christian life and follow Jesus on the path of discipleship. Stories are helpful, but they are not the primary way people learn such truths. The best, primary, and most effective way for people to actually learn what they need to *know* and *do* is through clear, straightforward, step-by-step, point-by-point communication.

I know this seems to contradict what I wrote earlier about the Bible being a story, but I am not contradicting myself. I previously stated that the Bible is a story and should be approached as a story. I said that we should not seek to cut it up, rearrange it, and make it more palatable to modern minds. I also said that stories truly do change people. I agree with everything I previously wrote.

But here in this section, I am not talking about the

Bible itself, but about *teaching* the Bible. There is a difference between reading the stories of Shakespeare and studying and explaining the stories of Shakespeare. There is a difference between reading and enjoying poetry, and seeking to analyze and understand what the poet is saying. In both cases, the teaching activity only tends to amplify the beauty and power of the story or poem. With greater understanding comes greater appreciation. If all we do is dissection and analysis, we end up killing the poetry, the play, or the story, but if we use the analysis and explanation to amplify our understanding of the text so that we can better enjoy the poem, play, or story, then we have studied the text successfully. It is the same with Scripture. The Bible is a story, and we study, analyze, and teach it to understand the demands it makes on our lives. There is a difference between recognizing that the Bible is a story and teaching people what the story of the Bible means. When we preach and teach the Bible, we explain the story of the Bible to people so they can learn how to live within the ongoing story that God has prepared for us.

But note that you would never seek to explain tricky sections of Shakespeare or the insightful twist of a phrase by John Donne through telling a story. You might use some illustrations or examples as a small part of a more logical and fuller explanation, but you would not think to explain such literary masterpieces with an overemphasis on stories. People do learn from stories, but they primarily learn through careful and logical presentations of facts and truths. So this is how we should present the truth of Scripture to them as well.

As for the parables of Jesus, He was quite clear that He told parables so that people *wouldn't* understand what He was saying (Luke 8:10). Therefore, the only time we should say, "Jesus told stories, and so should we," is if we want to confuse our hearers the way Jesus did. And why did Jesus tell confusing stories? There were numerous reasons, but chief among them was the fact that He wanted to invite people to follow Him, and telling confusing stories was a way to invite them in closer so that He might then transition to actually teaching them in a logical and orderly way. In other words, the parables of Jesus were not meant to inform and instruct others, but were instead ways to invite people to come to Him *so that* He might *then* inform and instruct them through careful and logical presentations of truth.

The point is this: Use illustrations and stories in your sermon as needed, but don't force them because of some misguided idea that you need stories to truly teach someone. You don't. And whatever you do, don't include a story to play with people's emotions or manipulate them into a desired response. Such use of stories only detracts from the powerful truths presented in a biblical sermon.

Once you have cut and organized your notes, and

added any stories, illustrations, and application you think are appropriate, it is time to write out what you want to say in your teaching or sermon. Many pastors and teachers believe that writing out, or manuscripting, a sermon is unnecessary, unimportant, or even unspiritual. But the exact opposite is true.

When you write out a sermon or teaching, it forces you to think through the logical flow of what you will be teaching. You are better able to see where the holes in your logic and explanations might be, and you will also be able to anticipate and address any possible objections. Furthermore, you will be able to develop proper transitions between sections of your sermon that are sometimes difficult to think up on the fly. At this stage, you can also add an appropriate introduction and conclusion, something that is thought-provoking or challenging, and which wraps your teaching together in a coherent way.[1]

Manuscripting also helps determine the length of your sermon. When people don't manuscript, they often think they have enough material for thirty minutes, only to discover five minutes into their sermon that they've come to the end of their notes, and have nothing left to say. Then they ramble pointlessly for the remaining time. The opposite can also happen, so that a teacher talks for thirty minutes, only to discover that they never

---

[1] Eventually I want to write a book about preaching the Bible. It will explain the importance of introductions and conclusions in greater detail.

progressed past the introduction. Manuscripting helps clear away all such problems. And don't worry, you will *not* be reading your manuscript. By the time you are ready to teach your sermon, you will barely need your manuscript at all.

As for it being "unspiritual" to write or type out what you plan to teach others, it is actually "unspiritual" *not* to properly plan and prepare. It is form of spiritual neglect for a pastor to come to the pulpit without having properly prepared a decent spiritual meal for those who have gathered to hear it. Just as God, through His Spirit, plans and prepares for all eventualities throughout all of human history, so also, it is a healthy spiritual practice to plan and prepare what we will teach to others. A pastor who steps up to the pulpit without proper preparation, thinking they will just "let the Spirit" provide something to say, is no better than the parent who refuses to shop or cook a meal for their children, thinking that they will magically pull something out of the empty cupboards at mealtime. God speaks more powerfully through a well-prepared spiritual steak dinner than through a lazy and haphazardly arranged "whatchyagot" stew. So study hard, prepare well, and write out your manuscript so that you can present your flock with a hearty meal that feeds their souls and informs their minds.

Once you have written out your sermon, it is best to let it marinate for a couple of days. If I am going to teach on Sundays, then I will try to have my sermon completed by Thursday so that I can take advantage of this "marinating" process. There is something about letting my sermon "gel" in my mind for a few days that allows me to present it with more passion and excitement than I might otherwise have done. It also gives me time to think through and meditate further upon the ideas I present in the sermon. Frequently, there will be a section or an illustration that doesn't sit quite right with my spirit. It is not that these sections are "wrong," but that there is just a feeling I have that I should pull this section out. I call these the "red flag" sections. As I think about what I will be teaching, little red flags pop up in my mind about specific sections, and I have learned over the years not to try to justify their inclusion, but to simply cut them out. Two or three days are required for this process to occur properly.

But don't wait more than a week between studying your text and teaching it. The best time to teach others is when the Word of God is a fire in your bones that you cannot hold in (Jer 20:9). You must preach your text when it is fresh in your mind, and when you are still excited about what you have learned. If you are overjoyed and overcome by what the Spirit has taught you in the text of Scripture, this excitement and passion will shine through your voice and body posture when you stand in front of others to teach the Word of God. If you wait too long, this fire will go out.

Within 24 hours of preaching, you should review your manuscript aloud at least three times, preferably with at least one other person who can offer critical feedback and make observations about what you are saying. Reviewing it out loud allows your ears to pick up on awkward parts of the sermon, and also helps you practice your rhythm and pacing. And since most people are faster at reading silently than when they read out loud, the practice of reading your sermon will also give you an idea of how long it will be. It is also just good practice. When you get in front of people to preach, you should be so familiar with your sermon you barely need to glance at manuscript. You will know your message forward and backward and will be able to present the truth of God's Word with clarity, conviction, and passion.

The very last step to teaching God's Word is taken the moment you step up in front of the people. Quietly, between yourself and God, in the time it takes to utter a silent sigh, ask God to bless the work you have done in seeking to understand Scripture, and pray for boldness and power to teach His Word in ways that will bless, encourage, instruct, edify, and even correct those who have gathered to hear from Him. My prayer is usually little more than this: "Father, I've done all I can. Give me boldness as I speak, for the rest is up to you." Then open your mouth, and teach the Word of God.

Teaching Scripture to other people is a solemn duty and must be approach with utmost care (Jas 3:1). However, it is also the greatest thrill and privilege that any spiritual leader can undertake. And in fact, many teachers report that they learn more from teaching a Bible passage than they ever learned from studying it without an intent to teach. The need to share truth with others drives our minds and spirits to glean more from the text than we ever would otherwise. So as you seek to study and understand what God teaches in Scripture, pray that God allows His Word to be accurately conveyed through your words, so that the people who hear will understand and obey.

DISCUSSION QUESTIONS

1. Why is it important to ask God to help you understand Scripture?

2. Even if you pray for God's help and the Spirit's illumination, does this guarantee that the results of your Bible study will be accurate? Why or why not?

3. What are some ways to gain a big-picture overview of the passage you are about to study? Why is this important?

4. When you are seeking to discover the big-picture over-view of a passage, what are the *only* books and resources you should allow yourself to read and consult?

5. Why is it helpful (though not required) to study books of the Bible starting with chapter 1, verse 1, rather than diving into the middle or end of the book to study a particular passage?

6. Reading and consulting commentaries is the *last* step you should take in studying a particular passage of Scripture. List some reasons why it is important to save this step for last.

7. Why is it important to teach others what you have learned from a passage of Scripture? How does this part of the process help you solidify what you have learned and apply Scripture to real life?

FIVE BEHAVIORS OF BIBLE STUDY

There is a story about a wealthy farmer who was one of the richest men in Africa. Hafid owned a large farm with fertile soil, herds of camels and goats, and orchards of dates and figs. One day he heard that some men around the country were rapidly becoming richer than him by discovering and mining diamonds.

Hafid, eager to increase his fortune, sold his farm, herds, and orchards. He placed his family in the care of someone else and set out to find his fortune. Hafid's travels took him all over Africa. Finally, in deep despair he threw himself off a mountain and died a frustrated, broken, and poor man.

The farmer who bought his farm was watering his camels one day and noticed a pretty rock in the river, because it sparkled. He took it home and put it on a shelf where the sun would strike it and splash rainbows of color across the room. One day, a holy man entered the house, saw the rock on the shelf, and exclaimed, "That's a diamond! Where did you find it?"

The farmer, somewhat confused by the flurry of excitement, explained that it came from down by the river. "Show me," insisted the holy man. The two of them went out to the river, and there, in the white sands, they found a larger diamond, then another, and many more diamonds, large and small. In fact, the land which Hafid sold to pursue his fortune elsewhere turned out to be acres and acres of diamonds. It became the Kimberly, the richest diamond mine in South Africa.

You are sitting on a diamond mine of the written Word of God. And God has provided it to you so that you can dig deep into its wonders and discover the greatest treasures of the universe. But the pages of Scripture are not immediately clear or accessible to all. Scripture study involves more than just putting a pretty verse on your wall. When digging into Scripture to see what gems it contains, there are five behaviors that you must maintain. These behaviors are ways of approaching Scripture that will allow you to glean from it what God wants you to learn. These behaviors are the mindsets or manners you must have as you delve into the divinely inspired Word. We begin with humility.

STUDY HUMBLY

Humility is the first attitude or behavior you must maintain in Bible study. Since you will never know everything about any particular text, every conclusion you draw from a text must be a tentative conclusion. Stay humble! Keep learning. Always be open to being proven wrong if someone presents compelling evidence and a better explanation for a particular text. Never consider your understanding of a text to be "settled." Rather, always be willing to reevaluate and reconsider previously studied passages in the light of new information. Hold the results of your study lightly, with an open hand, allowing the ideas and insights of others to change your mind as needed.

This requires great humility about the "conclusions" of your Bible study. In Bible study, recognize that there's no such thing as a final conclusion; there are only rest stops on your journey toward deeper understanding. Thinking about Bible study as a journey can be very helpful. If you think of studying the Bible like traveling all the roads of the world, then you know that just because you drove down a road and arrived at your temporary rest stop or city at the end of that road, this does not mean that you saw everything on that road or will not want to drive down it again sometime in the future to see more of the sights or to take one of the turns and seek a new destination.

Bible study is also like our lives. Just as none of us have

perfect lives, so also, none of us have perfect theology. But since nobody knows where they are wrong in their theology, you must maintain humility in everything you believe. Indeed, you can only discover where you are wrong by consulting the teachings, commentaries, and studies of people with whom you disagree. Only by reading the perspectives of others will you grow in your knowledge of the truth. If you only read books by people who share your perspective, you will never be challenged or stretched to see things differently.

And there is no danger in reading the views of others, for truth can withstand any challenge. If you are correct in your views, then by consulting the opinions of others you will only strengthen your beliefs. But you will only discover where you are wrong if you seek out the ideas of others to let them challenge you. But pride will never allow you to take such steps. Only humility grants the courage to accept being proven wrong. So read, study, and teach with conviction, but also hold your conclusions with a healthy dose of humility.

STUDY PRAYERFULLY

When you study Scripture, remember that you are reading and studying the written Word of God. Though the Bible can be read and studied like any other book, it is *not* just any other book. It is divine revelation. As such,

God Himself wants to speak to you through the text and teach you want you need to know. Therefore, study prayerfully, asking God to open the truths of Scripture to your heart and mind.

George Whitefield had a similar practice and wrote this in his journal:

> I began to read the Holy Scriptures upon my knees, laying aside all other books, and praying over, if possible, every line and word. This proved meat indeed and drink indeed to my soul. I daily received fresh life, light, and power from above.

The same thing will happen when you approach Scripture prayerfully.

The Holy Spirit is given for this purpose, among many others. The Spirit helped guide the writing of the text, the transcription of the text over time, its translation into various languages, the understanding of the text to our minds, and the application of the text to our lives. The Holy Spirit is *not* a substitute for proper Bible study, but instead works with our minds as we use good Bible study methods to understand the text and apply it to our lives (1 Cor 2:12-13).

It is helpful to begin your study with a quick and simple prayer for understanding. I like to use a quote from Scripture, such as "Speak Lord, for your servant is listening" (1 Sam 3:9-10, NIV) or a verse out of Psalm 119, such as "Open my eyes, that I may see wondrous things from your law" (Ps 119:18). The Bible is full of such prayers for understanding, wisdom, and spiritual enlightenment.

But do not stop with just a quick prayer at the beginning of your study. Study prayerfully all the way through. As you study Scripture, continually ask God to open the truths of Scripture to you. Listen for what the Spirit is saying to you from the text. Imagine yourself sitting at the feet of Jesus as He shows you how the Scriptures speak of Him. Ask God to lead you to the right resources, books, blogs, or podcasts that will help you understand the truth of Scripture. If you plan on teaching what you have learned to other people, pray for insight and understanding into the questions and issues they are facing so that God's Word can be helpful to them.

In my own Scripture study, I often remember the account of Jesus visiting the home of Mary and Martha, and how Mary sat at the feet of Jesus to listen to Him teach (Luke 10:38-42). As I sit down to study the written Word of God, I like to imagine that I am sitting down at the feet of Jesus, the living Word of God, who will then teach me what the Bible says. Or I imagine that I am one of the two disciples on the road to Emmaus who were privileged to walk with Jesus as He explained the Scriptures to them (Luke 24:13-35). So as I study the Bible, I prayerfully imagine myself in these sorts of situations, allowing Jesus to teach me from Scripture through His indwelling Holy Spirit. You can do this too, as you study Scripture prayerfully, letting God open His Word to your heart, mind, and soul (cf. Job 33:15-17).

For myself, I find it extremely helpful to engage in a literal conversation with Jesus as I read and study any text of Scripture. In my book, *What is Prayer?*, I suggest that prayer is nothing more (and nothing less!) than talking to God as you would talk to any other friend or loved one. I would like to expand on this, suggesting that prayer and prayerful Scripture study should not be a monologue with Jesus about the text, but a dialogue. When praying about the meaning and significance of a text, we must ask Jesus for help in understanding it, and then must leave room for Him to respond. In my experience, Jesus can and will show up to talk with you about Scripture.

These prayerful Bible studies with Jesus occur in the form of an inner dialogue, and my rational, theological mind often argues with me that I am just talking to myself. But I have come to believe that since Jesus is alive, since Jesus loves me, and Jesus wants to have a genuine relationship with me, this loving relationship includes conversing with me about life and Scripture. Furthermore, I know that my conversations with Jesus about the text cannot come from my own imagination alone, for Jesus often points out things from the text that I never would have considered, had never learned previously from anywhere else, and would never have seen on my own.

I encourage you to give it a try next time you study Scripture (or just need someone to talk to about life). Seek in Jesus in prayer, sharing your questions and needs with Him, and then stop talking and give Him room to respond. Jesus, through the indwelling Holy Spirit (John 16:14-15), will declare the truth of Scripture to you and will explain it to you as, like Mary, you sit at His feet and learn (Luke 10:38-42).

The danger with this practice, of course, is the assumption that if we hear something from Jesus, then the explanation given by Jesus is infallible. This can then lead to arrogance and heresy if what we *think* we heard from Jesus actually came from our own imagination instead. Care must be taken to constantly remind ourselves, therefore, that it is entirely possible to confuse our imagination with the voice of Jesus, just as it is possible to confuse an explanation of Scripture with Scripture itself. The safeguard is to remember that the authentic voice of Jesus, like any proper explanation of Scripture, will never contradict the written Word of God found in Scripture. Therefore, we can never abandon the careful and diligent study of Scripture.

STUDY DILIGENTLY

Along with studying the Bible humbly and prayerfully, it is critical to study the Bible diligently. It is no exaggeration to say that a properly performed study of Scripture is one of the most challenging tasks you will ever undertake. Studying the Bible demands immense discipline, effort, and patience, and causes significant fatigue to the mind and body. Those who regularly spend six to eight hours in the serious study of Scripture often find themselves emotionally, mentally, spiritually, and physically exhausted at the end of the day. Wrestling with the eternal principles of Scripture takes more stamina and discipline than nearly any other task.

Therefore, just like any other pursuit, engaging in serious Bible study is not something that you can just start doing. Like any skill, it takes consistent practice to keep your mind focused on Scripture and your nose to the tools of the trade. But if you are going to study Scripture, you must learn to toil and sweat over the words of the Bible, as you diligently develop the discipline of discovering the truths of God's Word. This means you cannot be sporadic in your study. Just as with working out the physical body, you should engage with Scripture daily.

One of the things that will help you remain consistent is having a set place and set time every day for reading and studying Scripture. Ruth Bell Graham once offered this advice:

It could be merely a piece of plywood stretched across two sawhorses. But have a special place for Bible study that doesn't have to be shared with sewing or letter writing or the paying of bills. For years, mine was just an old wooden table between an upright chest of drawers and a taller desk. This year I fixed myself a permanent office upstairs and my Bible study in the bedroom is now a big roll top desk I have had for years.

But on this desk I have collected a number of good translations of the Bible for reference, a Bible dictionary, a [fine-point pen that writes on thin Bible paper] without smearing or going through. When we were in school, we always kept a notebook handy to take notes of the professor's lecture. How much more important it is to take notes when God is teaching us.[1]

Don't neglect the Bible. Study it diligently and consistently. Just as Jacob wrestled with the angel of the Lord all night long, and did not let go until he received a blessing (Gen 32:22-32), so also, wrestle with Scripture, and do not let go until you are ready to shout with conviction and clarity, "Thus saith the Lord!"

STUDY COMMUNALLY

This fourth attitude of Bible study may be the one that is

[1] Ruth Bell Graham, "A Devotional." https://billygrahamlibrary.org/a-devotional-by-ruth-bell-graham/ Last Accessed February 1, 2019.

most often neglected in modern Western civilization. In our highly individualistic society, we pastors and theologians often retreat to our studies, surrounded by piles of books, emerging from our ivory tower only to deliver from a white pulpit what we have learned in private. But genuine Bible study is not best performed in such a fashion. We must, instead, spend some of our study time in a community of other people. Since all effective Bible study is for the purpose of instructing, encouraging, edifying, and even correcting other people, we must study Scripture with other people before we can hope to teach it to them.

In previous years, I used to say that I always studied Scripture with others … most of whom were dead. What I meant by this is that the community of saints with whom I studied are the dead pastors, theologians, scholars, and Bible teachers of bygone eras. I listened to their insights and thoughts about Scripture by reading their books. And this is true. When you read a commentary, you are engaging in Bible study with a scholar who has passed away, or who may live in some other part of the world. And there is value to this. But it is not the same as studying Scripture with a community of living people who are in the same room with you, from whom you can gain insights into Scripture you might have missed, and who can question or challenge some of the conclusions of your own private study.

Since Scripture is meant to be lived out in community with others, it must be studied in a living community as well. Scripture must be learned in community and lived out in community so that our community can grow and develop into a world-redeeming community. I believe this is partly what Peter is talking about when, in 2 Peter 1:20-21, he wrote that "no prophecy of Scripture is of any private interpretation." Though this passage also relates to the writing of Scripture under the inspiration of the Holy Spirit, Peter is also referring to the interpretation and explanation of Scripture. Some believe this verse refers to the "exposition" of Scripture, meaning preaching.

> No prophecy should be expounded according to private opinion. ... *idias* [one's own] refers to the expositor, not the *propheteia*.[2]

> As the prophecies do not owe their origin to the resolve of man, so their exposition is not left to human caprice. There can be true interpretation only through God Himself or through the Holy Spirit.[3]

Peter is saying that while God does speak to us through Scripture, He speaks to us in the context of community. We are to study, learn, and think about Scripture with others. Yes, we can study Scripture on our own, but

[2] Kittel, ed. *TDNT,* IV:337.

[3] Ibid., VI:833.

whatever we think we learn must be measured against what others have learned and taught as well, and must be lived out and practiced in a community.

Since the Holy Spirit primarily works in the community of believers, the Spirit often illuminates Scripture in communal study in ways that wouldn't occur in private. There are a variety of ways this can happen. Some pastors have a preaching team that helps the pastor plan, study, and prepare the sermons. Others use online forums and blogs to get feedback and questions from others. Still others request input and advice from family members or spouses, who are usually very good at pointing out the hypocrisies and errors that might be in the explanation of the text.

It might also be a good idea to include some non-Christians in your Bible study community. One of the most rewarding Bible studies I have ever been a part of was one in which I was the only Christian. The rest of the group included a diversity of peopleL an Atheist, a Muslim, a Rastafarian, and a Jew. We studied and discussed the Gospel of John together. The insights they had on the text and the questions they asked of the text were refreshing and illuminating to me in a way no other Bible study had ever been before. Listening to their feedback on the text helped me better address their needs, issues, and questions. It also helped me understand what the text communicates to non-Christians, as well as how the Holy

Spirit was actively drawing them to Jesus through it.

So include people in your Bible study. Include Christians and non-Christians, dead and alive, near and far. Studying the Bible in community is something to be pursued and practiced, not only for yourself, but for your hearers as well.

STUDY OBEDIENTLY

The final behavior of Bible study is to study obediently. We cannot teach others what to be and do until and unless we have incorporated the truth of Scripture into our own lives first. This is not only to avoid being hypocritical, but also so that we can advance to further truths and deeper insights into Scripture. Though many understand the importance of obeying Scripture, few recognize that obeying Scripture *is a means* to understanding Scripture. I am convinced that obedience to previously learned truths is one of the prerequisites for receiving more truths from God about Scripture. God will not reveal more of His will and His Word to you unless you have been obedient to what you have already learned.

This, I believe, is what Jesus is teaching in passages like Matthew 13:12, Mark 4:25, and Luke 6:38. When Jesus talks about giving to others what we have been given so that we can be given even more, He is not talking about money or wealth, but about the riches of the truths of Scripture. If we want to gain more insight and understanding into what God has said in Scripture, then we need to be responsible with what we have already been given, by obeying it and teaching it to others. Only by obeying what we've been taught will we receive further teaching.

If the Word of God is "living and active" (Heb 4:12), it must be lived and acted, which begins when we study. Until we live out and act on what we have learned, we have not truly learned. Scripture, when it is fully understood, will call us to obey. And only when we obey will we finally learn the truth of Scripture. There is no such thing as theoretical theology, for it is all practical and demands a response.

CONCLUSION

Do not let your Bible collect dust on the shelf or sit neglected in a drawer. Take it off the shelf and study the words within, for it is a gem of inestimable worth. On its pages are found the very ideas and thoughts of God. As such, it must be approached humbly, prayerfully, diligently, communally, and obediently, giving it the respect it deserves. But don't neglect Bible study because it is difficult, for reading and studying the Bible is one of the most valuable pursuits a person can undertake. After all, the Bible holds the riches of God's truth, which transforms lives and redeems the world. This is the truth we learn in the final chapter.

DISCUSSION QUESTIONS

1. Why is pride such a danger when studying and understanding Scripture? What sorts of things can be done to ward ourselves from pride when studying the Bible?

2. Some challenge the idea that the Holy Spirit helps us understand Scripture. They say this because some teachers use the Holy Spirit as the "trump card" to resolve disagreements about Scripture. (e.g., "I'm right because the Holy Spirit taught me!") How can we study prayerfully (with the illuminating help of the Holy Spirit) while avoiding this trap?

3. "Much study wearies the body" (Eccl 12:12). If you have ever spent extended periods of time studying Scripture, describe how you feel at the end of the day or the end of the week. What are some tips and strategies for allowing your mind and body to study Scripture for longer periods of time?

4. Why do you think so many pastors and teachers avoid and neglect the communal aspect of Bible study? What are some possible ways you can add community to your

study?

5. We often quote the cliché, "Practice what you preach." But there is truth to it. How can you ensure you obey what you learn from Scripture before moving on to study a new section?

6. Of the five behaviors discussed in this chapter, which one will be most important for you to implement? Which one will be most difficult? Why?

CHAPTER 6

THE ONE GOAL OF BIBLE STUDY

Before you set out to study the Bible, you need to know *why* you are studying the Bible. You need to know the goal of Bible study. The goal of Bible study may not be what you expect. The goal of Bible study is not merely to learn about the Bible or accumulate scriptural knowledge. In 1 Corinthians 13, Paul's famous love chapter, he writes that even if he were to gain all knowledge, but lacks love, it amounts to nothing. The same is true for you and Bible study. If you can recite the Bible forward and backward, can argue theology with the best theologians in the world, can read (and understand) Karl Barth, and can debate about infra-, supra-, and sub-lapsarianism, but have not love, then you have nothing. Studying the Bible is wonderful, and gaining knowledge of the Scriptures is a worthy endeavor, but if you seek knowledge solely for its own sake, it would be better not to have studied the Bible at all. Winning at Bible trivia is not the goal of Bible study.

So what is the goal? The goal of Bible study is not the accumulation of knowledge, but the actualization of the kingdom. The goal of Bible study is to transform lives, culture, and the world to reflect Jesus' likeness and the kingdom of God. In a word, the goal of Bible study is love. The following chapter will unpack this idea in two ways. First, it will show why simply learning what the Bible says is not enough. Increasing biblical literacy among Christians is not a worthy goal. Instead, the goal of all Bible study is something I call "Incarnational Redemption," which is a fancy way of saying that we practice the Scriptures in our lives so that we can transform the world through loving presence.

Let us begin with the truth that biblical literacy is not the goal of Bible study.

BIBLICAL LITERACY IS NOT THE GOAL

As I have attempted to make clear in this book, I love to study the Bible. I study Scripture for hours nearly every day. I study Scripture for pure enjoyment, but I also study it for my books, for my teaching and preaching, and for my podcast and website. I study the Bible because I enjoy it, it helps with my job, and it is one way I practice my spiritual gifts.

But not everybody needs to study the Bible as much as I do. Most do not. And this is completely fine. In fact, most Christians already know enough about the Bible. Most Christians do not need to study the Bible further. What they already know is sufficient for a lifetime. This may be a shocking idea, but it's true. Most Christians don't need more Bible knowledge; they need to put into practice the Bible knowledge they already have.

You will sometimes hear pastors bemoan the fact that most Christians are biblically illiterate. They will point to studies and statistics which reveal that the majority of Christians are ignorant of many basic Bible stories, rarely read their Bibles, and cannot find verses in the Bible without using a Table of Contents or the Bible index tabs. Pastors see this biblical illiteracy as the primary reason for the poor state of modern Christianity.

I do not deny that most Christians are biblically illiterate. What I do deny, however, is that increasing the biblical literacy of the average Christian is going to solve the problems that face the church today.[1] The issue isn't a lack of biblical literacy but a lack of biblical living and loving. And to be honest, you don't need to know much about the Bible to live and love like Jesus.

In fact, the opposite is often true. It usually seems that those who know the most about the Bible live it the least. There is frequently a noticeable lack of love among self-

---

[1] I once wrote an article titled "15 Reasons Biblical Illiteracy is NOT a Problem in the Church." You can read it here: https://redeeminggod.com/15-reasons-biblical-illiteracy-is-not-a-problem-in-the-church/

proclaimed "Bible experts," such as pastors, professors, and Ph.D. authors. It sometimes seems there's an inverse relationship between biblical literacy and love, so that as Bible knowledge goes up, the practice of love goes down. Greater Bible knowledge doesn't always foster love but can sometimes lead to hate, judgmentalism, pride, and hypocrisy.

Some people hesitate to serve others, fearing they don't know enough, or won't be able to answer questions when they arise. As a result of this fear, they keep their noses in their Bible and their bodies in the pew, rather than getting out into the lives of people in their community. One reason some pastors, professors, and Ph.D. authors promote this behavior is that their livelihoods depend on it. Church leaders need people to show up on Sunday, listen to their teachings, and buy their books, and so they tell people that biblical illiteracy is the most significant problem facing the church today.

But it isn't.

The reality is that with Bible knowledge, you'll never feel you know enough. Bible knowledge is like an addiction: you always need just one more hit. It is also like wealth: "How much is enough? Just a bit more than I have now." So don't wait until you "know enough" before you step out and put into practice what you already know. If that is what you are waiting for, you will never get around to loving and serving others. It is better for people to take what little they do know and start living it than to neglect the practice of what they know because they feel like they need to know more. You will always need to know more, so you might as well start practicing what you do know.

Bible knowledge, therefore, is like Brylcreem: "A little dab'll do ya." Most Christians know enough about Jesus to live like Him. And so if Jesus is inviting us to put down our Bibles so we can follow Him into the world, who are we to disagree? In our day, God is leading people away from pews and Bible studies, and out into the real world where we can love, and serve, and laugh, and cry with the people who are out here.

Should we know and study the Bible? Yes, of course. But knowing the Bible is never the goal of Bible study. Most of us don't need to know more about the Bible; we need to love more in accordance with the Bible. The true sign of a disciple is not that we can quote hundreds of Bible verses and win at Bible trivia, but that we will be known by our love for one another (John 13:35). If our reading, studying, and teaching of Scripture is not leading us to look, act, and love more like Jesus, then we are not properly understanding or reading the Scriptures and should probably just put them away for a while until we learn to love others more like Jesus.

My friend LeRoy is literally illiterate. He is in his late seventies and never learned to read. Furthermore, because his wife has a certain illness, he has not attended church since he was six years old. He hasn't been to church in seventy years. Because his wife is highly sensitive to noise, he cannot listen to Christian radio. So he cannot read his Bible, cannot attend church, and cannot listen to sermons or preaching on the radio. In our many conversations, I've learned that he knows only what he recalls from Sunday school as a child. He remembers the basic story about Jesus. That's it.

But LeRoy is one of the most kind-hearted, loving people I have ever met. Is he biblically illiterate? Of course! No matter which definition you use, he knows next to nothing about the Bible. But he loves others like Jesus, and when I talk to him, I see Jesus. He has hardly any money, but he cuts and delivers firewood for free to others who need it. He hands out pears from his pear tree to people who are hungry. He has faithfully remained in a challenging marriage for over fifty years. But he doesn't read the Bible. He doesn't gain Bible facts and Bible knowledge. He can't recite the 66 books of the Bible. Nor can he list the Ten Commandments or name the Twelve Apostles. He knows what he learned about Jesus in kindergarten, and that has sufficed for the seventy years since.

The complete opposite of LeRoy is the Bible experts in our own day, as well as those in the days of Jesus. The most biblically literate people in the days of Jesus were the Pharisees and Sadducees. Yet Jesus repeatedly tells them in the Gospels that even though they are Bible experts, they know nothing about God, loving others, obeying the law, or the true meaning of the Scriptures themselves. He says, "You search the Scriptures daily, because in them you think you have eternal life, but these Scriptures speak of me" (John 5:39). It is as if Jesus is telling them (and us) to put down their Bibles and stop studying Scripture so that they can follow Him into a life of loving others. Few of them listened. Will you?

LIVING LOVE IS THE GOAL

It is one thing to say that living love is the goal of Bible study; it is quite another to understand what this love looks like. After all, despite the fact that non-Christians often say that most Christians lack love, no Christian thinks they are unloving toward others. Even the harshest Christians believe they're showing love when they confront others with Bible verses and threaten them with eternal torment in hell. "If someone is walking off a cliff," they say, "it is more loving to warn them than to keep silent and let them fall."

This sounds legitimate, but is it true? Is it loving? What does true love look like for the Christian who seeks to obey Scripture and follow Jesus into the world? For me, the phrase "Incarnational Redemption" is the best way to define the love that Jesus wants from those who are His disciples. A less theological way of saying this is that we actually live and act like Jesus. But again, since all Christians think they act like Jesus, it is important to try to define what this looks like. The phrase "Incarnational Redemption" seeks to do just this.

Jesus was the incarnation of God. He embodied the nature, character, and attributes of God. He was God in the flesh, in human form. Through His words and actions, Jesus showed us exactly what God was like. Jesus said, "If you've seen Me, you've seen the Father" (John 14:9). The goal of the incarnation was redemption. Jesus sought not only to redeem humanity from sin, death, and the devil but also to transform how humanity views God. By revealing God to us, Jesus sought to correct and redeem all of our false ideas about God, ourselves, and what is happening in human history.

Scripture is provided to us so that we can both see how Jesus did this, and also so we can learn how to do similar things in our own lives. We, too, can be incarnational. We are the physical Body of Christ on earth. The church is the hands, feet, and voice of Jesus on earth. Just as Jesus was God in the flesh, so also, the church is Jesus in the flesh. Just as Jesus revealed God's nature, the church, by embodying Jesus, shows the world what God is like.

The goal of such incarnational living is that we redeem and reconcile all things to God through Jesus

Christ (Col 1:20). And "all things" doesn't just mean "all humans." It also includes cultures, traditions, locations, holidays, memories, and historical events. Yes, even these things can be redeemed. Scripture reveals that nothing and nobody is beyond the scope of redemption. And while not everything will be redeemed, everything is redeemable.

Such redemption is not automatic. God accomplishes redemption through incarnation. Not just the incarnation of Jesus, but the incarnation of Himself into all things. God takes a person, place, culture, nation, practice, or event and infuses it with His presence. When this happens, beautiful new creations emerge. The original element—whether a person, place, culture, nation, practice, or event— does not cease to exist, but is transformed into something entirely new.

This is what Paul talks about in Ephesians 2, where the Jews and Gentiles, who were formerly at enmity with each other, have now been redeemed and brought together into one body, the church. In so doing, Jews and Gentiles do not lose their identity, culture, traditions, and customs. Instead, all such things, along with the people themselves, are renewed, reformed, reconciled, and redeemed through the indwelling power of the Holy Spirit and the direction of Jesus Christ.

Scripture is given to us to show how this redemption has taken place in other times, in other cultures, and with

other people. Genesis 1–2 shows how mythological creation stories from Babylon and Egypt were redeemed to
present the Hebrew people with a brand new vision of
God. The story of Abraham shows how an idol-worship-
ping pagan was redeemed by God to become the forefa-
ther of a nation. The stories of Isaac, Jacob, Joseph, the
Judges, David, Solomon, Ruth, and Esther all show how
God takes the mess of human lives and civilization and
redeems them for His own good purposes and goals.

The Gospels show how Jesus accomplished this with
the apostles, not only with the people themselves, but
with many of the Jewish customs, teachings, and holidays. Jesus changed and transformed the meaning and
significance of many of the Jewish traditions so that they
became more loving toward others, and so that they
pointed the minds and hearts of people toward Himself.
So when Jesus says at the Last Supper, "do this in remembrance of Me" (Luke 22:19), He was not primarily referring to the meal *itself*, but to *what Jesus did* with the Last
Supper.[2] And what did He do? He redeemed it. He took
an important Jewish tradition, the celebration of

---

[2] It is so tragic that in the ancient debate about how to practice
the Lord's Supper, we have missed the entire meaning. It is not about
the words we say, or what happens (or doesn't happen) to the bread
and wine. When Jesus said, "Do *this* in remembrance of me," He
wasn't talking about the meal, but rather the *redemption* of the meal.
He was saying, "See how I have taken this central Jewish tradition and
pointed it to me? Now go do that with other human traditions. Find
them, practice them, and point them to Me."

Passover, and incarnated Himself into it, so that whenever and wherever His Jewish followers practiced Passover, the meal would now point to Jesus and remind them about Jesus.

And then Jesus sent them out to do similar things for others. This does not mean that the apostles were sent out to copy exactly what Jesus said and did. No. Instead, they were to follow His example of living within (incarnation) the human traditions, cultures, customs, and holidays of the people they visited, and then finding ways to redeem these things so that they no longer pointed to violence and pagan teachings, but rather to Jesus Christ Himself. The Book of Acts shows how the Apostles began to accomplish this incarnational redemption through their own lives and ministries. They did not force everyone to become Jews and follow Jewish traditions, but instead allowed their incarnational presence to help redeem the people, places, traditions, holidays, and practices of the people they encountered. They reincarnated the incarnation so that redemption could occur.

> They handled the traditions about [Jesus] with creative but responsible freedom, retaining those traditions while at the same time adapting them. If we take the incarnation seriously, the Word has to become flesh in every new

context.[3]

> We can neither apply Jesus' words and ministry on a one-to-one basis to a fundamentally different world nor just deduce 'principles' from his ministry. Rather ... we are challenged to let Jesus inspire us to prolong the logic of his own ministry in an imaginative and creative way amid changed historical conditions.[4]

As we seek to follow the story of Scripture and find our way within the flow of redemptive revelation, we can be doing similar things in our own time. We must discern our role in the story of incarnational redemption that is unfolding all around us. Rather than attempt to replicate the redemptive actions recorded in Scripture, we must seek creative redemption of our own lives, times, and cultures through new and unique incarnational activities today. Scripture helps us accomplish this by revealing what has been done in the past.

God does not intend for us, 2000 years later, two continents away, with numerous cultural differences, to duplicate the life and ministry of Jesus, or the life and ministry of the apostles and early church. No one can be Jesus. Only Jesus can be Jesus. Jesus was the Christ and did what He did as Christ. Similarly, no one can be Paul, or Peter, or John, nor should we try. To "be like Christ,"

---

[3] David Bosch, *Transforming Mission: Paradigm Shifts in Theology of Mission* (Maryknoll, NY: Orbis, 1991), 21.

[4] Ibid., 34.

therefore, or to "imitate the early church," means to do what they did. And what was that? They lived and acted as themselves! Jesus was effective because He lived up to what God wanted Him to do. The early church was effective because they followed what God wanted them to do. Today also, we will be effective for the gospel only when we do what God has called and gifted us to do. Trying to duplicate the ministry of Jesus Christ or the early church—aside from being an impossible exercise in futility—is nothing more than abandoning our calling.

We are given the teachings and stories in the Bible as *examples* of how others lived and where they succeeded and failed, not so that we can copy them, but so that we can learn from them and then make our own informed choices today for how we should live our own lives in our own cultures (1 Cor 10:11). We must look at what the people in the Bible did, asking ourselves why and how they acted this way, and then follow similar (but different) routes for being Jesus in our time and our culture. This requires Spirit-inspired creativity and intuition.

We are to lovingly incarnate Jesus in fresh ways today, becoming familiar with the times, traditions, customs, and culture of our own day, so that we can creatively seek redemption of such human practices. In so doing, they will no longer pull people away from God toward sin and death, but will instead point people toward Jesus and what He is doing in our midst today.

The cross of Jesus is the perfect example of how this is done. The cross used to be a symbol of oppression, death, torture, and violence. It was the means by which the Roman Empire dehumanized its foes and defused rebellions. By crucifying the leaders of their enemies, the Romans exerted their dominance and reminded all people who saw the crucified victims to surrender and obey. But Jesus, by giving Himself up to death, and specifically death on a cross, and then triumphing over it through the resurrection, redeemed the symbol of the cross. Today, people display the cross on buildings and wear it on gold chains around their necks. Today, it symbolizes victory over darkness and life over death. Today, the cross symbolizes the exact opposite of what it used to symbolize. Jesus has redeemed the horrible and ghastly symbol of the cross.

The holiday of Christmas is another example. Most people today do not realize that Christmas originated as the pagan holiday of Saturnalia. But the early church, seeking to follow what Jesus taught about redemption, and noticing how popular Saturnalia was with the people, set about to redeem this holiday and point it to Jesus. Today, few know or remember that Christmas has pagan origins. Most, even non-Christians, view Christmas as a holiday with Christian roots. But this is because it has been redeemed, which means that Christians can and should celebrate Christmas, for it shows that we serve a redeeming God.[5] Such redemption can occur with every person, place, holiday, event, and thing in this world.

The goal of Scripture, therefore, is to show us how to lovingly accomplish incarnational redemption. Too often, Christians use Scripture to condemn cultural elements that God wants us to redeem. We consign people to hell whom He loves and forgives. We picket places Jesus wants to enter. We boycott businesses and institutions when Jesus wants to transform them for kingdom work. The goal of Scripture study is to teach us to look at sinful places, people, events, holidays, traditions, and customs in our culture, not so that we can condemn them, but so that we can see the potential in them and what they can become through incarnational redemption.

We can neither bring Scripture straight over from what we read in the text (as in some churches that try to "get back to the New Testament church" or others that try to follow all the commands of Scripture without regard for context), nor find the objective truth kernels within the text to bring over into our own culture and context. Instead, we read to see how they solved their dilemmas and lived for God in their context, then use similar strategies today. I believe that historical and cultural background studies are most beneficial in this area, and so that will always be my primary focus. If the text is a

---

[5] For more on this topic, see my book, *Christmas Redemption* (Dallas, OR: Redeeming Press, 2012).

record of God redeeming the elements and people of a particular culture, we must understand the culture itself before we can understand how God redeems the people, events, and places of that culture, and how He is redeeming people and cultures today as well.

> The Bible ... is designed to function through human beings, through the church, through people who, living still by the Spirit, have their life molded by this Spirit-inspired book. ... God sends the church into the world ... to be and do for the world what he did for Israel.[6]

If you want to follow the teachings of Scripture, look into your neighborhood, town, city, and country and find the places, people, and events that most seem to detract from the glory of God and are most reliably drawing people away from Jesus. Then, through the inspiring creativity of the Holy Spirit and what you have learned from Scripture, seek to enter into these places and events so that you can redeem and transform them into something that brings glory to God and points people to Jesus Christ.

This is the loving goal of Scripture study. Scripture teaches us to love all that is in the world, not only the people but everything else as well. We can love the traditions, histories, cultures, and customs of people, as well as every place and structure. It is all a strange mixture of

---

[6] Wright, "How Can the Bible Be Authoritative? ": 12.

beauty and depravity. And so we love these things by entering into them to rescue and redeem them from the inside out, just as Jesus showed us.

The goal of all Scripture study, therefore, is the loving, incarnational redemption of all that is in this world. We study Scripture to learn how this redemption has occurred in the past so that we can find our own way in bringing about similar re-creations of redemption in our own time and culture as well. When we love in this way, the people, places, and events we love only grow in beauty and splendor, pointing all people to the glory and majesty of Jesus Christ.

So take up your Bible and read. Study and learn. Teach and obey. Only in this way can you change yourself and change the world.

DISCUSSION QUESTIONS

1. Have you heard a pastor claim that the biggest problem in the church today is a lack of biblical literacy? Perhaps they have quoted Hosea 4:6, "My people are destroyed for lack of knowledge." Why do pastors say this?

2. How much biblical literacy is "enough"? Must every Christian be a Bible expert? How much of the Bible should a person learn before they can begin obeying what they have learned?

3. Jesus was the incarnation of God. He was God in the flesh. How can the church be the incarnation of Jesus?

4. What do you think of the idea that everything on earth is redeemable? How is this different than saying that everything will be redeemed?

5. How do redemption and incarnation work together? In other words, how can we live as the incarnation of Jesus to work toward the redemption of all things?

6. Think of the worst person, place, and event in your town or city. Do you think these can be redeemed so that they no longer belong to the kingdom of darkness, but are brought into the kingdom of Jesus Christ? If so, try to creatively imagine how you can be the hands, feet, voice, or presence of Jesus to this person, in this place, or at this event to bring about this redemption.

CHAPTER 7

THE LAST STORY

This is the end of the book. Or maybe it is just the beginning. But that is precisely the point of all genuine Bible study. No study of Scripture ever ends. It is always only the beginning. You never arrive at the end of Scripture study but are always stepping out into the grand adventure of discovery into the deep mysteries of God's truth that He has made available for even the simplest mind to grasp.

Indeed, as we come to the end of Bible study and discover that it is just the beginning, we also discover that the end of Bible study is the beginning of a story. It is the first and last story. A story with no beginning and no end. A story in which you star as a seemingly insignificant character of infinite importance. It is a story of adventure, romance, and danger unlike any ever told. Your story is already a best-seller, yet it has not yet been published.

The Bible, which is not your script, contains the accounts of those who have traveled this road before. It tells some of their trials and tribulations, as well as their triumphs. It shows you some of what you can expect to encounter in your adventures. But don't follow in the steps of your fellow adventurers too closely; your path is your own. Also, the conclusion of your story will be unlike any ever told. It will be far, far better than anything you can ask or imagine.

In the end, which will be just the beginning, you will discover that all the bits and details of Bible study didn't matter at all. All that matters is the story. The secret truth about Bible study is that if you are able to grasp the story of Scripture and your role in that story, then there is no real need for Bible study. Just as analyzing Shakespeare can shed additional light on the characters and genius of Shakespearean plays while at the same time destroying the stories of Shakespeare, we Christians too often diminish Scripture's story by overanalyzing it. By analyzing the text, we kill the text. We study the Bible to death—its death and ours.

I do not want you to kill the text, to dissect it unto death. So although a "system" or "framework" has been presented in this book, I want to note in conclusion that there is no substitute for creativity and imagination. Make sure that when you seek life from the text, you keep life in the text. The following quote, though it originally applied to the process of dream interpretation, guides the process of Bible study as well:

> The interpretation of dreams and symbols [or the

understanding of Scripture] demands intelligence. It cannot be turned into a mechanical system and then crammed into unimaginative brains. ... No experienced worker in this field will deny that there are rules of thumb that can prove helpful, but they must be applied with prudence and intelligence. One may follow all the right rules and yet get bogged down in the most appalling nonsense, simply by overlooking a seemingly unimportant detail that a better intelligence would not have missed. Even a man of high intellect can go badly astray for lack of intuition or feeling.[1]

So toward that end, I want to conclude this book with imagery and poetry, intuition and feeling. Never stop feeling the awe within the text. The profound wonder of what Jesus did to rescue us from ourselves. Below are two versions of the story of Scripture. This is the first story, the last story, the only story. It is the story that must never be forgotten.

This is your story. And it is epic.

Before time wove its tapestry, God existed—eternal, unchanging, a boundless wellspring of love. This love, pulsing within the divine heart, yearned to spill beyond itself, to embrace something new. And so, from the void, God spoke, and creation unfurled like a scroll: galaxies spun, seas sang, and humanity stood upright, crowned with the gift of freedom.

[1] Carl Jung, "Approaching the Unconscious," in *Man and His Symbols* (London: Aldus, 1964), 92.

For love, to be true, must be freely given, and God desired a world that could choose to love in return.

But freedom, like a wild river, can carve treacherous paths. Humanity, enchanted by its own power, strayed from love's warmth. We built walls of pride, thinking they would shield us, but they became a prison, locking us in with shadows of our own making. We forgot the melody of love, lost in the clamor of our self-crafted chains.

Yet God's love did not waver. Through ages, God called out to us, a steadfast voice in the wilderness. Through chosen souls and nations, God wove a story of devotion, painting miracles across deserts, etching laws on mountain stone, and sending prophets, priests, and kings to bear the message of an unbreakable bond. Poetry and tales of old carried whispers of this eternal love, a beacon for a world adrift.

Still, we turned away, deaf to the call, convinced our walls were wisdom. So, in a daring act of grace, God stepped into our story as a man—Jesus, the embodiment of divine love. He walked among us, His life a mirror reflecting God's heart and humanity's potential. He showed us the prison we'd built, its cold bars forged from our loveless choices, and revealed the monsters we'd unleashed within.

Jesus, the Rescuer, slipped into our shadowed cell, bearing the key to freedom. But we, clinging to our familiar chains, rejected the rescue. We seized him, nailed Him to a cross, and declared our prison home. "These walls are ours," we cried, "cold but comforting." And so we killed Him. His mission, it seemed, had failed.

Yet God's love defies defeat. The grave could not hold Jesus; God raised him, a radiant victor, to heaven's throne. Many thought the tale ended there, a fleeting spark snuffed out. But it was only the dawn of a greater story. His death, a sacrifice of love, cracked open hearts. Some began to see— eyes wide with wonder—questioning why God would brave our darkness. Could there be truth in Jesus' words? Could life, love, and freedom await beyond the walls?

A few daring souls climbed the ramparts, peering over to glimpse a world ablaze with beauty—fields of endless light, horizons humming with promise. Others wandered the prison's corridors, finding the gates flung wide, and stood awestruck at the vista beyond. Yet, they did not flee to those vibrant hills. They lingered, bound by a single name: Jesus.

Those who saw the truth became torchbearers, choosing to stay within the gray walls to guide others out. "As long as one remains captive," they vowed, "we will remain." They plead, they serve, they teach, their lives a living echo of Jesus' love. Some fall, like him, their blood mingling with the earth, but even death is not the end. This story, ever unfolding, whispers eternally, "To Be Continued…"

And now, a more artistic version for those who long to hear the music beyond the walls:

In the beginningless dawn,
where eternity whispers its name,

God abides—pure, boundless Love,
a trinity of hearts entwined in divine dance.
Yet Love, in its aching fullness, yearns to overflow,
to kiss the void with creation's breath.
From the canvas of nothingness, God paints the cosmos:
stars as lovers' eyes, earth a cradle of dreams,
And humanity, crowned with freedom's fragile flame,
invited to mirror Love's eternal embrace.

But oh, the shadow falls—freedom's gift twisted
into chains of self-woven despair.
We, the beloved, wander lost in fog-shrouded gardens,
forgetting the warmth of the first light,
Building towers of illusion, walls of stone-cold pride,
where thorns of envy choke the blooming rose.
Our hearts, once rivers of joy, harden to arid deserts,
echoing with the hollow cry of isolation.
Yet Love remembers, unyielding as the tide—
God woos the wayward soul through veils of time.

Through chosen vessels, like vessels of clay kissed by fire,
God scatters seeds of redemption:
Miracles blooming as desert flowers after rain,
laws carved on thunderous peaks like promises etched
in stone.
Prophets' voices rise as wild winds,
priests' incense curls heavenward in silent pleas,
Kings wield scepters shadowed by divine grace,
while psalms weave tapestries of longing and lament.
Stories unfold like ancient scrolls,
poetry drips as honey from the comb—
declarations of a Love that weeps for the estranged.

Still, we turn away, eyes veiled by the glitter
of our own forged idols,
Whispering, "We know the paths of our own making,"
blind to the abyss yawning beneath.
So Love descends, veiled in flesh—a man named Jesus,
the Word made heartbeat, the Light in human form.
He walks our dust-strewn roads, healing the fractured,
feeding the famished souls with bread of truth,
Revealing God's tender gaze in every glance,
and humanity's hidden glory,
a spark divine within the clay.

He unveils our prison:
not bars of iron, but fortresses of fear,
labyrinths of lies we ourselves have raised.
Walls meant for shelter become tombs of the spirit,
where inner demons prowl in the dim, devouring hope.
We huddle in shadows, clutching keys we dare not use,
prisoners of our own shadowed throne.
But Love, undaunted, storms the gates—
Jesus, the daring intruder,
slips into our night with arms outstretched,
A rescuer bearing the lantern of liberty,
calling us from chains to the wild, waiting dawn.

Alas, we recoil in terror, seizing the Savior in claws of
betrayal, nailing Love to a cross of our crafting.
"We cherish our captivity!" we cry,
as blood stains the earth like tears from heaven's eye.
The rescue falters in the roar of rejection;
the Light extinguishes in the grave's cold embrace.
Yet death's grip shatters—God, in triumphant surge,
awakens Jesus from slumber's abyss,

Ascending Him to glory's throne,
a beacon piercing the veil between worlds.

And in that resurrection's echo, a miracle stirs:
the slain Rescuer's cry awakens slumbering hearts.
Eyes flutter open to wonder,
imaginations ignite like stars in the velvet sky.
"Why this risk, this plunge into our peril?"
they ponder, hearts swelling with awe.
Perhaps beyond these grim bastions lies
a realm of radiant meadows, rivers of living joy,
Where love flows unchecked, liberty dances on winds of
grace—more than fable, a fierce, living truth.

Brave wanderers scale the parapets,
peering into infinity's embrace;
others trace forgotten halls to gates flung wide.
Gasps escape at the vision: horizons alive with color,
symphonies of souls in harmonious flight.
Yet they linger, feet rooted in the gray expanse,
voices weaving tales of the splendor unseen.
"Why tarry in twilight?" the unseeing inquire,
brows furrowed in confusion's fog.
The reply, a sacred whisper: "Jesus."
He who unveiled the divine, unlocked the captives'
chains.

Those illumined by His truth—torchbearers now—
choose the prison's chill to kindle fires for the lost.
"As long as one soul lingers in shadows," they vow,
"we abide, mirrors of His sacrificial flame."
They plead with passion's poetry,
serve with hands scarred by empathy,
teach with wisdom's gentle glow,

And through every act, Love pulses—
eternal, fierce, a river carving canyons in stone hearts.
Some fall, like Him, to the blade of indifference,
yet even in death, their story spirals onward,
A tapestry unfinished,
threads of hope weaving into the infinite:
"To Be Continued ..." in the symphony of forever.

Go. Play your part in this eternal story. The universe waits with bated breath.

APPENDIX I:
TEN THINGS TO STOP SAYING ABOUT BIBLE STUDY

As I teach and write about studying the Bible, I often encounter some strange ideas about Scripture. Sometimes these ideas come from people who haven't carefully considered their statements, but other times these statements are made by pastors and theologians who teach large audiences of people about how to approach the Bible. This Appendix reveals ten of these statements, and why they do not accurately reflect a proper approach to the study of Scripture. Let us begin with a statement I hear most often (and which I used to say as well).

1. I READ THE BIBLE LITERALLY

People who believe in the inspiration and inerrancy of Scripture often claim to "read the Bible literally." They argue for a "literal reading" of Scripture, and frequently accuse people with whom they disagree of not reading the Bible literally. The problem with this, however, is that the word "literally" can be easily misunderstood by other people. The word "literally" gives some people the idea that there are no figures of speech or symbolic language in the Bible. If the word "literally" does not allow for figures of speech and metaphorical language, then it is impossible to literally "read the Bible literally."

For example, Jesus once said, "I am the vine, you are the branches" (John 15:5). But Jesus is not literally a vine, and His followers are not literally branches. Elsewhere, Jesus said He was a door (John 10:9), bread (John 6:35), and a mother hen (Matt 23:37). Likewise, God is described in Scripture as a shield, a rock, and a fire (Deut 4:24; Ps 18:2; 28:7). But God is not *literally* any of these things. The Bible uses figures of speech just as we do in our own conversations.

I am fine with saying that the Bible must be read literally, *as long as* we understand that Scripture contains many symbols, metaphors, similes, allegories, and even some mythical language and terminology, and that all such literary elements must be understood as the figures of speech that they are. A truly "literal" reading of Scripture must allow for figures of speech that do not get interpreted literally.

To avoid confusion, instead of saying we read the Bible literally, we could say we read the Bible *seriously*, or naturally. Such terminology allows us to read the Bible the way we do any other book, listening for the intent and purpose of the author while allowing the symbols and figures of speech to add to and amplify the truth that is being conveyed. Scripture is a beautiful revelation from God, and when we approach it seriously, it changes lives and changes the world. So let it naturally speak as God intends.

2. THE BIBLE SAYS IT; I BELIEVE IT; THAT SETTLES IT

Pastor Peter LaRuffa once said this:

> If somewhere in the Bible, I were to find a passage that said 2+2=5 then I wouldn't question what I'm reading. I would believe it, accept it as true, and then do my best to work it out and understand it.

From one perspective, I understand what LaRuffa is saying. The Bible contains many hard and difficult teachings, and if we were to deny as true or reject as error anything that we didn't like or immediately understand, there is very little of the Bible that we would keep. So in one sense, it is true that we should believe and accept all of Scripture while we seek to understand what it is saying.

However, we must also recognize that since all truth is God's truth, the truth of God's Word will never contradict truth that is found elsewhere. The truth of Scripture never contradicts the truth of archaeology, history, math, or science. If the Bible said that 2+2=5, we would be right to reject it, for this would be a clear contradiction with mathematical facts. Thankfully, we don't need to reject anything in Scripture in this way, for (despite what some say) it does not contain any clear contradictions with factual statements from other sources of truth.

Yes, some statements in Scripture appear to contradict factual statements from other sources. But if we carefully study what Scripture actually says, we eventually recognize that the Bible is entirely true in everything it says. The five areas of contextual studies discussed previously in this book always help the serious student of Scripture reconcile the truth claims of Scripture with the truth claims of other fields of study.

Nevertheless, we should avoid saying the Christian cliché that "The Bible says it; I believe it; that settles it." The initial premise is the problem. Yes, "The Bible says it," but what exactly does the Bible say? There is not a single Christian alive today, or in all of human history, who has gained a perfect understanding of everything the Bible says. We all misunderstand vast portions of Scripture. Therefore, we don't really *know* everything the Bible says. We *think* we know, but often, we are mistaken. There is a difference between what the Bible says, and what we *think* the Bible says. This is why we continually study the Bible. By studying Scripture, we try to find the holes in our understanding and bring our knowledge of what we *think* the Bible says into better alignment with what it *truly* does say.

Is the Bible correct in everything it says? Yes, of course. But the trick is knowing what the Bible actually says. Something like the following statement is closer to reality: "The Bible says things; I am trying to learn what the Bible says and believe what I have learned; that doesn't settle it, because I could still be wrong."

3. JUST READ THE BIBLE; DON'T READ OTHER BOOKS

It is uncomfortable for Christians to be confronted with ways of understanding Scripture that challenge some of our core beliefs. Some Christians respond to this experience by condemning the practice of reading books other than the Bible. They say things like "Just read the Bible; don't read other books." The implication is that other books about the Bible lead Christians astray. But if Christians read *just* the Bible and nothing else, then they would all have sound doctrine and correct beliefs. This approach to Scripture sounds pious, holy, and spiritual, but it is entirely illogical, quite hypocritical, and nearly impossible to practice. Let me explain why.

This approach to Scripture is illogical because while I agree that everything in the Bible is true, this does not mean that all truth is in the Bible. Yes, all truth comes from God, and yes, the Bible is all true, but all of God's truth is not in the Bible. The equation 2+2=4 is true, and therefore, originates with God, but this truth is not taught in the Bible. You must learn this truth from other books. In fact, more truths are taught outside the Bible than within it. This is not just a fact for scientific and historical truths, but spiritual and theological truths as well. The Bible is a limited source of truth that helps guide and direct us into the rest of the limitless truths from God.

Furthermore, when someone says, "I just read the Bible," the question can always be asked, "Which Bible?" Most of the time, people who say such things are reading an English version of the Bible, usually the King James Version. But such versions are only translations of the original Greek and Hebrew text of the Bible. So if someone says they only read "the Bible," they better be reading the "original" Bible as penned by the original authors in Greek and Hebrew (and maybe some Aramaic). Of course, such a Bible doesn't exist, so these authors cannot ever read such a book. This also makes their position illogical.

But it is also quite hypocritical. These pastors always have numerous church services and Bible studies for the people in their congregations to attend each week. And without fail, the pastor will get in front of them and say all sorts of things that are not specifically stated in Scripture. Oh yes, they claim to be teaching or preaching what Scripture says, but unless they do nothing but read from the text of Scripture, they are speaking words to others that are in addition to the biblical text. There is no difference between this and reading words that are in addition to the biblical text.

For example, the statement "Just read the Bible; don't read other books," is not found in the Bible. So if a pastor teaches this to his people, he is teaching them something that is not found in the Bible. Even if he thinks this idea can be inferred from Scripture (which it can't), it still is a statement that is not explicitly stated anywhere in Scripture. The same is true with nearly every word he speaks in every sermon and Bible study. A sermon and Bible study, after all, is nothing more than a person attempting to explain the Biblical text with additional words that are not found in the Bible. If a pastor can *speak* words that seek to explain the biblical text, then there is no reason that he or the people in his congregation cannot *read* words that seek to explain the biblical text. It is utterly hypocritical for a pastor to tell his congregation, "Listen to my explanation of the biblical text, but don't read any books or articles about the biblical text." After all, a written explanation of the biblical text is nothing more than a written record of what someone once said about the text. There is no real difference between hearing an explanation of the text and reading an explanation of the text. To claim otherwise is pure hypocrisy. Indeed, even the teaching, "Only read the Bible" is not itself found in the Bible, but comes from outside source, usually an egotistical spiritual leader who doesn't want anyone to question him.

Finally, this idea of "reading only the Bible" is nearly impossible to practice. It is impossible to go through life and read nothing but the Bible. Such a person could not ever drive to work, for they have to read traffic signs. They could not perform their job, because nearly all jobs require some reading. Nor could they stay home, because even if their house contained no books or magazines whatsoever, there would still be words on nearly every container and appliance. If a person can read, it is impossible to go through life and read nothing but the Bible.

A while back, a pastor wrote to me on Facebook, saying that I was sinning by writing about Scripture and theology on my website at RedeemingGod.com. He said that I should not be doing this, because people shouldn't read anything except for the Bible. I pointed out the fact that he must read words and ideas every day that are not found in the Bible, such as when he drives, goes to the grocery store, or even reads posts on Facebook. He responded that it is okay for people to read "non-spiritual" words like traffic signs and grocery lists, but only the Bible should be consulted for spiritual truths.

I respond by saying, "If that is true, then why are you reading things from me on Facebook, and why are you writing a message to me about the Bible that you expect me to read? The words of your message are not the Bible, but you expect me to read it?" After I sent this message, I checked his Facebook profile to see what sorts of things he wrote about. Nearly every single post had some sort of spiritual concept, encouragement, or idea in it that was not a direct quote from Scripture. I sent him a second reply pointing out that even he wrote things on his Facebook page that contained spiritual ideas that are beyond the very words of Scripture. I never received a response. Maybe he saw that his approach to Scripture was impossible for anyone (including himself) to follow. (I doubt it, but one can hope.)

Yes, you should read the Bible. But you should *also* read other books, because only in this way will your thinking be challenged, your wrong ideas be corrected, and your bad theology fixed. Furthermore, there is *no other way* to gain knowledge about all five forms of context than by reading other books. You cannot learn about the history and culture of Bible times without reading other books. You cannot understand literary genres and the proper rules of grammar without reading other books. You cannot gain insight into the theological and

Christological contexts of Scripture without allowing your thinking to be exposed to the ideas found in other books. So read diligently, and read widely.

4. JESUS IS THE WORD OF GOD; THE BIBLE ISN'T

Some people say that "Jesus is the only Word of God; the Bible isn't." This claim is stated in other ways as well, such as "When God sent us His Word, He didn't give us a book," or "The Word of God has come in the flesh, not as a book." This claim is a reaction to the tendency of some Christians to idolize the Bible, in which they also make the Bible the fourth member of the Trinity. Yet this view is an overreaction. It is also an attempt to undermine the authority of Scripture.

It is an overreaction in that while Jesus is certainly the Word of God (John 1:1, 14; Rev 19:13), the Bible is also the Word of God. There are numerous texts in Scripture, many of which are quotations from Jesus Himself, which clearly indicate that the Bible is also the Word of God. For example, in Mark 7:13, Jesus accuses the religious leaders of "making the Word of God of no effect through your tradition which you have handed down." Jesus is clearly speaking about the Hebrew Bible, which we call the Old Testament. In Luke 4:4, Jesus says, "It is written, 'Man shall not live by bread alone, but by every Word of God.'" If Jesus were referring to Himself when He spoke about the "word of God," He would not have talked about "every" Word of God. If Jesus is the "only" Word of God, then there is no such thing as "every" Word of God. Again, in John 10:35, Jesus clearly equates the Word of God with Scripture when He says, "If He called them gods, to whom the Word of God came (and the Scripture cannot be broken) ..." So Jesus Himself believes and states that the Bible is the written Word of God (cf. Luke 5:1; 8:21; 11:28).

The apostles believed similarly. For example, in Acts 6:2, the twelve apostles said, "It is not desirable that we should leave the Word of God and serve tables." The context indicates that they were thinking primarily about their responsibility to teach and preach the Bible to others. In 1 Corinthians 14:36, Paul asks the Corinthians, "Or did the Word of God come originally from you? Or was it you only that it reached?" The written revelation from God about Jesus went out to all the churches, not just the Corinthian church, and it did not originate in Corinth, but in Jerusalem with Jesus and the apostles. Paul clearly thinks that the Bible is the Word of God. And while the Apostle John does say that Jesus is the Word of God (John 1:1, 14; Rev 19:13), he also indicates that the Bible is the Word of God, as a written testimony about Jesus Christ (Rev 1:2).

So we must not say that the Bible is not the Word of God. It is. I like to say that Jesus is the *living* Word of

God while the Bible is the *written* Word of God. And the two work together. For while Jesus is the ultimate revelation from God, so that if you want to see what God is like all you need to do is look at Jesus, the fact of the matter is that we would not have this revelation about Jesus unless we had the Bible. In this way, the revelation of God in Jesus depends upon the Bible to carry that revelation to us.

Yet the Bible itself focuses upon Jesus as well, for Jesus is the interpretive lens through which we read and study Scripture. Without Jesus, we would not know how to understand the Bible. Jesus is the guiding hermeneutic; the trump card of all Bible study. But without Scripture, we couldn't know anything for sure about Jesus. We need Scripture to be an inspired, inerrant, and authoritative record about Jesus so that Jesus can guide and direct our interpretation and application of Scripture.

The relationship between Jesus and the Bible is a bit like the relationship between truth and love (Eph 4:15). You cannot have one without the other. You cannot speak the truth hatefully, because truth, by definition, is loving. And you cannot speak lies in love (though many often try), for love, by definition, speaks only what is good and helpful, neither of which is true of lies. It's the same with Jesus and Scripture. Jesus is revealed in Scripture, and Jesus helps us understand Scripture. You cannot have one without the other.

All Scripture points to Jesus, and so when we teach the written Word of God, we should point people to the living Word of God, but this does not mean that the written Word of God is not the Word of God. It is. So stop saying that Jesus is the Word of God and the Bible is not. Both are the Word of God.

5. A VERSE A DAY KEEPS THE DEVIL AWAY

This is an old Christian cliché that I used to hear more in previous decades, but which—thankfully—has almost entirely dropped out of usage. It is based on the old Johnny Appleseed saying, "An apple a day keeps the doctor away." The idea is that if we keep Bible verses ready at all times and spend a few minutes a day reading Scripture, we will be well-prepared to stand against all the wiles of the devil when he comes prowling around. In the words of Martin Luther, "One little word shall fell him!" But whether we are talking about the Bible or apples, the statement is false.

The idea that Bible reading and Bible quotations can ward off the devil is based on the Gospel accounts of Jesus quoting Scripture to defend Himself against the temptations of the devil in the wilderness (Matt 4:1-11; Luke 4:1-13). In this account, Satan tempts Jesus in three different ways, and rather than use logic, emotion, or strength of will to defeat the temptations, Jesus quotes

Bible verses. At the end of the temptations, the devil departs. So it is sometimes taught that when temptation comes, if we can just find the right Bible verses to quote, we too can defeat the devil and protect ourselves against temptation.

In this way, the Bible is viewed as a six-shooter pistol from a Western movie, with us squaring off against the devil on a dusty road of an old desert town. We squint at the devil, and he grimaces back at us, with our trigger fingers twitching by the pistols at our side. When we draw with lightning-fast reactions, the devil shoots temptations our way, and we shoot Bible verses back at him. If we are quick on the draw, our Bible verses knock the devil flat on his back so we can ride off into the sunset.

But Satan doesn't work that way, temptation doesn't work that way, and the Bible doesn't work that way. After all, Satan himself quotes Scripture at Jesus in the temptations (Luke 4:10-11). Satan isn't scared of the Bible. Bible quotes are not Satan's kryptonite. To the contrary, Satan loves it when people quote verses at him, because then he gets to quote verses right back. We can't beat Satan at the Bible quotation game. For even if we can quote ten, a hundred, or even a thousand verses, Satan can quote the entire Bible. No human can beat that.

The Bible is not a magic book that helps set up invisible shields around us. It is not a book of secret power. Verses are not spells. It is not a book by which the full might and power of God is placed at our disposal if only we can say the right words at the right time. It is not a book where the ability to quote a few verses will help you defeat all temptations, persevere under every trial, and break down every stronghold.

A similar idea to the "Verse a day keeps the devil away" approach to Scripture is the practice of randomly opening your Bible and stabbing your finger down on the page to get your daily dose of wisdom from God. There is an old joke about a man who did this. He opened his Bible, stabbed his finger randomly on the page, and read "And Judas went out and hung himself." Thinking that this wasn't very inspirational, the man tried again. This time, he read, "Go and do ye likewise." A little nervous now, the man tried a third time. His finger landed on the verse that said, "Whatever you do, do quickly."

This story is obviously a joke, but it is not too far from the truth for how some people read the Bible. I personally know a man who moved his family across the country because he followed this "stab your finger on the page" approach to Scripture. He performed this practice daily, and one day, he read about God commanding Abraham to leave his home and go where he led. So he packed up his belongings and started driving. He eventually drove across the country, ending up bankrupt and nearly homeless. His children rebelled against God because of how "God" had ripped them away from their friends, school, home, and life. Do not use the "Verse a Day" approach to reading Scripture. It is dangerous and unhelpful.

The Bible is not a bottle of daily vitamins that keep us healthy, wealthy, and wise. You cannot develop a relationship with God or learn how to follow Jesus by spending one minute a day in the Bible. The "Daily Dose of God" or "One Minute Bible" approach to Scripture severely undermines the power and purpose of Scripture and guides us into the life God wants for us. Imagine the idiocy of an approach to marriage or parenting called "The One Minute Marriage" or "One Minute Parenting." You cannot have a good marriage or be a good parent in one minute a day. So also, you cannot understand Scripture and develop a relationship with God in one minute a day.

The key to properly using Scripture against temptation is not found in the ability to quote Bible verses, but rather in the ability to properly understand the Bible and use biblical truth to help us follow Jesus and obey God. A misunderstood Bible verse quoted out of context plays right into the devil's hands. Therefore, it is better for you to study and understand one Bible text than to memorize ten. The serious and diligent study of Scripture is part of what it takes to grow in a relationship with God. Don't just be able to quote Scripture; study and learn what it says so that you can properly obey it.

6. BUT IN THE *GREEK* IT SAYS ...

The ability to read and study the Bible in the original languages is helpful and important. I myself study the Bible in Greek and Hebrew. Without scholarly research into the Greek and Hebrew texts of Scripture, we would not have good English translations of the Bible. So use of Greek and Hebrew are essential.

But a knowledge of Greek and Hebrew can easily be abused. I often find that the phrase "But in the Greek it says ..." is wrongly used in two ways. First, it is sometimes used as a trump card to shut down disagreement. When there is theological disagreement between two people, and one of them knows Greek (or Hebrew) while the other doesn't, the person who knows Greek will often pull out the Greek trump card to refute and discredit the ideas of the other person. The implication is that the person who knows Greek and Hebrew is automatically correct *because* they know Greek and Hebrew.

The truth, however, is that studying the Bible in the original languages is not that much different from studying it in English. As long as a good English translation is used (e.g., the NKJV, NAS, or NRSV), there is very little that the Greek or Hebrew can say which the English does not. Words in any language have a variety of meanings, and the best way to determine which definition of the word is correct is *not* by referring to what the word was in some other language, but rather by looking at the context in which the word is found, regardless of which language it is in. Yes, sometimes the English translation is *so bad* that you have to go back and see what was originally written, but this is only the case in about 0.01% of the Bible. In general, you can perform word studies in English almost as well as you can in Greek and Hebrew. This is especially true if you compare one English translation with another.

The second way the original languages are abused is when they are used to prop up a Bible teacher in a position of power and control. When a pastor or teacher refers to the Greek or Hebrew in their lessons, it is sometimes true that they do this simply to appear smarter, wiser, and more knowledgeable about Scripture and theology than they really are. Frequent references to Greek and Hebrew can indicate arrogance and pride on the part of the person who uses them in this way. They constantly refer to the Greek and Hebrew as a way of making their listening audience dependent upon the teacher for what the Scriptures really say. It is an issue of power and control.

In May 2018, I posted a question on Facebook about how to translate Matthew 25:41. I found it puzzling that God would prepare a place of fire *for* the devil and his angels, given that fire cannot burn or harm them. So I wondered if there was a different way of translating the text, and proposed one on Facebook. (I have since rejected that proposal. The traditional translation is fine, as I explain in my book, *What is Hell?*).

A reader was startled by what I suggested and wrote a comment in which they tagged their pastor to read my post and weigh in on the discussion. The pastor left a comment later that day in which he attempted to refute my post by referring to Greek participles and genitive articles. The member of his church then thanked his pastor profusely for pointing out my error and then said to this pastor, "You are the expert in this area ... I totally agree. Thanks for your help."

Later that day, I read this comment exchange and was a little shocked by it, because what the pastor said about the Greek from the text was completely and demonstrably false. It was clear from the pastor's comments that had an extremely limited understanding of Greek, for he had referenced rules of Greek grammar that were either nonexistent or incorrect. He then drew conclusions from these fabricated grammar rules to "prove" that I was wrong. I pointed out these errors to the pastor in the comment thread, and he backpedaled a little bit by saying that he "mistyped." His parishioner responded however, by saying that I was arrogant and wrong to correct his pastor, for his pastor was a Greek expert and I was not.

This is the sort of thing that can happen when a pastor uses Greek and Hebrew to prop himself up as an authority when it comes to understanding the text. Gullible

Christians are sucked in by these fine-sounding arguments from the Greek and Hebrew, and since they themselves don't know any Greek and Hebrew, they have no way of verifying if what their pastor says is true. So they trust their pastor—sometimes blindly—to teach them what the Bible *actually* says. And often, these pastors are flat-out wrong.

Back in the Middle Ages, one of the ways the church maintained control over the masses was by only allowing clergy members to read and study the Bible. The church used the Latin Vulgate (a Latin translation of the Bible) and since the average person could not read or understand Latin, the clergy had complete control over what the average Christian heard and believed from the Bible. It is because of this abuse that the Protestant Reformers sought to give the Bible back to the people in their own language so that they could read and study it for themselves. Yes, this has also created all sort of problems for the church, including numerous heresies, but it is far better for the people to have the Word of God for themselves to study on their own than to entrust such spiritual riches into the hands of a few powerful (and power-hungry) people at the top.

Yet the pastor or Bible teacher who constantly refers back to the Greek or Hebrew in their teachings is guilty of returning to the position of Middle Ages, in which the Bible can no longer be properly read or studied by the average Christian. Instead, the masses are once again becoming dependent upon a few people at the top who have been properly educated and trained in the "spiritual languages" of the Bible. This should not be. The Word of God is for all the people of God to read, learn, and understand.

It is completely fine if you know Greek and Hebrew and use these languages in your study of Scripture. But be very careful about how and when you use references to the Greek and Hebrew in your teaching and writing. I will occasionally refer to them, but only when it is absolutely necessary to bring clarity to a confusing text. I also frequently refer to study tools and guides that allow people with no knowledge of Greek and Hebrew to verify my work for themselves.

7. THE SPIRIT WILL GUIDE ME INTO ALL TRUTH

When I teach others about how to study the Bible, someone occasionally objects by saying that they don't need to study the Bible because "the Spirit will guide me into all truth." This idea comes from John 16:13, where Jesus promises His disciples that He will send the Holy Spirit to them, Who will guide them into all truth by speaking to them the things He hears from God. Along with John 16:13, people also tend to refer to Luke 12:11 (cf. Matt 10:19; Mark 13:11) where Jesus tells His disciples that when they stand before synagogues, rulers, and authorities, they should not worry about what they will say, but will be given the right words at the right time. Such passages are then used to say that we don't need to study the Bible, for God will give us what we need to know when we need to know it.

This perspective on Scripture is also found by those who disagree with you by saying, "Well, you just have head knowledge; I have heart knowledge. You use logic; but I follow the Spirit." I always wonder if they really understand that such a statement accuses the Holy Spirit of being illogical. The truth is that there is no difference between head knowledge and heart knowledge, just as there is no difference between head faith and heart faith (see my book, *What is Faith?*). Knowledge is knowledge, regardless of how you gained it or where it came from. So people who say such things are simply trying to refute others by discrediting their factual and logical arguments by claiming that they were taught by the Holy Spirit.

All of this sounds super spiritual, but is actually the opposite of what the Holy Spirit wants. We know this for three reasons. First of all, John 16:13 is in the context of the Upper Room Discourse, which contain the final instructions of Jesus to His disciples before He went to His crucifixion. A large portion of these instructions contains details about the coming Holy Spirit, and before Jesus told the apostles that the Spirit would guide them into all truth, Jesus told them that the Spirit would be given to them to help them recall what Jesus had taught (John 14:26). So clearly, the disciples could not be guided into all truth or remember the truth unless they first heard and understood it. You cannot recall something you never heard. The disciples had been with Jesus for three years, following Him around Israel and listening to His teachings, and Jesus is saying that the Holy Spirit will help them remember the truth of what they heard. This was for the purpose of teaching these truths to others and writing them down in Scripture.

Jesus is not saying that the apostles did not need to read and understand Scripture or listen to the teachings of Jesus. They did and they should. Jesus is saying that *after* listening to Jesus and understanding the truth of Scripture, the Holy Spirit will guide them into the truth of what they have heard and learned. The same is true for us today. The Holy Spirit does not help us *in the absence* of Scripture reading and study, but in connection with such activities. The Spirit guides and speaks to us through the text of Scripture, not in the absence of it.

Second, it is foolish to think that those who refuse to study Scripture and prepare biblical lessons for others are more spiritual than those who do study and prepare. The passages in the Gospels about God giving us the words we should speak are said in reference to being put on trial for our beliefs. These texts are not about whether or not pastors should study and prepare for their sermons or even about proper preparation for regular legal battles in court. Those passages refer only to the situations when followers of Jesus are questioned and challenged by the authorities about their commitment to follow Jesus. Those texts do not apply to any other situation.

Furthermore, it is not true that a lack of planning and preparation is extra spiritual. After all, God Himself plans and prepares (cf. Jer 29:11). It is good and godly to plan and prepare. Those who just "trust God" to give them words to say when they preach or teach the Bible to others are simply lazy. They are also not behaving properly as pastors or shepherds, for they are not caring enough about the people who have gathered to learn to properly plan and prepare a good spiritual meal for them to eat. When a parent sets out to make a meal for their children, they do not just wait until supper time and then sit at the table hoping that food shows up. Menus must be planned. Groceries bought. Food must be cut, cooked, and prepared. Only in this way will the children be properly fed and nurtured so that they can grow and develop into healthy adults. The same is true for feeding spiritual food to the people of God.

Thirdly and finally, such an approach to Scripture ignores the fact that the Bible frequently calls us to diligently study the Bible (2 Tim 2:15) and praises those who do so (Acts 17:11). It is spiritual and praiseworthy to diligently study Scripture so that the truth of God's Word can be properly taught to others. The Spirit works with our minds and spirit as we study Scripture to illuminate the Word of God to us so that the Spirit can then speak through us when we teach Scripture to others. The Spirit will guide you into all truth as you study the truth of Scripture.

8. THE BIBLE IS NOT A BOOK, BUT A LIBRARY

It is becoming increasingly common for some scholars and Bible teachers to remind others that the Bible is not a single book but is instead a small library of books that have been bound together into one volume. Technically, this is not wrong. The Bible consists of 66 books written over the span of roughly 2000 years by over 40 authors from three different continents and speaking three different languages. So yes, there is no denying the fact that the Bible is a small library.

However, the doctrine of the inspiration of Scripture teaches that God superintended the entire process of writing these various books, helping guide the various authors to write what He wanted Scripture to say. Therefore, it is also not wrong to say that the Bible is an individual book which has been directed by a single author, God.

The reason this is important is that the people who say that the Bible is not a book but a library of books are generally searching for a way to explain the apparent contradictions and inconsistencies in Scripture. Just as you would not expect all the books in a library to agree with each other, so also, if you view the Bible as a library of 66 books instead of a single volume, then you can expect to see that the authors of these 66 books have different views on various issues, and feel free to disagree with or contradict the ideas of other authors.

While I agree that the single volume of the Bible is made up of 66 different books, written by about 40 authors, it is also true that God is the ultimate divine author of every individual book. God inspired the authors to write the text of Scripture. Therefore, it is not wrong to say that while the 66 books of the Bible are individual volumes in the "library of Scripture," God is the single guide and overseer of Scripture, who made sure that the ideas and truths of Scripture form a coherent volume with consistent truths. All of the various voices of the human authors were guided by the single voice of the divine author.

This does not deny the reality of progressive revelation, of course. It is true that various Old Testament authors did not have as much insight and understanding into what God was doing in the world than do New Testament authors. There is a progress to revelation that takes place over time, but this is not the same thing as saying that the later authors contradict the earlier authors.

Since God guided the entire process, all Scriptures are true in what they reveal, and no passage of Scripture contradicts any other Scripture. This is partly what makes the Bible one of the greatest books ever written.

9. BUT IN *MY* BIBLE IT SAYS ...

This statement is most often heard by someone who is using a Study Bible, though it is occasionally said by someone who has a different translation of the Bible than the one that is being used by the teacher. In the case of a different translation, the person who makes this statement is usually disagreeing with what the teacher said because their Bible translation has a different word or phrase than the translation used by the teacher, and the student thinks this word disproves what the teacher is saying. The simple solution to this, of course, is to simply point out that there are different translations of the Bible, and where one translation disagrees with another, our job as students of Scripture is to perform a contextual word study on this verse in question and discover which translation is best.

When the disagreement comes from a person who is referring to the notes at the bottom of the page in a Study Bible, it is often because the person does not know that the study notes are not inspired or because the person does not realize that good Bible teachers can disagree on what the Bible actually says. In either case, the disagreement provides an opportunity to explain how the Bible works, where the study notes come from at the bottom of the page, and why there is a difference between what the Bible says and what we *think* the Bible says. The notes at the bottom of the page are nothing more than one person's opinion on what the Bible says. The notes can be a helpful guide, but they can also lead us astray. Our job is to perform our own study of Scripture so that we can learn what the Scriptures say for ourselves.

When two Bible teachers, Bible translations, or Bible textual notes disagree, this is not a problem with the Bible, but with our own understanding. A proper study of Scripture in its various contexts can help us determine which teacher, translation, or textual note is most likely correct.

10. THE BIBLE IS A ROADMAP TO LIFE

This way of approaching Scripture was briefly discussed earlier in this book, but it is worth considering here again, since many people say something like this about Scripture. Along with calling the Bible a roadmap to life, they might also say that the BIBLE is "Basic Instructions Before Leaving Earth." But this is not what Scripture is.

First of all, even if the Bible contained instructions and guides for how to live life, it would not be about leaving earth, but about living on this earth. Yet even then, it does not give us clear-cut instructions or steps to follow. As discussed previously, the Bible was not primarily written to us, but to other people from other times and other cultures. It does not contain specific instructions to people in our time in our culture. Yes, Bible study can lead us to some guidelines and principles that apply to everyone everywhere, but there are no clear "how-to" guides or step-by-step instructions for navigating life.

Remember, the Bible is a story, and it inspires and guides us the same way any story does, by showing us what has been said and done in the past, and how these words and actions influenced the lives of these people. Since the Bible is a story, it is not a rule book, recipe, road map, to-do list, or instruction manual. The Bible is a story that shows what God has done in the past, and therefore, what sorts of things He *might* be doing now. Our job is to read the story of Scripture so that we can discover our role today in the ongoing and unfolding story of God.

So do the Scriptures tell us what to do and how to live in life? Yes, but only as inspired, inerrant, and authoritative accounts of what has already occurred. Scripture provides us with examples of how God and people have interacted in the past, and in this way, provide us with a template for what this present interaction between God and man may look like (cf. 1 Cor 10:1-11; Heb 3:5-

4:13).

If you have ever gone to Scripture for help on some of life's biggest decisions (who to marry, where to live, what job to take, etc.), you have probably been disappointed. The Bible is not much of a roadmap to life. But that is because God did not intend it to be our guide. He wants to be our guide and friend, the one who walks with us and talks to us on our journey. If we're too busy studying the map while we're driving on the road, we're likely to get in an accident. It's best to let Him give us the directions as we drive.

So we don't go to Scripture to find out what Jesus did or the early church did so that we can parrot their actions and words in our own time. We don't ask "What did Jesus do so I can do it too?" or "What did the early church do so we can do it too?" but instead, "If Jesus were here today (which He is), what would He want me to do?" The question walks a fine line, but it's a line that matters. God wants us to live our lives in a similar way to how He wanted biblical authors to write Scripture. I don't believe in the "dictation theory," and I don't believe in "dictation living." Scripture was written by human authors as they were carried along in the flow of the Spirit, and that is how we are to live our lives as well. God did not override the emotions and personalities of the authors, and He doesn't override ours either. We must live our lives within the Scripture-directed flow of the Holy Spirit.

Reading and studying Scripture in this way allows the Bible to be a guide into the most exciting and liberating experience of a lifetime. We discover that we are invited to play a starring role in God's work in this world, and that He is so confident in our ability to play our part, He hasn't given us any clear instructions for what to do or lines to say, but invites us to improvise along with the Holy Spirit. Living this way with Scripture is creative, beautiful, and thrilling. So what are you waiting for? Take up the Bible and read!

DISCUSSION QUESTIONS

1. The phrase "I read the Bible literally" can lead to misunderstandings about figures of speech in Scripture. Have you ever struggled to interpret symbolic or metaphorical language in the Bible? How can reading the Bible "seriously" or "naturally" help you better understand its message?

2. The cliché "The Bible says it; I believe it; that settles it" assumes we fully understand what the Bible says. Reflect on a time when your understanding of a biblical passage changed through study or discussion. How can humility in Bible study help us grow closer to God's truth?

3. Some Christians advocate "just read the Bible; don't

read other books" to avoid being led astray. Why might this approach be appealing, yet problematic? How have books, commentaries, or conversations outside the Bible deepened your understanding of Scripture?

4. The idea that "Jesus is the Word of God; the Bible isn't" emphasizes Jesus as God's ultimate revelation. How do you see Jesus and Scripture working together to reveal God? How can we balance honoring both as the Word of God in our study and teaching?

5. The notion of "a verse a day keeps the devil away" can reduce Scripture to a quick fix. Have you ever approached the Bible this way? How can we shift from treating Scripture as a spiritual vitamin to engaging it as a story that shapes our relationship with God and others?

6. The Bible is described as a story, not a roadmap to life. How does viewing Scripture as a narrative rather than a rulebook change the way you apply it to life's big decisions (e.g., relationships, career)? How can we discern God's guidance through Scripture without expecting step-by-step instructions?

APPENDIX II:
WHAT THE BIBLE IS NOT

For much of my life, I approached Scripture as a puzzle to be solved, a divine textbook that, with the right interpretive keys, could be unlocked to reveal all the answers to life's questions. I treated it like a scientific specimen—something to dissect, categorize, and systematize.

But over time, I've come to see that this approach often misses the heart of what Scripture is. The Bible is not a cold, mechanical manual; it's a living, breathing story that invites us into God's redemptive work. To understand what the Bible is, we must first clarify what it is not. Below, I outline seven misconceptions about Scripture that I once held, each of which subtly distorts its purpose and power.

By letting go of these ideas, we can better embrace the Bible as God's inspired, inerrant, and authoritative revelation—a story that transforms lives and redeems the world.

A MIXED-UP THEOLOGY BOOK

I used to think the Bible was a jumbled theology text-book, as if God had given us a disorganized collection of truths that needed to be sorted and reassembled to be useful.[1] I believed it was my job to sift through its pages, gather scattered fragments on a topic, and piece them together into a coherent "biblical" doctrine. Individual passages were true, but I thought they were incomplete without the rest of Scripture to fill in the gaps. In my mind, God's Word wasn't quite "right" in its current form, and it was up to me to make it more practical or systematic.

This approach, while not entirely wrong, risks missing the point. God gave us the Bible in its present form—narratives, poetry, letters, and prophecies—because that's how He wanted it. Treating it as a mixed-up puzzle implies we know better than God how His Word should be presented.[2] The Bible's diverse genres and voices aren't flaws to be fixed; they're intentional. Stories, not systematic lists, shape worldviews and inspire transformation.[3] Our task isn't to rearrange Scripture into a theology textbook but to immerse ourselves in its narrative flow, asking why God chose this form and how it speaks to us today. By embracing the Bible as it is, we discover its power

---

[1] Cf. Wright, "How Can the Bible Be Authoritative? ": 4-6.

[2] Ibid., 6.

[3] Ibid., 13-14, 17.

to change hearts and cultures through story, not just facts.

INSPIRED (BUT CONFUSED) AUTHORS

Another assumption I held was that I sometimes understood biblical truth better than the authors themselves. In my preaching and writing, I'd say things like, "What Paul was trying to say here is ..." or, "John says this, but other passages clarify what he *really* means."[4] This implied that the biblical authors, even under divine inspiration, were muddled or incomplete in their expression, and I could articulate their intent more clearly.

This mindset betrays a lack of humility. While it's true that the biblical authors, guided by the Holy Spirit, may not have fully grasped the scope of what they wrote (1 Pet 1:10-12), it's equally true that we may not fully understand their words either. Approaching Scripture with the assumption that we know better risks distorting its message. Instead, we should strive to hear what the authors were saying in their context, resisting the urge to impose our own theological frameworks.

The "analogy of faith"—using other Scriptures to interpret a passage—can be helpful, but it's often overused as a shortcut. I think that "the analogy of faith" is the lazy man's way of understanding a difficult text. It's best, if possible, to avoid cross referencing other passages until all

---

[4] Ibid., 14.

other Bible study methods have been exhausted. Cross-referencing should confirm our findings from diligent study of the text, not replace the study of the text. Let's approach each passage humbly, trusting that the Spirit-inspired authors said exactly what God intended.

THE ROADMAP TO LIFE

As discussed in Appendix I (Item 10), I once viewed the Bible as a divine "Roadmap to Life," a guidebook that, if studied enough, would provide clear answers to every question—whom to marry, where to live, what job to take. I thought it was a rulebook or a step-by-step manual for navigating existence. But this noble idea fell short. The Bible is both more and less than a roadmap.

Scripture isn't a how-to guide but a story of how God has worked in the past and how His people have responded—sometimes faithfully, sometimes not (1 Cor 10:1-11; Heb 3:5–4:13). It reveals the consequences of following or ignoring God's guidance and shows how Jesus' followers transformed cultures by injecting His presence into them (from the book of Acts onward). While Scripture contains many commands that all people can follow (e.g., love your neighbor, Matt 22:39), it primarily offers examples of God's interactions with humanity, providing a template for our own engagement with Him today.

In *The Wounded Healer*, Henri Nouwen tells the tale of a young fugitive who comes to a town where the people are willing to take him in. When soldiers arrive seeking the fugitive, the townspeople admit to knowing nothing about him. Suspecting their lie, the soldiers warn that unless the fugitive is turned over by morning, the entire town will be burned. In deep consternation the people rush to their pastor for counsel.

The pastor, greatly troubled, retreats to his study to search the Scriptures. All night he reads, but finds nothing. Just before dawn his eye falls on a passage: "It is better that one man should die for the people than that a whole people be lost." The minister goes to his people with the news of his discovery. The soldiers are informed and the young man is taken away. A great festival commences, lasting far into the night, celebrating their miraculous deliverance.

But the pastor returns to his study, still troubled. That night an angel appears to him. "Why are you troubled?" the angel asks. "Because I have turned the fugitive over to the enemy," he replies. "But did you not know that he was the Messiah?" the angel inquires. "How was I to know?" the pastor replies in great anguish. The angel responds, "If, instead of reading your Bible you had visited the young man and looked into his eyes, you would have known."[5]

---

[5] Retold by Wayne G. Rollins, *Jung and the Bible* (Eugene: Wipf &Stock, 1983), 93.

VERSE OF THE DAY

This topic was also discussed in Appendix I (Item 5), and so not much more needs to be said here. I used to think a daily Bible verse was like a spiritual vitamin, keeping the devil at bay and ensuring health, wealth, and wisdom. The "One Minute Bible" or "Verse a Day" approach seemed like a quick fix for spiritual growth. But this mindset undermines Scripture's power and reveals a self-centered desire for easy answers rather than a deep relationship with God.

Imagine a book called *The One Minute Marriage* or *One Minute Parenting*. The idea is absurd—relationships require time, effort, and presence. Similarly, Scripture study isn't a daily pill but a lifestyle of engaging God's story to grow closer to Him. A verse plucked out of context, like a random quote from a novel, often distorts the narrative. Instead of seeking quick spiritual boosts, we must immerse ourselves in Scripture's flow, letting it shape our hearts and actions over time. The goal isn't to ward off evil with a verse but to live out God's love in community, as Jesus did (John 13:35).

THE VOICE OF GOD

This one is tricky, and I risk being misunderstood, but let me try. I used to approach Scripture to "hear God's voice," praying for divine insight through its pages. I thought the ink and paper themselves carried God's voice, almost like a magical oracle. Looking back, this feels idolatrous, as if I were treating the Bible like a witch doctor views bird intestines. I was seeking divine guidance through a physical object.

Yes, the Bible is God's Word, inspired and authoritative (2 Tim 3:16). But God's Word is not the same as God's voice. If I write a letter, it captures my thoughts, not my living voice. A written account is nothing more than a record of my past thoughts. It shows the reader the way I think and the kinds of things I would say if I were speaking to them in person.

Similarly, Scripture records what God has said to others in the past—Israelites, early Christians, apostles—not directly to us. Scripture is not so much "God's Word to us" as a document written to others, through which, we can learn to recognize and hear God's Word to us. It helps us recognize the voice of God so that we can hear what God is saying to our generation today. As His sheep, Scripture helps us learn to hear and recognize His voice (John 10:1-5).

Scripture is like a musical score, showing us the melody of God's work in history so we can join the song in our own time. Reading and studying Scripture provides a "divine trajectory"[6] to follow—a plan, a goal, a characteristic direction to travel in, guiding us toward

---

[6] Wright, "How Can the Bible Be Authoritative? ": 9.

redemption, reconciliation, and resurrection. We're not seeking new revelation but fresh ways to live out God's existing revelation. As we study Scripture, we're pulled into the Spirit's flow, learning to think, act, and pray in alignment with God's purposes. The Bible doesn't speak God's voice directly; it equips us to hear Him in our lives and world.

Scripture reading pulls us into the whirlpool of divine direction, so that when we think, act, speak, and pray, we are doing so within the Spirit's flow. So we are not looking for new revelation, but new directions and actions, based on existing revelation. We are looking for "fresh covenant tasks" of redemption, reconciliation, and resurrection.[7] "As we let the Bible be the Bible, God works through us—and it—to do what he intends to do in and for the church and the world."[8]

THE ONLY SOURCE OF DIVINE REVELATION

The Protestant doctrine of *sola Scriptura*—Scripture alone as the source of divine authority—has shaped much of Christian thought since the Reformation. I once held this view tightly, believing the Bible was the sole channel of God's revelation. But this perspective, while well-intentioned, doesn't fully align with Scripture itself. The

[7] Ibid., 12.

[8] Ibid., 14.

Bible reveals that God speaks through many avenues: nature (Ps 19:1-4), conscience (Rom 2:14-15), other people (Heb 1:1), angelic messengers (Luke 1:26-38), and even dreams and visions (Acts 2:17). We Christians are not "people of a book." We are people of a living God, and our God speaks to us in many diverse ways, including to our hearts, minds, and souls.

To those who say that it borders on dangerous heresy to say that God speaks directly to humans today, I would argue that the exact opposite is true. In his essay, "Introduction to the Religious and Psychological Problems of Alchemy," Carl Jung wrote, "It would be blasphemy to assert that God can manifest himself everywhere save only in the human soul." Wayne G. Rollins agrees:

> The restriction of God's speaking to the pages of a book or to the pages of the past is repugnant to Scripture itself. Nowhere in Scripture is God ever conceived of as one who expresses Himself primarily in print. He is to be found in the storm, in the whirlwind, in the cataclysmic events of history, in the healing presence of His Son, in the ongoing proclamation of the church. For Paul, the prophets, the Gospel writers, and the spirit-baptized Christians, it was unthinkable to suggest that God's speaking could ever be restricted to written form and it is their ongoing expectation that God continues to speak and manifest his will through the power and presence of the Spirit, in all ages

and in all times.[9]

This doesn't diminish Scripture's authority. The Bible is uniquely inspired, inerrant, and authoritative, serving as the primary record of God's revelation and the lens through which we test other forms of revelation (1 Thess 5:21). But claiming it's the only source risks silencing God's living voice. To hear God, we must study Scripture while remaining open to His voice in creation, community, and personal experience, always testing these against the Bible's testimony. This approach keeps us humble, preventing us from boxing God into pages while embracing His dynamic presence.

AN INDIVIDUAL STUDY BOOK

As a pastor, I used to retreat to my study, surrounded by books, to uncover God's message for the week, emerging only on Sunday to deliver it from the pulpit. I saw Scripture as a text for solitary scholars, not a communal story. But this approach misses the Bible's purpose. If the Word of God is "living and active" (Heb 4:12), it demands to be lived out in community, not just studied in isolation. Knowledge that isn't lived isn't truly learned; there's no such thing as theoretical theology.

---

[9] Wayne G. Rollins, *Jung and the Bible* (Wipf & Stock: Eugene, 1983), 96.

> The Bible ... is designed to function through human be-
> ings, through the church, through people who, living still
> by the Spirit, have their life molded by this Spirit-inspired
> book. ... God sends the church into the world ... to be
> and do for the world what he did for Israel.[10]

The Bible functions through people who, guided by the Spirit, embody its story in their lives and relationships. As God sent the church to be for the world what He was for Israel, we must study Scripture together—Christians and non-Christians alike—to discover how it calls us to love and transform our world (John 13:35; Col 1:20). Solitary study has its place, but it's incomplete without communal engagement. By sharing Scripture's story with others, we grow into a community that reflects Jesus' incarnational redemption.

CONCLUSION

The Bible is not a mixed-up theology book, a roadmap, a daily vitamin, or a solitary study guide. It's not a confused text, a direct oracle of God's voice, or the only way He speaks. It's a divinely inspired story, inviting us to join God's redemptive work through humility, prayer, diligence, community, and obedience. By letting go of these misconceptions, we free Scripture to be what God intended: a living narrative that draws us into His love and

[10] Ibid., 12.

mission to redeem the world. Take up the Bible, not to dissect it, but to live its story, becoming the hands, feet, and voice of Jesus today.

DISCUSSION QUESTIONS

1. How have you viewed the Bible in the past—as a roadmap, a theology book, or something else? How does seeing it as a story change your approach?

2. Why might we be tempted to rearrange Scripture into a more "useful" form? How can we resist this urge and embrace its current form?

3. Reflect on a time when you sought a specific answer from Scripture for a life decision. Did it work? How might God's guidance through relationships or other means complement Scripture study?

4. How can studying Scripture in community (with Christians and non-Christians) deepen your understanding of its message?

5. If Scripture isn't the only source of divine revelation, how do we discern God's voice in nature, conscience, or other people while staying grounded in the Bible?

6. Which of these seven misconceptions is hardest for you to let go of, and why? How can you begin to approach Scripture differently?

APPENDIX III:
THE BIBLE MIRROR

Note: This appendix is the first chapter of a book I am writing titled *The Bible Mirror*. However, based on my current slate of writing projects, it appears that I will never finish that book. Yet the central idea of that book is so critical to correctly reading and understanding the Bible, I decided to include the first chapter here so that the central idea of that book might help others even if the book never gets published. I believe that the central idea I present in that book may be one of the most overlooked and neglected ideas in all of biblical hermeneutics.

§

For if anyone is a hearer of the word and not a doer, he is like a man observing his natural face in a mirror; for he observes himself, goes away, and immediately forgets what kind of man he was.
–James 1:23-24

I recently spoke with a young man who wants to become a college professor. He told me that as part of his coursework, he is taking some classes on sociology, psychology, and anthropology. "I bet that is fascinating," I told him.

"You have no idea," he said. "I grew up Pentecostal, and we were told never to study sociology, psychology, and anthropology because they contradict the Bible. It's true that I am learning a lot of things that go against what I was taught growing up, but I am also learning a lot about how humans are wired to do certain things, why people behave the way they do, and what systems and structures make society and culture work. And to be honest, what I am learning in these classes helps me see things in the Bible I have never seen before! I understand why certain events happen in the Bible the way they do, why certain battles and wars occurred, and why Israelite culture developed within Mesopotamia the way it did. I may not agree any longer with everything written in the Bible, but I certainly understand it better than I ever did before!"

I congratulated him for seeing something that few Christians see or understand: that studying human development, the human psyche, cultural change, and societal evolution does not decrease or endanger our love for Scripture, but only enhances it. Since the Bible was written by humans and for humans (with divine involvement, of course), understanding human development and human culture can only help us understand the Bible as a human book.

But far too often, Christians tend to ignore the Bible as a human book, as well as the historical and cultural events that were taking place at the time when the Bible was written, and focus only on the Bible as some sort of timeless manifesto dropped out of heaven by God to our individual edification. When we have a moral or theological question, we go to the Bible for answers as if the Bible were directly written by God *to us today* to address every question we have and provide direction on every issue. When we do this, we completely miss the true message of the Bible because we ignore the original historical, cultural, *human* contexts. We are so busy treating the Bible like a book of magic incantations that reveal mysteries of the divine, we miss out on the true power and beauty of this book.

When we think that the Bible is God's revelation of Himself to us, we miss what God is *actually* revealing to us in this book.

Do not misunderstand the words "to us." One of the basic mistakes in how most Christians read and think about the Bible is that they think it was written "to us." It wasn't. We Westerners have a very egocentric view of life, thinking it is all about us, and we sometimes approach the Bible as if God wrote it as a "love letter" just to me. We think God wrote the Bible to give *me* guidance and instruction for *my* needs and *my* questions, and to help *me* get through my day.

Such a way of viewing Scripture has led to most of the abuses and misuses of Scripture throughout the history of Western Christianity. For example, when a king (in England, France, or Spain) thinks the Bible was written to him, to guide and instruct him, he takes some of the commands and instructions in the Bible that God gave to other kings at different times, as things that he and his nation should be doing in their own time. This mistake has led to some of the greatest horrors of human history. Even Hitler often quoted the Bible as an explanation and defense for his actions.

But it is not just kings and tyrants at fault. We do the same thing. For example, we use God's biblical instructions on how to build the temple as both guidelines and justifications for building massive and expensive church buildings. We use prophetic condemnations of other people groups to justify our wars and our own hatred of others who are not like us.

The fact of the matter is that we cannot, we *must not*, take what the Bible says and apply it directly to our lives. Why not? Because the Bible was not written to us. The various books of the Bible were written to other people. These people lived at different times, in different cultures, in different places, who spoke different languages, had different beliefs and values, and faced different issues and challenges. The books of the Bible were written to them, not to us.

This doesn't mean the Bible is worthless for us. It is of inestimable value. As Paul writes in Romans 15:4, the Bible can teach us many important truths. But there is a big difference between learning from the truths and examples that are recorded in Scripture, and thinking that the Bible was written to us today so that we must follow it exactly.

The Bible provides an example of how to live. It is a "guide" of sorts, showing us how people lived and thought, what they did, what God thought of such beliefs and behaviors, and also what the consequences were of these beliefs and behaviors. It is descriptive, not prescriptive. Rather than prescribing what we must do, it describes what happened.

Though we live in a different time and culture, we can assume that many of the similar behaviors and beliefs will lead to similar consequences, but such is not always the case. So instead, we learn from the lives of those who went before us, and then, with our minds filled with Scripture, and with an understanding of our times and culture, and not neglecting the gentle leading of the Holy Spirit, we try to do our best to live our lives within the "stream" or "flow" or "trajectory" of biblical revelation.

God has a different will for you and me in our time and culture than He had for a Jewish person living in the

Babylonian captivity 2500 years ago. And that's a good thing. I work with a lot of different religions, and I see all of them (Christians included) trying to follow commands and ideas that made a lot of sense 2000 years ago, or 1000 years ago, or even 100 years ago, but which today are pointless and purposeless.

When we treat the Bible as God's Holy Book of personal instructions, or as God's Love Letter to you and me, we miss out on what the Bible really is for.

Which is what? To teach you and me about you and me.

This brings us back to the comments made by the college student. He discovered that by learning about humanity, society, and culture, he actually gained a deeper understanding of, and appreciation for, the message and content and truth of Scripture.

In telling me this, he touched on what I believe to be one of the most significant problems in Christian theology. The greatest deficit in Christian theology is not that we have failed to understand God, but that we have failed to understand ourselves. Nearly all theology is built upon the premise that the Bible was inspired by God so that we might learn about God. But this faulty premise has led to much faulty theology. While the Bible does contain much that reveals the character and nature of God, the Bible was not primarily written for this purpose. The Bible was not primarily written to reveal God to us, but to reveal us to us. It is divine book about humans, not a divine book about God.

The Bible is a book from God to humanity about humanity.

This idea may seem shocking to some, since most of us think we have a pretty good understanding of ourselves. We think God is the mysterious One, and it is He that we need to understand. But this is not true. The greatest unexplored aspect of all creation is the human soul. We know far, far less about ourselves than we think. As many people are only now beginning to understand, the inner world of human consciousness, thoughts, emotions, and the subconscious remains the most neglected and overlooked frontier in both science and theology. We know far, far less about ourselves than we imagine.

Furthermore, most people already know enough about the nature and character of God, for nature, conscience, and reason reveal pretty clearly what we need to know about God. If you were to ask the average person on the street what they think God is like, or what they *want* God to be like, the description you receive will be quite similar to the description of God as He is revealed in Jesus Christ. This reveals that we inherently know the basics of what God is like and what God wants from us.

What we do not know, however, is what we are like. While we think we are experts on ourselves and ignorant about God, the truth is that we instinctively know and see God and are completely blinded to the reality of the human condition. Knowing this to be true, God inspired the authors of Scripture to inerrantly write what they did so that we might receive a revelation of ourselves that we could not have received in any other way.

If we look to Scripture to see what it tells us about God, we will come away with some interesting ideas, but we are in danger of misunderstanding God if we take these ideas as factual truths about God. It is better, wiser, and truer to Scripture to see what the Bible says about God not as facts about God, but as facts about human ideas about God. Such a view enables us to learn from and argue with the authors of Scripture (as they did themselves) about what they thought, rather than take everything we read as unassailable, authoritative factual statements about what really is.

So am I saying the Bible is not true? No! I am saying it is more true than we ever thought, for it reveals a truth to us that we mostly ignore. The Bible reveals to us the one thing we should all be able to see, but the one thing we all choose to ignore. The Bible reveals to us the truth of our own hearts. Through the aid of Scripture, we humans can finally come to "Know thyself," which is the first step in truly living as ourselves. God created us and calls us to be who we truly are, but we cannot be ourselves until and unless we first know ourselves.

Yet when we approach the Bible as a revelation about

God rather than a revelation about ourselves, this allows us to ignore and avoid the one truth that the Bible actually wants to unveil: the truth of the condition of the human heart.

This way of reading Scripture also helps us understand many of the difficult sections of Scripture that portray God and violent and bloodthirsty. These, as we will see below, are wrong descriptions of God. But this does not make the Bible *itself* wrong, for what it reveals in the passages that are wrong about the nature and character of God is the critically important truth about the nature and character of man. When we ignore what the Bible says about man so that we can accept what the Bible says about God, we end up using Scripture to make the same mistakes about both man and God that our forefathers made. As long as we think the Bible is primarily about God, we fail to perceive the truth the Bible reveals about both God and man. But once we see that the Bible is a mirror into our souls, we grasp the truth of the condition of our hearts, and this in turn helps us see the face of God for the very first time. As Carl Jung once wrote, "Your vision will become clear only when you can look into your own heart. Who looks outside, dreams; who looks inside, awakes."

Let me back up and tell you how I got here.

STUDYING THE VIOLENCE OF GOD

The impetus for this idea came from an attempt to write a book on how to understand the violence of God in Scripture. I spent several years researching the various views and developing a theological hypothesis, which I then intended to test on the violent passages of the Bible, such as the flood, the Canaanite genocide, the imprecatory Psalms, and the book of Revelation. For those who are not aware, the issue of the violence of God in the Bible is a major problem for theology. If God is loving, kind, forgiving, and gracious, then how can there be so many examples in Scripture of a God who appears to be hateful, vengeful, and full of wrath and anger? How can God both say, "Let the little children come unto me," and also, "Happy is he who seizes your infants and dashes their heads against rocks"?

In studying this critical issue, I thought I had come up with a way to maintain the inspiration and inerrancy of Scripture while at the same time allowing the violent texts to be understood in light of Jesus Christ and Him crucified. So I set out to write a book on the topic. Things went quite well initially. I began by defining the problem and presenting my proposal. When I was done with that, I planned to take several tough texts from the Bible and show how my proposal helped better explain and understand the text.

But as my initial presentation progressed, it became

far too long. 200,000 words long. To give you an idea, this current book you are reading is 80,000 words. So 200,000 words for an "opening chapter" was much too long for anyone to realistically read. But I knew that I could simplify it later after I tested and proved the hypothesis through a detailed study of all the violent texts in the Bible.

I next set out to write explanations for the violent texts of Scripture. I started in Genesis 4 with the murder of Abel by Cain. You can hear the results of this study in my podcast episodes on Genesis 4 from several years ago. And my proposal worked perfectly in explaining that text. I was excited; things were going swimmingly.

But then I encountered the flood in Genesis 6. My parade ended in a flood of rain. All my work, all my writing, and all 200,000 words drowned in the flood account of Genesis 6–8. I tried my best to keep my head above water. I dog-paddled around for numerous months, coming up with one contorted explanation after another for how to understand the flood account as described in Genesis 6–8, while maintaining my belief in inerrancy, but also while seeking to understand these chapters in light of Jesus Christ, who dies for His enemies rather than drowning them. I ultimately failed, and the entire project was swept away by the waters of the flood.

But I didn't stop thinking about the problem of the violence of God in the Bible. Eventually, I came to realize that it was a good thing that my proposal drowned in the flood. My proposal was so convoluted and contorted, I myself couldn't keep straight all the twists and turns of my own theory. If I couldn't remember it all and keep it all straight, how could I ever expect any reader to do so? Even if the theory had been correct, it might as well have been wrong. If a method of understanding Scripture cannot be grasped, understood, remembered, or applied by the average Christian reader of Scripture, then it is a worthless method. Thus, even if my method had worked, it was still worthless.

So I set out to find Ockham's razor for this problem. In theology, as in science, the simplest explanation is often the correct explanation. I asked myself what the simplest explanation was for the violence of God in the Bible. As far as I could tell, there were only two simple explanations:

1. God committed these acts of violence.
2. God did not commit these acts of violence.

If we go with Option 1, as most conservative Christians do, we are able to maintain a belief in the inspiration and inerrancy of Scripture, but we somehow have to explain how Jesus Christ, who Scripture hails as the supreme and perfect revelation of God, never acted to harm another human being nor instructed His disciples to do so. We need to explain how Jesus fully revealed God to us during His earthly ministry ... without the violent side of God. Suppose we believe that God is violent but Jesus wasn't. In that case, we must conclude that the violent side of God was hidden in Jesus, which means that Jesus was *not* the full revelation of God which Scripture claims Him to be, and therefore, Scripture is in error and the revelation of God in Jesus is based on a lie.[1] So this view is self-defeating.

That left only Option 2. The problem, however, is that Option 2 seems to require that we abandon any belief in the inspiration and inerrancy of Scripture. This, for a variety of logical, theological, and personal reasons, I am not able to do. Thus, this view was also unacceptable, for it contradicted other central theological beliefs.

I was stuck. Ockham's razor and the revelation of God in Jesus Christ led me to believe that God did not commit the acts of violence that are attributed to Him in the Bible, but my commitment to the inspiration and inerrancy of Scripture would not allow me to accept the Bible was wrong in what it said about the violence of God. I had a

---

[1] Christians point to the book of Revelation as the answer. They say that the bloody and violent Jesus will show up in His Second Coming. But even if this is a correct way of reading Revelation (it isn't!), the texts in Scripture which tell us that Jesus fully reveals God to us (cf. John 14:9; Col 1:15; 2:9; Heb 1:3) refer to His three-year earthly ministry, not to some future Second Coming. We cannot point to Revelation and say "There's the violent Jesus!" And while we're at it, the "Get a sword" instructions (Matt 10:34; Luke 22:35-38) and cleansing of the temple events (Matt 21:12-17; Mark 11:15-18; John 2:13-17) don't qualify as violent either.

pile of pieces to a seemingly unsolvable puzzle.

THE SCAPEGOAT MECHANISM

Then someone introduced me to the writings of a French historian and philosophical anthropologist named René Girard. I do not really recommend his books, for they are extremely difficult to read. But as I labored through six or seven of his more popular works, something clicked in my mind that made all the pieces of the puzzle fall into place. In various ways and in various places, Girard wrote about "the scapegoat mechanism" that is found in nearly all literature of all cultures and all religions throughout all of time around all the world.

The scapegoat mechanism is something that two people groups (either two individuals or larger groups of people, such as families, cities, or entire countries) unconsciously use to create peace between themselves when violence or war seems inevitable. The two groups essentially make peace between themselves by uniting together against a third outside party—a scapegoat.

Gregory Anderson Love aptly summarizes the Girardian insight this way:

> Anthropologist René Girard argues that when rivalry over a limited desired object leads to escalating violence between multiple groups, the crisis of violence is surprisingly solved when a figure (or minority group) is singled out by

any arbitrary mark of difference or weakness, and warring parties find commonality in attacking this one. The brutalization of the surrogate deflects attention from the previous object of desire and brings peace. The startling peace is felt as holy, and the sacrificial death of the surrogate deemed "sacred," the will of God who brought about peace through those violent means.[2]

Let me unpack this summary statement and describe the process in more detail. To understand how the scapegoat mechanism works, you first have to understand how two parties come to be at odds with each other in the first place. René Girard explains that humans are all born with the innate ability to imitate each other. This is not only how we learn everything we think and do, but is also how we learn what is valuable and important. Imitation is critically important for all levels of human development and civilization.

The problem with imitation (the term Girard uses is *mimesis*) is that it often leads to violence. When two parties are imitating each other, one or the other party notices an object of desire, something they want to own or achieve, and the other party then imitates this desire, and seeks to own or achieve that thing for themselves. A competition ensues to see who can own or achieve the object of desire first. Thus, the imitator and imitated become

[2] Gregory Anderson Love, *Love, Violence, and the Cross* (Cascade: Eugene, OR, 2010), 44.

rivals, and depending on the situation, some level of violence between the two will likely result.

For example, it is not uncommon to see two children fighting over one toy in a room that is filled with toys. Though there are plenty of toys to occupy both of them all day long, both children tend to fixate on *one* toy which they *both* want. When one child picks up a random toy, it instantly becomes more valuable and desirable to the child who does not have it. This is mimesis. So the second child tries to take it from the first child. "It's *mine!*" he or she might say. "I saw it first!" But the first child, seeing that what he has is now desired by the second child, now believes that the toy in his hands is more valuable than ever, and does everything he can to keep it. Eventually, this mimetic rivalry results in violence to one or both of the children, and maybe even to the toy itself.

We are all familiar with this scenario, having seen it play out a thousand times over in our schools, playgrounds, and living rooms. What we fail to recognize, however, is that this same scenario often gets played out in our work places, courtrooms, and government offices. Almost all human aggression and violence has some sort of mimetic rivalry at its root. And when this rivalry escalates out of control, it can quickly lead to war or a contagion of violence that threatens to destroy all of the involved parties.

This is where the scapegoat mechanism enters the

scene. Two warring parties who are caught in a violent contagion of mimetic rivalry can create peace with each other if they mutually (and often unconsciously) agree to turn their aggression on an innocent third party. The two, who were previously at war with each other, unite together in the common purpose of blaming an innocent outsider for causing the problems in the first place. The two warring parties create peace with each other by blaming and then destroying an innocent third party.

The tricky thing with the scapegoat mechanism is that nobody except the condemned third party recognizes what is going on. The two warring parties truly believe that the third party is guilty of the things for which they are blamed. Protests and cries of innocence from the scapegoat only serve to further convince the accusers that condemnation is justified. And when the innocent person (or group) dies, and peace between the two (formerly) warring groups occurs, this provides the infallible proof to the original two parties that the third-party outsider truly was guilty of the crimes for which they were accused, condemned, and killed.

Often, the two formerly warring parties who are now at peace, give praise and thanks to God for revealing to them that the problem was actually the wicked and evil third party, whom God has now enabled them to destroy. This last step is important. When the warring groups turn their violence upon the outsider and achieve peace, they truly think that the outsider was the guilty one who causes the conflict in the first place. The fact that peace results when this outsider is killed provides proof that killing them was the right thing to do and that this killing was *the will of God.* The truth that the outsider was actually an innocent victim is hidden from their minds. Since the death of the scapegoat is the mechanism that brings peace, this death is seen to be the will of God.

Of course, the divine peace never lasts. Mimesis and rivalry always return, and with it, the mimetic cycle of violence begins again.

When Girard turned to study the literature of the Bible to see if his proposal was true there as well, Girard says he was shocked to discover that not only was the scapegoat mechanism present everywhere in Scripture (which was no surprise), but that it was unmasked and unveiled everywhere in Scripture. For Girard, this made the Bible *unique* among all the literary works of world history. The scapegoat mechanism, while *present* in all aspects of life and literature, is usually hidden to those who practice it and write about it. Outside victims are always scapegoated, but they are also always thought to be truly guilty of the crimes for which they are accused. That is, we think our scapegoat victims truly are guilty. But, Girard says, the Bible lays the entire process bare for all to see and read. The scapegoat victim is revealed to be innocent. The scapegoat process is most clearly revealed, says

Girard, in the arrest, trial, and crucifixion of Jesus Christ.

Eureka! The insights of René Girard helped me see the truth of Option 2 above. My thought process went like this:

1. René Girard points out that Jesus is perfect example of a scapegoat. He was clearly innocent of all wrongdoing, but He was killed and condemned by two warring groups so that there might be peace. Though there was rivalry between Jews and the Romans, both banded together to accuse and kill Jesus. In this way, the death of Jesus starkly reveals the scapegoat mechanism for all to see.

2. Jesus perfectly reveals what God is like. This is especially true on the cross. But what do we see in Jesus on the cross? We do not see God killing Jesus. Rather, we see two warring parties, the religious Jews and political Romans, uniting together to condemn and crucify an innocent third party, and they justify their actions by stating they are just doing God's will. And if Jesus fully reveals God to us by becoming a scapegoat to create peace, then this must also be what God has always been doing. God becomes a scapegoat for two warring parties to create peace. Since Jesus serves as a scapegoat for the sinning Jews and Romans, God serves as a scapegoat for the sinning groups of the world.

3. The scapegoat always appears guilty to the outside observer. To the normal observer in Jerusalem that day, the scapegoat Jesus appeared to be

318 HOW DO I STUDY THE BIBLE?

a guilty criminal condemned by both the religious and the political powers. Similarly, to the normal reader of Scripture, the scapegoat God appears to behave in ways that would get Him condemned as "criminal" by most religious and political powers if such things were done against them. Commanding genocide? That sounds like Hitler. Killing babies? Evil. Drowning millions? Satanic. Oh ... but "God did it"? God certainly appears guilty. Just like Jesus appears guilty hanging on a cross. But Jesus wasn't guilty of the things for which He was charged.

4. Therefore, just as Jesus was not guilty of the things He was accused of doing but served instead as a scapegoat *to reveal the scapegoat mechanism*, so also God is not guilty of all the things He is described as doing, but serves instead as a scapegoat *to reveal the scapegoat mechanism.* So also, just as Jesus reveals that it was the religious Jews and political Romans who are the *real* guilty ones, for they were the ones who committed murder in God's name, so also, in human history (and in biblical history), the *real* guilty ones are those who commit violence in God's name. God does not do the things for which He is accused. He is a scapegoat for the wicked humans who do them, and who justify their actions by saying, "God told me to."

Once I saw this, the truth of Option 2 bowled me over. *God did not commit the acts of violence* that are attributed to him.

As stated above, I was reluctant to accept Option 2 because I believed that doing so would require me to abandon my belief in the inspiration and inerrancy of Scripture. I thought that accepting Option 2 would require me to say that the Bible was not true. But by seeing the truth of what Jesus revealed on the cross, I was able to see that this was the *same* truth that God had always been revealing throughout Scripture.

Jesus did not do the things he was condemned for, but He willingly went to the cross and accepted the sin and blame placed upon Him. Why? So that He might (1) create peace, and (2) reveal to us how complicit we are in the ancient practice of scapegoating innocent victims. So also, throughout history, we humans blame God for things He did not do, but He willingly accepts the sin and blame placed upon Him. Why? So that He might (1) create peace, and (2) reveal to us how complicit we are in the ancient practice of scapegoating innocent victims.

Jesus fully reveals God to us!

The violent portrayal of God in Scripture is no less true than the criminal portrayal of Jesus on the cross. From the perspective of the outside observer, both parties appear guilty. But for those "in the know," for those with a personal relationship with the God revealed in Jesus Christ, we see through the accusations and condemnation, and see that out of His great love for us, God gladly bore the blame and the shame for our sin so that He might deliver us from it and expose sin for what it really is.

The point is this: one primary saving function of the cross is that it is *revelatory*. It reveals to humans the way we murderously blame and scapegoat others. But it is also *revolutionary*. If we see the sinful scapegoat practices that Jesus revealed on the cross, then we are called to abandon such practices in the future. If Jesus did not retaliate against those who wrongfully accused, condemned, and crucified Him, but forgave them instead, then this is what we humans must start doing instead. Christlike forgiveness will bring a peaceful revolution to all human interactions. Jesus revealed this on the cross, just as God has been revealing this through His actions all along. By accepting the blame for our violence, God was pointing out to us that we ourselves are the source of our violence and was calling us to abandon such practices in the future.

THE VIOLENCE OF GOD IS THE VIOLENCE OF MAN

In the end, I saw the stark and shocking truth of Option 2 to be this: God did not commit the acts of violence that are attributed to Him. *The violence of God in the Bible is actually the violence of man which we commit in God's name.* This does not make the Bible less true, inspired, or inerrant, but more true than ever imagined. For when we read the Bible and recognize that God is not doing what the Bible says He is doing, it is then that we first get a glimpse into the truth of the human condition, the truth that has been hidden since the foundation of the world, the truth that we hide from, that we ignore, and that we do our best to cover under the rituals of religion and the policies of politics. What truth? That *we* are guilty of great violence, and we justify this violence by blaming God for it.

This is the great truth of the violent portions of the Bible. When we recognize this truth, we see that the Bible is more inspired and inerrant than we ever imagined, for the Bible reveals a truth which no religion and no politician has ever seen or heard. The Bible reveals a universal condition of the human heart which few recognize or admit. The truth is this: God is love and in Him there is no violence at all. You and I are the violent ones, and we justify our violence by blaming it on God. This is the inspired and inerrant truth to which Scripture testifies on nearly every page.

And this is what makes the Bible more of a book about humans than a book about God. The Bible is an inspired and inerrant book in which God seeks to reveals us to us. While Jesus is the greatest revelation of the Bible, the most overlooked truth in the Bible is the revelation it contains about the humankind. The mystery that has been hidden since the foundation of the world, and which remains hidden to most people to this very day, is that God is love and in Him there is no violence at all. All so-called "divine violence" is actually human violence that we justify in our own mind by blaming it on God. We humans use the scapegoat mechanism to kill and blame others, and when we use it, we make God the ultimate scapegoat for our violence. When rivalry occurs in life, we use the scapegoat mechanism to bring peace between warring brothers, and when we kill an innocent third party to bring this peace, we always do so in the name of God, thus making Him the ultimate innocent scapegoat for *our* sin.

GOD AS THE ULTIMATE SCAPEGOAT

The process for making God the scapegoat for our violence unfolds in six basic steps. In nearly every divine vengeance text in Scripture, most of these six steps are either present or implied.

1. I hate my enemies.
2. God is on my side.
3. God hates my enemies.
4. God kills His enemies.
5. God wants me to kill my enemies.
6. It is God's will for me to kill my enemies.

Through this process, we "turn God into the divine

victim/scapegoat."[3] Because we love God and God loves us, and because we hate our enemies, God also must hate our enemies. After all, they are the sinners. They are evil doers. They are in rebellion against God. They have shamed us and cursed His name. They worship false gods and harm women and children. Therefore how could God feel anything but hatred for them just as we feel hatred for them? In light of such obvious facts, God must be on our side against our enemies. And since we hate our enemies, God must hate them too. And since we often see God destroy His enemies in history (which, in reality, is just other recorded accounts of this same process), He must want to destroy our enemies today as well. And he wants to use us as His instrument of divine vengeance.

However, such logic cannot be found anywhere in the Gospels from the words or actions of Jesus. To the contrary, Jesus taught and lived the exact opposite. When His disciples wanted to call down fire from heaven upon those who rejected Him, Jesus strongly rebuked them for such thinking (Luke 9:54-55). When Jesus set out to minister to sinners, Gentiles, women, and worst of all, sinful Gentile women, the disciples tried to dissuade Him, but Jesus always corrected them and said that it was for such people that He came. In His famous Sermon on the Mount, Jesus instructed His disciples to love their

[3] Robert G. Hamerton-Kelly, *Sacred Violence: Paul's Hermeneutic of the Cross* (Minneapolis: Fortress, 1992), 98.

enemies and pray for them (Matt 5:43-48), rather than condemn them and try to kill them. On the cross, when Jesus was being wrongly condemned and crucified, He called out to God, not for vengeance, but forgiveness (Luke 23:34). Of all the major human characters in biblical narratives, Jesus is the *only* one who never called for violence and never practiced scapegoating, either of another human being or of God Himself. Moses did. David did. All the prophets did. Peter, Paul, and John did (though in much less significant ways than with Old Testament writers).

But since Jesus never did any scapegoating or called for any violence, and since Jesus perfectly reveals God to us (John 1:14, 18; 14:9-11; 2 Cor 4:4; Php 2:6; Col 1:15; Heb 1:2-3), then we must say that God also never does any scapegoating or calls for any violence. There cannot be a "hidden side" of God that did not get 'revealed in Jesus, for if there is, then the biblical revelation of Jesus is incomplete and the Bible is wrong.

We do, however, see religious and political leaders in the Gospels claiming that they are doing God's will when they arrest, condemn, and crucify Jesus. They place the blame for their murder of Jesus squarely on the back of God Himself. They make Jesus a scapegoat, thereby creating peace between the Jews and Rome, and they also make God a scapegoat by blaming Him for the murder of Jesus.

In this way, Jesus reveals to us what we have always been doing, not only in our tendency to scapegoat others, but also in our tendency to scapegoat God. While Jesus is a scapegoat for the religious and political problems of His day, the real scapegoat in the crucifixion of Jesus is God Himself. He is blamed for the crucifixion of Jesus. Both the religious and political authorities believed they were doing what God (or the gods) wanted so that peace might come to their land. By blaming God for the death of Jesus, God becomes the ultimate scapegoat. The death of Jesus reveals that humans have always blamed God for our own violence and evil. God did not *need* Jesus to die so that sins could be paid for and grace extended.[4] And since Jesus was innocent of all wrongdoing, there was no legal or moral reason for Jesus to die. But we humans killed Jesus anyway *in the name of God*, because this is what humans have done since the foundation of the world. We kill and destroy our enemies and then claim that we did it in obedience to God's will. But God never commands such a thing! We humans *put* commands of violence in the mouth of God so that we can kill our

---

[4] Grace, by definition, requires no payment to anyone, either by us, or by God. If sin was "paid for" by the death of Jesus, then grace is not required. A debt can either be paid off or freely canceled. But not both. If you pay off your mortgage, the bank does not send you a certificate saying they canceled your debt. No, it was paid off. Similarly, if a bank does cancel a debt, then it was not paid off and does not need to be paid off. See the entries on Grace, Forgiveness, and Sin in *The Gospel Dictionary* (forthcoming) for more.

enemies and feel justified in doing so.

This raises a significant question. Which is the greater evil? To do an evil thing, or to do that exact same evil thing, but do it in the name of God? The answer is obvious. The latter is a far greater evil. If one person murders another out of rage or jealousy, it is a great evil. But if a person murders another and says, "I did this because God told me to," this is a far greater evil. Why? Because they have taken an act of great evil and turned it into an act of seeming righteousness, thus blaming God for the evil they themselves commit. Furthermore, they turn the righteous God into a monstrous God.

Yet this is what we humans do. Especially religious humans. One of the great "benefits" of religion is that it allows us to behave just as wickedly as the non-religious, but we get to call our wicked behavior "righteous" because "God told me to do it."

Francis Bacon commented on this very thing in his essay, "Of the Unity of Religion." Here is what he wrote:

> It was great blasphemy when the devil said, "I will ascend and be like the Highest," but it is greater blasphemy to personate God, and bring him in saying, "I will descend, and be like the prince of darkness." How terrible it is to make religion descend to the cruel and abominable actions of murdering princes, butchery of people, and subversion of states and governments! Surely this is to bring down the Holy Ghost, instead of in the likeness of a dove, in the shape of a vulture or raven, raising on the ship of the

Christian church a flag of pirates and assassins.[5]

By blaming God for our own violence, we commit a double sin, and the second is worse than the first. The sin itself is bad enough, but to blame the sin on God is to turn the holiness of God into the spawn of Satan.

This revelation about the human tendency to blame God for our own human vices is not found *only* in Scripture. Those who have eyes to see can also discover this revelation in numerous other sources as well. Sometimes it is quite obvious. For example, in *The History* by Herodotus, we are told of a time when King Cyrus of the Persians became alarmed at how his soldiers were becoming rich from plundering cities they conquered. He was afraid that some of them might rebel if they became too rich. However, he couldn't just take the plunder from them, because then they would certainly rebel. To avoid this problem, one of his counselors told Cyrus to do the following:

> Let some of thy bodyguards be placed as sentinels at each of the city gates, and let them take their booty from the soldiers as they leave the town, and tell them that they do so because the tenths are due to Jupiter. So wilt thou escape the hatred they would feel if the plunder were taken away from them by force; and they, seeing that what is

[5] Francis Bacon, *Essays*, "Of the Unity of Religion." Minor changes in wording were made to make the quote more understandable to modern readers.

proposed is just, will do it willingly.[6]

Cyrus followed this advice and was able to take a tenth of all the plunder for himself, while saying it was Jupiter's will that the soldiers do so. Throughout the rest of Herodotus, numerous other acts of war, greed, and violence are attributed to the will of the gods, when in reality, the causes were human greed and pride.

The Netflix series "Peaky Blinders" has numerous similar examples. The show is an English television crime drama set in 1920s Birmingham, England, in the aftermath of World War I. It depicts how the "Peaky Blinders" street gang rose to power through robbery, violence, racketeering, illegal bookmaking, and the control of gambling. In Episode 3.5, the leader of the gang, Thomas Shelby, hosts a meeting between himself, his brother Arthur, and a man named Alfie Solomons, who is the leader of a rival Jewish gang. In a previous episode, Alfie Solomons betrayed Arthur and had him arrested, and so the scene begins with Alfie apologizing to Arthur for this betrayal. The dialogue unfolds as follows:

Alfie: "Arthur! Shalom! ... I owe you a little something. I do. Come. Sit down. Sit down. Listen, Arthur. I want you

---

[6] Herodotus, *The History*, I:89. This "tithe to Jupiter," which actually ends up in the hands of leaders, sounds suspiciously like a similar practice in the church today. See my book, *Church is More than Bodies, Bucks, & Bricks.*

to know that whatever happened between us back then, that was business. It was just business. And I also want you to know that I have made my apologies by my own God for abusing a very holy day to get you clinked up and battered, which I did. And now I would also like to extend my personal apologies unto you."

[Arthur stares at him as says nothing.]

Alfie: "I hear you have allowed Jesus to come into your life! Eh?"

Arthur: "Oh, you heard that?"

Alfie: "Yeah, that's beautiful. That's wonderful. That's lovely, isn't it? That's lovely. But I was wondering … how does that work for you on a day-to-day, considering your line of work, mate?"

Arthur [grimacing]: "Your apology is accepted."

Alfie: "Cause I heard you're a right f****** nuisance with it."

[Arthur seethes with anger and reaches over to grab a heavy, crystal bowl and prepares to smash Alfie in the face with it.]

Alfie: "You see, all I'm saying is that every man, he craves certainty, doesn't he? He craves a certainty, even if that certainty of yours, right … well, I mean … It's f****** fanciful mate, isn't it? … Eh?"

Arthur puts down the bowl and pulls his face in close to Alfie and growls: "I'm Old Testament."

Alfie: "F****** hell. Look at that. Now, that ... that scares me more. Yeah." [He looks over at Thomas.] "Congratulations, Tommy. You now have the finished article right here, don't you? See, that man, right, he will murder and maim for you with God on his side. Yeah. You don't want to let him go."

Do you see? Alfie Solomon gets it. Arthur, though he "has Jesus" in his life, follows the Old Testament, and this allows him to murder and maim in the name of God. His enemies are God's enemies, and since Arthur wants his enemies dead, God does too. When Arthur kills and hurts people, he is only doing God's will, just like the people in the Old Testament. For Arthur, God is the perfect scapegoat. God is the perfect victim on which to lay blame for all the wrong that he does.

But it's not just Arthur. It's all of us. This is what we humans do. Whether its war and violence, we lay the blame on God and said, "He did it. He wanted those people dead." All violent and accusatory texts in Scripture reveal something similar. When we see violence in Scripture, even when it is attributed to God, these texts are not there so that we can nod our heads in agreement with what was done, thinking to ourselves, "Well, they were evil; they deserved it," nor to see such texts as a permission to treat our enemies in similar ways. Rather, we are to follow the universal love and forgiveness of Jesus Christ, while sensing the inner nonviolent voice of the Holy Spirit, and condemn such texts. We do not condemn them as "errors in Scripture," but as perfectly inspired and inerrant revelations of the great problem in the human heart. We are to turn away from such texts in disgust, because in them, we see the violence of our own hearts.

This is also true of the texts about "natural violence" in Scripture, such as the flood in Genesis 6–8. The Bible tends to record natural violence as also being divine violence from God meted out on the wicked and evil groups of people. But we must remember that all accounts of "natural divine violence" in Scripture were recorded after the event had occurred, by human authors who were trying to explain why such a terrible thing had occurred to a particular group of people. Natural disasters in biblical history, just like natural disasters now, are horrible events in search of an explanation.

The typical explanation offered in biblical history is the same explanation that is typically offered now. Why did that hurricane wipe out so many homes and kill so many people in New Orleans? Well, they're given to drunkenness and the occult, and God wants them to repent. Why did the tsunami kill over 200,000 in Indonesia? Well, most of them aren't Christian and God wants them to convert. Why did my neighbor's house burn down? Well, if only they had come to church like I asked them to, God would have spared them.

And similar explanations are found in the Bible. Why did the flood occur? Because the people were evil continually. Why the earth swallow up some of the Israelites? They were rebelling against Moses. Why did famine come upon the land? Because the king and the people are worshipping idols.

Is any of this true? No. These are not the *real* explanations for why these things happen. But they are the explanations that we humans give. We blame all violence on God, including the violence of natural disasters. And how do we know that God did not actually send or cause these natural disasters? Once again, Jesus shows the way. In His day, there was a man who was blind since birth, and the disciples wanted to know if the man was blind because he had sinned or his parents. Jesus said it was neither (John 9:1-7). Later, the tower of Siloam fell and killed some other people. Again, the disciples wanted to know (showing how humans think) if the people who died in the collapse were greater sinners than everyone else. Jesus answers and says that everyone is equally sinful and so we should all repent (Luke 13:1-5). In other words, Jesus teaches the truth about natural disasters and diseases: They do not come upon those who are worse sinners than everyone else. Sadly, these things just happen in this world. God does not send them or cause them.

The *only* activity of God in such disasters is to save people from them. And He calls us to help Him in this task. We are not to condemn those who suffer from disasters, but to rescue as many as we can.

So again, whether it is human violence or natural violence, regardless of what the Bible records as the "source" of such violence, Jesus reveals that the source is not God. So when the Bible tells us that the source *is* God, we know that the Bible is not revealing God to us, but is revealing us to us. The Bible is serving as a mirror of the human heart, showing us how we wrongly rope God into our violence, blaming Him for our own murderous intentions, and how we wrongly blame God for all the other ills that occur in this world. By revealing our hearts to us in this way, as in a mirror, Scripture calls to see the evil in our own hearts and turn away from such behavior.

SCRIPTURE AS THE MIRROR OF MAN

This imagery of the mirror of Scripture comes from Scripture itself. It is found in James 1:23-24. James writes, "For if anyone is a hearer of the word and not a doer, he is like a man observing his natural face in a mirror; for he observes himself, goes away, and immediately forgets what kind of man he was." Most Bible scholars believe that the book of James is the earliest New Testament letter, and that it was written by James, the half-brother of Jesus, who was also a prominent leader in the Jerusalem church (Acts 15:13-21; Gal 1:19).

Many scholars also believe that the book of James has the Sermon on the Mount in Matthew 5–7 as its foundation. This certainly seems to fit in the opening chapters of each, as both James and Jesus begin by encouraging others to rejoice in their trials and difficulties (cf. Matt 5:1-12; Jas 1:1-20). James adds some additional comments about how just as God cannot be tempted by evil, so also He does not tempt anyone. And while we humans are often tempted not only to sin, but also to blame God for putting us into situations where we are tempted, James wants his readers to understand that God only brings good gifts into our lives; He does not bring sin, evil, or temptation. Such an idea is already preparing us for what James wants us to see: that violence and evil and the temptation to do both, comes not from God, but from within ourselves.

Following the discussion of seeing trials and blessings, both James and Jesus move on to talk about the conditions and consequences of violence (Matt 5:21-48; Jas 1:15–2:13). It is interesting that both begin with the concept of desire, and how desire leads to sin, which results in death (Matt 5:21-22; cf. 1 John 3:15; Jas 1:15-20). Desire, of course, is the foundational idea in René Girard's mimetic theory. Humans are hard-wired for desire. We want what we see, and we only want it more when we see that others also want what we want. Desire is only amplified by a similar desire in other people. This desire then leads to rivalry, which can lead to violence and death. Of course, as we see in James 1:14-15, James was writing and teaching about this idea long before René Girard was ever born. This does not make desire wrong, for imitative desire (or mimetic desire) is how God hardwired humans to learn. Mimetic desire is responsible for helping us learn to walk, talk, behave, and interact with other human beings.

The first readers of James would have certainly made the connections that James alluded to in these opening statements of his letter. He wrote about the blessings of trials, clarifying that while trials and testing can be beneficial, those that stem from temptation do not originate with God but rather with human desire. "God only gives good gifts," James says. "All sin and violence comes from man."

The logical question, then, is, "What then are we to do with the violence of God in the Hebrew Scriptures? God is angry, wrathful, and violent all over in Scripture, is He not?"

The response to this implied question begins in James 1:19. After James reiterates that anger and wrath come from man (not God), he states that anger and wrath do not accomplish the righteousness of God (Jas 1:20). Why would James say this? Isn't it blatantly obvious that human wrath and anger do not accomplish the righteous will of God? To be honest, no, it is not obvious. Why not? Because most people, especially religions people, believe that when they get angry at something, they get angry with a "righteous anger." They get angry at what they see, and they lash out with violent words and violent actions, believing that God is on their side, and that He is just as angry as they are at the injustice that has been done. James points out that human anger and wrath does not accomplish the righteousness of God because human anger and wrath is always and *only* human anger and wrath. Despite what we so often tell ourselves, the righteousness of God cannot be carried out through human anger and wrath.

But what about divine anger and wrath? Cannot God command wars, death, and violence to punish sin or to accomplish His will? James answers these sorts of questions in the rest of his letter. He talks about various forms of injustice that occurs in the world, and shows point by point how each of these are to be laid at the feet of mankind. Favoritism and injustice to the poor comes not from God blessing some people over others, but because we humans judge with evil thoughts and treat others with dishonor (Jas 2:1-13).

When it comes to telling those in need that God will provide for them, it is not enough to tell them that God will provide, for God has set this world up so that He provides for those in need through the generosity and kindness of you and me (Jas 2:14-26). So when someone goes hungry or sick, it is not because God has cursed them or abandoned them. No, it is because we are not doing our part to take care of them.

The violence of the tongue takes up all of chapter 3. James points out that what we say has consequences, and that when we say things that are hurtful, rude, and mean, these things do not come from God, but come from an evil, poisonous heart (Jas 3:8, 14). Any words that come down from heaven to the earth through our tongue will be words of wisdom, grace, mercy, love, and kindness (Jas 3:17). Any words that do not fit such a description can safely be assumed to have originated in the fires of hell rather than from God (Jas 3:6, 15-16). So once again, violence, even in the form of words, is seen to have nothing to do with God, but instead come from the human heart fueled by evil.

The first verse of chapter 4 deals with the question of physical violence itself, and specifically the question of wars and fights. And again, as with everything else James has been saying, he reveals that such things have nothing to do with God, and do not come from Him, but instead come from desire, just as they did in 1:14-15. The rest of the letter continues in this theme by circling back around to address once more the themes that were already discussed.

But over and over again in this short letter, James is revealing his belief that there is no violence of any kind in God. All types of violence, including verbal violence, physical violence, and the violence of unjustly judging others, come not from God, but from the heart of man, which is overcome with desire.

And since James was the earliest New Testament book to have been written, the only Scriptures James had at this point with which to teach others were the Hebrew Scriptures, which were filled with example after example of how God seemed to act and behave in ways that were exactly the opposite of what James was writing here. Yet by carefully reading what James has written, we see that he is providing his audience with a hermeneutical lens on how to read the Hebrew Scriptures. He wants them to see that whenever they read about hate, violence, war, bloodshed, envy, judgment, and condemnation, they should read these as having come from the human heart. But whenever they discover the wisdom of Scripture that invites them to peace, purity, gentleness, mercy, and equality (Jas 3:17), then these can safely be assumed to have come from God.

Ultimately, one of the truths that James wants his readers to see is the truth he states in James 1:23-24. The purpose of Scripture, James says, is so that when we look into it, we see our own face, and seeing the faults and blemishes that are there, we do something about what we see and correct them. If we see the reflection of our heart in Scripture, and go away without remembering what we have seen or doing anything about it, then we deceive ourselves and all our religious beliefs and practices become useless (Jas 1:26).

In other words, James is instructing his readers (and us) that to understand Scripture properly, we must read it as if we were looking into a mirror. And what do we expect to see when looking into a mirror? Not the face of God, but our very own face. And what we see in the mirror determines what we should do about what we see. We may need to straighten our hair, pop a zit, or take some food out of our teeth. The worst thing is to look into the mirror, see the problems that are there, and then turn away without doing anything about what we see. The mirror of Scripture is given to us by God to reveal to us our human blemishes and sinful ways. And as James points out repeatedly in his letter, the primary human blemish in Scripture is the blemish of violence in all its forms, and for which we blame God. The statements in the Bible about God committing violence are not statements about God committing violence, but are statements about how humans blame God for the violence we ourselves commit. Only when we see this human blemish for what it is can we then correct it and be blessed in what we do (Jas 1:25).

We believe we need the Bible to reveal God to us. And

we do need it for that, but we fail to realize is that we also need the Bible to reveal us to ourselves. In fact, humanity is in a greater need of a revelation of ourselves than we are in need of a revelation of God. We humans think we understand ourselves pretty well, but we don't. We barely know the first thing about us. We know as little about ourselves as we know about the infinite God. We have shrouded ourselves in myth and mystery, so that we do not know the things we do. In the words of Jesus, we know not what we do. Our true character, our true nature, is a mystery hidden since the foundation of the world. And it goes on being a mystery to us as long as we think the Bible is about God.

God looks at how we read the Bible to learn about Him, and says, "No, no! It's about you! I know you Christians like to say, 'It's not about me' but in this case, it is! It's all about you. So pick it up, read, learn, and see yourself in the mirror that I have provided to you. Only once you have eyes to see your own faces will you then have eyes to see me as well." We err when we think the Bible was written about God. The Bible is about God in the same way that nature is. Yes, both can point us to God, but are not "about" God. Seeking to learn about God from the Bible will lead us astray as surely as seeking to learn about God from nature.

In his sermon, "The Weight of Glory," C. S. Lewis said this:

> I read in a periodical the other day that the fundamental thing is how we think of God. By God Himself, it is not! How God thinks of us is not only more important, but infinitely more important. Indeed, how we think of Him is of no importance except in so far as it is related to how He thinks of us.

Yes. And most of us read the Bible for the first purpose: to learn about God. We want to learn to think properly about God. But God did not give us the Bible for that reason. He gave the Bible so that we would know what He thinks of us. As Lewis states, this is infinitely more important. The great Roman philosopher Seneca once wrote to Nero Caesar to encourage him toward rule based on clemency. In the first sentence of this essay, Seneca tells Nero that he writes "in order that I may serve as a mirror to you."[7] Seneca knew, as did Lewis, James, Jesus, and, of course, God, that there is no greater need in a life of a human being than a mirror which reveals to him the darkness in his own soul. Thankfully, we have this greatest of all mirrors within the pages of Scripture. The Bible serves as a mirror of the human soul, revealing to us that which could not be seen in any other way.

The father of all philosophy, Thales of Miletus, taught that the most difficult task for a human being, and thus the most important, was to "know thyself." How sad it is that so few humans have sought to learn anything real

---

[7] Lucius Annaeus Seneca, "On Clemency," I.I.

about ourselves. Thankfully, God has sought to remedy this and provide a clear insight into the condition of humanity by providing us with the Bible.

Viewing the Bible as a mirror that reveals to us our very own face is the key to understanding Scripture and understanding the violent portrayals of God in Scripture. Till we see our own faces, we can never be who we really are.[8] If you do not keep this key in mind, you might be tempted in the chapters that follow to think that I am denying the inerrancy and inspiration of Scripture. I am simply pointing out the human blemishes that the Scripture mirror inerrantly points out to us. We humans love to blame God for our own sin and for all that goes wrong in this world. We not only see this in our own time and culture, but this behavior is also seen everywhere in Scripture. Scripture is a mirror that reveals ourselves to us, because without Scripture, we would never be able to see our own faces. We would never see ourselves as we really are.

But if Scripture is the mirror of man, then how can we know what God is like? There are numerous ways, but one of them is through the person and work of Jesus Christ, who, of course, is revealed in Scripture itself. Just as Jesus entered into the human world to reveal God to us and to reveal us to us, the words and works of Jesus

---

[8] This is the truth in C. S. Lewis' greatest novel, *Till We Have Faces.*

were written in the human book of Scripture both to reveal God to us (as He really is) and to reveal us to us (as we really can be). In this way, just as Scripture is the mirror of man, so also, Jesus is the mirror of God.

JESUS AS THE MIRROR OF GOD

To understand how Scripture reveals the face of man to us, it is helpful to see the parallel between the way God is portrayed in Scripture and how Jesus was presented to the people of Jerusalem on the day of His crucifixion. For those watching the crucifixion of three men that day at Golgotha, Jesus was just another criminal. He had been tried, convicted, and crucified by both religious and political authorities. If someone were to come along (as the early church did) and say that Jesus was in fact innocent of the crimes for which He was condemned, others would (rightly) object that this not only accuses the highest religious and political authorities of error, but also accuses God of making a mistake. After all, it would be pointed out, Jesus did not object to His condemnation. Jesus did not speak a word in His own defense, which proves that He knew He was guilty.

But Christianity believes Jesus was not guilty. So why did He remain silent? Why did God not send a legion of angels to defend the murder of His innocent Son? Some recent theologians have argued that the reason God did not defend Jesus and the reason Jesus did not speak in His own defense is because this had been their plan all along. According to this idea, God needed Jesus to die so that God could pour out His wrath upon someone else instead of sinful humanity, and so Jesus and God decided that Jesus would die in the place of mankind. Someone had to be punished for human sin, and so Jesus became a man so that He could become the substitute for humanity and suffer in our place for our sin.

There is another possibility, however. It is the possibility I explained and defended in my book, *The Atonement of God.* Briefly stated, this possibility is that God was never angry at humans for our sin, nor did He want to punish us for it. Instead, God was always grieved at how sin had captured and enslaved us, and rather than punish us for our sin, God wanted to rescue and deliver us from it. The incarnation of Jesus was not a way to punish humans for sin, but was a way to rescue humanity from sin. God has always loved, always accepted, always forgiven us, and His thoughts toward us have never changed or wavered. The death of Jesus on the cross resulted in the defeat of sin, death, and the devil, and revealed to humanity the depth of God's love for us as well as the depth and depravity of our own violence and evil.

This means then that Jesus remained silent in His own defense, not because He was agreeing with His accusers, but because He was revealing to us (through them) that the primary source of all evil and violence in this world is the way we accuse, condemn, judge, and kill others in the name of God. This revelation of our sin could *never* have happened if Jesus had defended Himself in court or called down legions of angels to carry Him to safety. Such actions would have instead served to fortify and justify our continued reliance the idea that we can use violence and power to overcome evil and injustice. Jesus wanted to show us that violence cannot be used to overcome evil and violence, and that while humans try to fight violence with violence, God has never acted in this way in history. Instead, the weapons of God are truth, love, grace, mercy, generosity, longsuffering, patience, and forgiveness.

Just as Jesus did not speak or act in His own defense, but let His accusers condemn and crucify Him as a blasphemer and a traitor, so also, God did not often speak or act in His own defense in the Old Testament when He was accused and condemned by Scripture as a violent murderer and traitor to the human race. Are the Scriptures wrong in what they say about the nature and character of God? Yes, just as those who accused and condemned Jesus were wrong about Him. But this does not mean that Scripture is wrong about God any more than it means that Jesus was wrong to not speak in His own defense. By remaining silent, God was revealing a deeper truth about Himself and about humanity that we could never have seen otherwise. By letting us blame Him, by allowing us to accuse Him of things He did not do but which we did in His name, both God in human history and Jesus Christ on the cross have revealed to us that we are the guilty ones, we are the one who condemns, we have the spirit of the accuser, and we can only break free of this sin by seeing an undeniably clear image of ourselves within the mirror of Scripture.

So is the Bible wrong about what it sometimes says about God? Yes. But what it gets wrong about God is what makes the Bible so right, for what it gets wrong about God is exactly the same thing that we get wrong about God as well. By making the horror so blatantly obvious, the Scriptures reveal the truth about humanity about which we are all blind and ignorant. In this way, Scripture proves beyond a shadow of a doubt that the Bible is inerrant and inspired revelation from God, for we humans would have never come to this revelation about ourselves if it had not come to us from God. Inspired Scripture inerrantly affirms the truth about God and about ourselves that no human would ever invent or imagine, unless God had revealed it to us.

And what is that truth? That sin leads to violence and death (Jas 1:15), and we humans justify this violence and death by blaming it on God. This is the truth we will see over and over in Scripture in the following chapters. Let us look intently into the mirror of the Bible and see our own face starting back at us from its pages. If we go away forgetting what we have seen, we do so at our own peril.

THE MONSTER AT THE END OF THE BOOK

As a child, my favorite "Sesame Street" story was *The Monster at the End of the Book*. In it, Grover is warned that there is a monster at the end of the book, and so he does everything he can to keep the reader from turning pages in the book. He builds walls. He tries to glue the pages shut. He attempts to tie the pages down with rope. Near the end of the book, Grover makes one last frantic plea for the reader to not turn the final page, only to discover on that final page, in a surprise self-referential plot twist, that the monster is himself. Grover, cute, cuddly, loveable Grover, is the monster at the end of the book.

The Bible also has a monster at the end of the book. Except that the monster in the Bible is truly monstrous (and cute and cuddly at times as well, I suppose) . The monster is you and I, and we have done monstrous things. Worst of all, we blame our monstrous behavior on God. We are the violent ones, and we have projected our violence onto our loving, gracious, forgiving, and compassionate God. Indeed, it is only because we are able to blame God for our violence that we are able to commit greater and more monstrous violence.

Many believe that the monster in the Bible is God. But as we read through Scripture, we begin to get a growing sense that we are mistaken about the identity of the monster in this book. A mystery develops about the nature and identity of this monster. As we turn page after page, with growing trepidation, we see God doing and commanding the more horrible things, but then we also see God behaving in the most loving and kind ways. And we begin to ask ourselves, "What is going on? What is God truly like? How can God behave in both of these opposing ways?"

But then Jesus shows up in the Gospels and claims to reveal God to us. And we like the God that Jesus reveals to us. The God revealed in Jesus does not appear to be a monster at all. He is gentle, kind, gracious, and forgiving.

And so we kill Him.

Why? Because part of us wants the violent God back, so that we can continue to kill our enemies in God's name. If God is just like Jesus, and Jesus is supremely nonviolent, then we humans can no longer march off to war with God's name on our lips.

And when we killed Jesus, we say it was because God told us to. Jesus spoke blasphemy, and as we all know, God wants to kill blasphemers. So although "we" killed Jesus, we didn't actually kill Him. God killed Him. Through us. It was God's will.

Sadly, this is still the mantra most people hear from Christian pulpits today around the world. As in the days of Jesus, it makes us feel better to have someone to blame for our own violent tendencies. Projecting our violent, monstrous tendencies onto God gives us an escape hatch for those violent tendencies. We not only can engage in such hateful acts, but we can do them with praise to God on our lips.

But a careful reading of Scripture reveals the truth. The violent portions of Scripture are little more than projections of our bloody violence onto the heart and hands of God. The monster in this book is not God, but humanity. You and I are the monsters at the end of the book.

We object, of course, that we are not monsters. We are just human. And we make mistakes.

That is true. In fact, calling someone a monster is one sign that scapegoating is taking place. We tend to dehumanize our scapegoat victims before we condemn and kill them. I am not seeking to dehumanize anyone, but rather to rehumanize everyone. But rehumanization begins by recognizing our own monstrous acts and deeds. And most of all, by recognizing that we cannot, we *must not*, continue blaming God for our monstrous deeds. We humans are not monsters, but God is not a monster either. And the truly monstrous occurs when we humans do monstrous things in God's name. *That* is the monster revealed in the Bible. The Bible holds a mirror up to our face and says, "Let me show you your heart. Let me reveal what lurks within. Look deeply. Do not turn away in horror.

Take a good, hard, long look. Do you see? Are you horrified? Good. Now turn away from what you saw, and begin to follow in the way of Jesus, who not only reflects the heart of God, but also reflects God's true goal for humanity."

In his epic fantasy novel, *The Bonehunters*, Steven Erikson writes this:

> There had been plenty of altars before which she had knelt over the years, and from them, one and all, Torahaval Delat had discovered something she now held to be true. All that is worshipped is but a reflection of the worshipper. A single god, no matter how benign, is tortured into a multitude of masks, each shaped by the secret desires, hungers, fears, and joys of the individual mortal, who but plays a game of obsequious approbation.

> Believers plunged into belief. The faithful drowned in their faith.

> And there was another truth, one that seemed on the surface to contradict the first one. The gentler and kinder the god, the more harsh and cruel its worshippers, for they hold to their conviction with taut certainty, febrile in its extremity, and so cannot abide dissenters. They will kill, they will torture, in that god's name. And see in themselves no conflict, no matter how bloodstained their hands.

Until you see the stains on your hands and the piles of mangled bodies at your feet, you will never properly see

God or understand the message of the cross.

THE EMPEROR IS DEAD

A different fantasy novel reveals a similar truth. In *The Way of Kings,* Brandon Sanderson includes a short story that is told to the main character, Kaladin. In this short story, a ship captain named Derethil sets sail to discover the origin of their ancient enemy, the Voidbringers. While they are on this journey, a giant storm overtakes them and their ship, the *Wandersail,* until they run aground. Here is how the story continues:

> The *Wandersail* ran aground and was nearly destroyed, but Derethil and most of his sailors survived. They found themselves on a ring of small islands surrounding an enormous whirlpool, where, it is said, the ocean drains. Derethil and his men were greeted by a strange people with long, limber bodies who wore robes of single color and shells in their hair unlike any that grow back on Roshar [the mainland].
>
> These people took the survivors in, fed them, and nursed them back to health. During his weeks of recovery, Derethil studied the strange people, who called themselves the Uvara, and People of the Great Abyss. They lived curious lives. Unlike the people of Roshar—who constantly argue—the Uvara always seemed to agree. From childhood, there were no questions. Each and every person went

about his duty.

One day, while Derethil and his men were sparring to regain strength, a young serving girl brought them refreshment. She tripped on an uneven stone, dropping the goblets to the floor and shattering them. In a flash, the other Uvara descended on the hapless child and slaughtered her in a brutal way. Derethil and his men were so stunned that by the time they regained their wits, the child was dead. Angry, Derethil demanded to know the cause of the unjustified murder. One of the other natives explained. "Our emperor will not suffer failure."

As Derethil began to pay more attention, he saw many other murders. These Uvara, these People of the Great Abyss, were prone to astonishing cruelty. If one of their members did something wrong—something the slightest bit untoward or unfavorable—the others would slaughter him or her. Each time he asked, Derethil's caretaker gave him the same answer. "Our emperor will not suffer failure."

The emperor, Derethil discovered, resided in the tower on the eastern coast of the largest island among the Uvara. Derethil determined that he needed to confront this cruel emperor. What kind of monster would demand that such an obviously peaceful people kill so often and so terribly? Derethil gathered his sailors, a heroic group, and they armed themselves. The Uvara did not try to stop them, though they watched with fright as the strangers stormed the emperor's tower.

Derethil and his men came out of the tower a short time later, carrying a desiccated corpse in fine robes and jewelry. "This is your emperor?" Derethil demanded. "We found him in the top room, alone." It appeared that the man had been dead for years, but nobody had dared enter his tower. They were too frightened of him.

When he showed the Uvara the dead body, they began to wail and weep. The entire island was cast into chaos, as the Uvara began to burn homes, riot, or fall to their knees in torment. Amazed and confused, Derethil and his men stormed the Uvara shipyards, where the *Wandersail* was being repaired. Their guide and caretaker joined them, and she begged to accompany them in their escape. So it was that Nafti joined the crew.

Derethil and his men set sail, and though the winds were still, they rode the *Wandersail* around the whirlpool, using the momentum to spin them out and away from the islands. Long after they left, they could see the smoke rising from the ostensibly peaceful lands. They gathered on the deck, watching, and Derethil asked Nafti the reason for the terrible riots.

Holding a blanket around herself, staring with haunted eyes at her lands, she replied, "Do you not see, Traveling One? If the emperor is dead, and has been all these years, then the murders we committed are not his responsibility. They are our own."

This is a beautiful and haunting story, partly because it is a picture of what is actually going on in human history, as revealed to us by Scripture. But there is a great danger in finding out that we are to blame for our own violence. The people of Uvara needed someone to blame for their monstrous cruelty, but when they found that they had no one to blame but themselves, they turned on each other in retaliation for all the crimes committed against one another. God is willing to act as our scapegoat, as our dead emperor, if the alternative is more and greater violence.

We humans are violent, and we maintain peace by committing violence toward others. Our violence is not random, however, but is carefully directed toward those whom we believe God has given us permission to hate and to kill. This makes us feel better about the violence we commit, for it is not "we" who are violent. We tell ourselves that we don't want to kill, but we have no choice, for we must follow the will of God. After all, "Our emperor does not suffer failure. Sinners must be punished. The enemies of God must be destroyed."

What is most shocking about the biblical revelation, however, is that God purposefully lets us blame Him for the violence we commit in His name. Why? Because, like the people on the island of Uvara, if we were to realize the true source of our violence, that it comes from our own heart rather than the heart of God, few would be able to handle the horror.

Think of it: Your hands, my hands, and the hands of

every human being are dripping with the blood and gore of countless victims, whom we murdered in the name of God.

Such a revelation will destroy us. When we see how we have willingly contributed to the murder of millions of innocent children, the slaughter of people who committed no "sin" but that of being different, and the genocide of entire civilizations, we should weep, mourn, and wail. We should call for the mountains to fall upon us, for the sun to shine no more, and for the world to burn away in ashes, for none of us deserve to live another second of another day after the great crimes against humanity of which we are all complicit. Most humans are unwilling and unready to see such a truth, and so we ignore it and hide from it. We do not want to know what we really are.

But God knows. He knows what we are. He knows the murderous violence that resides in the heart of every human. And He also knows that a true revelation of our blood-soaked human heart would destroy us. Furthermore, and inexplicably, despite the horrors of the human condition, God loves us, and does not want to see us destroyed.

So God did the only thing He could do.

God let us blame Him for the violence we committed. While we often scapegoat others as a way of blaming them for the violence we commit against them, God let

Himself become the ultimate scapegoat, letting us blame Him for the violence we committed against others. Rather than force us to face the darkness and cruelty in our own hearts, God let us blame Him.

But in the crucifixion of Jesus, God said, "Enough! It is finished." Through the crucifixion, God revealed to humanity what we have always been doing. We humans always kill others in the name of God. We make victims of innocent people while claiming that we only do such things because God wills it. This is exactly what happened to Jesus.

And if Jesus had stayed dead, the world would never have known the truth about the human condition. But Jesus did not stay in the grave. He rose again. And rather than retaliate against those who wronged Him, He forgave them. So we humans have now seen the double truth revealed by God through Jesus: We are the guilty ones, and we are forgiven. But now, we can both stop our murderous violence, and also forgiven others as we have been forgiven.

Forgiveness is the way out of the mess we find ourselves in. Though we have come face to face with the horror of our own hearts, we can forgive ourselves because God has already forgiven us, and we can also forgive others because God has also already forgiven them.

Violence need not destroy us. Violence need not be met with greater violence. Violence is not the answer. In

Jesus, there is a second, more powerful response to violence that keeps us alive even in the face of our great guilt and shame. It is the response of forgiveness. Though each of us is a Jeffrey Dahmer a million times over, God has forgiven us. We are forgiven. And if God forgives us for killing others, and doing it in His name, then maybe we can forgive ourselves as well.

When our Emperor, Jesus, died on the cross and rose again, He showed us a better way out of violence. Once our eyes have been opened to the reality of who and what we really are, and where violence comes from, we can then choose to retaliate against others who have wronged us, as the Uvara did, or we can choose to forgive them, as Jesus did.

Forgiveness is the only way of escape from the reality that Scripture reveals. We must accept who we are and what we have done, and then we must also accept the shocking, scandalous, outrageous, and completely "immoral" forgiveness of God. We do not deserve forgiveness. But God extends it anyway. It is unjust for Him to do so, but He still forgives.

RE-READING THE BIBLE

This revelation of Jesus on the cross about the origins and source of violence, as well as the way out of violence, sheds lights on every violent and questionable text in

Scripture. Whenever and wherever we see the people of God engaging in violence, or God Himself commanding or excusing violence, we can know that God has nothing to do with it. The description in the Bible is nothing more than an inspired and inerrant mirror into the condition of the human heart. Such texts do not reveal God to us; they reveal us to us.

All biblical authors and characters, except Jesus, engage in this hateful, scapegoating, violent tendency in various ways. We see it in Moses when he writes about the reasons for the flood, and how the Egyptians and Canaanites deserved what "God" did to them. We see it in Joshua and Judges with every violent encounter "commanded" by God. We see it in the behavior of all the kings when they set out to war to kill their enemies "in God's name." We see it in the imprecatory Psalms when the inspired author calls down curses upon his enemies. We see it in the Prophets, when they condemn and dehumanize the enemies of Israel and Judah.

We see it in the apostles and disciples of Jesus when they want to burn and destroy those who will not accept Jesus. We see it in Peter and Paul when they write about the evil, wicked Gentiles or the hard-hearted Jews who crucified Jesus. We see it everywhere in the book of Revelation when John writes about the destruction by blood and fire that comes upon the sinful people of earth.

And yet, with some sanctified eyes, we can see the

truth behind all these violent, scapegoating accounts. They do not reveal God. They reveal us. And we must have the courage to look. In addition, we must have the courage to condemn as "wrong" anything in Scripture that does not look like Jesus Christ. When we see events or behaviors in the Bible that seem to be commanded or condoned by God, but which do not match the character and actions of Jesus, we can condemn such texts as an errant portrayal of God but as perfectly inerrant portrayals of humanity. These passages show us that it is *we* who commit violence, and then we blame it on God. The Bible reveals us to us so that we can look more like Jesus and become who we truly are.

Scripture is a mirror into our own souls. And if we go away, after looking at our face in the mirror, and forget what we have seen, we will continue to misunderstand God, misunderstand Scripture, and also misunderstand ourselves. We will continue to engage in violence and encourage violence toward our enemies, thereby missing the entire point and message of our Lord and Savior, Jesus Christ.

He said from the cross, "Father, forgive them, for they know not what they do." We now know what we do. And we are forgiven for it. But hopefully, by seeing what we do, we will now turn from it and follow instead the loving, forgiving way of Jesus. Peace will never come to this world till we have faces revealed to us in the Bible mirror.

DISCUSSION QUESTIONS

1. The Bible is described as a mirror revealing our own hearts rather than primarily God's nature. How does this perspective challenge your current approach to reading Scripture? What might it look like to read the Bible as a reflection of your own tendencies and biases?

2. The appendix argues that violent portrayals of God in Scripture reflect human violence, not God's character. Reflect on a violent biblical passage (e.g., the flood, Canaanite conquest). How does seeing it as a mirror of human scapegoating change your understanding of the text?

3. René Girard's scapegoat mechanism reveals how we blame others, including God, for our conflicts. Can you recall a time when you or your community justified harmful actions by claiming divine approval? How can recognizing this tendency foster forgiveness and reconciliation?

4. James 1:23–24 compares Scripture to a mirror, urging us to act on what we see. What "blemishes" in your own heart (e.g., judgment, anger) has Scripture revealed to you? How can you respond practically to these insights in your relationships?

5. The appendix suggests that Jesus' nonviolent response

on the cross is the model for breaking the cycle of scapegoating. How can you embody Christlike forgiveness in a world prone to blame and violence? What might this look like in your community?

6. The story of the Uvara in *The Way of Kings* illustrates the chaos of realizing we're responsible for our own violence. How can the church help people face this truth without despair, guiding them toward God's forgiveness and a life of love?

ABOUT J. D. MYERS

J. D. (Jeremy) Myers is a popular author, podcaster, theologian, and Bible teacher who lives in Oregon. He primarily writes at RedeemingGod.com, where he seeks to help liberate people from the shackles of religion. His website also provides an online discipleship group where thousands of like-minded people discuss life and theology and encourage each other to follow Jesus into the world.

If you appreciated the content of this book, would you consider recommending it to your friends and leaving a review online? Thanks!

JOIN JEREMY MYERS AND LEARN MORE

Take Bible and theology courses by joining Jeremy at
RedeemingGod.com/join/

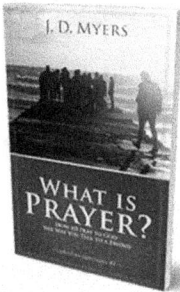

WHAT IS PRAYER? HOW TO PRAY TO GOD THE WAY YOU TALK TO A FRIEND

Stop worrying about how to pray, and just start praying!

This book reveals one simple truth: That you already know how to pray!

Once you discover that you know how to pray as revealed in this book, you will also discover that you already know what to pray for and how to see more answers to your prayers.

Read this book and find the freedom and power in your prayer life you have always longed for.

REVIEWS

I LOVE THIS BOOK! J. D. Myers has done such a great job of putting into clear words all the things about prayer that have been developing in my thoughts for years. If you wonder what praying means, if you wonder what praying should be like, or even if you wonder why on earth people should even pray, READ THIS. This is, so far, my favorite Jeremy Myers book. Not too deep, not too theological, not even too serious—though the subject matter is serious and is dealt with seriously. The tone of the writing is perfect, and the advice is genuine and extremely worthwhile. EXCELLENT BOOK. –B. Shuford

The book appears to be too simple but as you progress Jeremy covers many aspects of prayer in a way that is like a breath of fresh air. The book ends up being a natural encouragement to talking to God as a friend. I definitely recommend this book as the reader will definitely benefit from it. Not just intellectually but practically as well. Prayer will change from a chore or obligation to a pleasurable interaction with God. My heart was so filled with joy while reading this book. Jeremy you've reminded me once more that as you walk with Jesus and spend time in His presence, He talks to you and reveals Himself through the Scriptures. –Pete Nellmapius

When you finish this short book, you will know two things: 1) How easy it is to pray, and 2) How dangerous it is to pray! Prayer changes things, I used to hear. I heard in Jeremy's book, prayer changes me. I especially appreciated a page where Jeremy discusses how often we are the answers to our own prayers. I saw a "vision" of someone I am now praying for, and the Lord looking at him and looking at me, as if to say, "Well, I've put you in his life, haven't I?" A beautiful book. –Carol Roberts

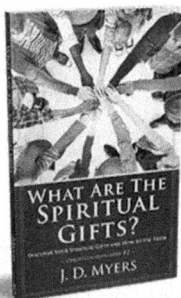

WHAT ARE THE SPIRITUAL GIFTS? DISCOVER YOUR SPIRITUAL GIFTS AND HOW TO USE THEM

Let's cut through all the nonsense about spiritual gifts.

Here is a down-to-earth discussion about what the spiritual gifts are, how to discover your spiritual gifts, and how to use them in the real world.

This book answers such questions as:

-Why did God give spiritual gifts?
-What are the spiritual gifts?
-How can I know my spiritual gifts?
-Are some spiritual gifts better than others?
-What are the dangers of the spiritual gifts?
-Have some spiritual gifts ceased?
-What about the spiritual gift of tongues?
-How can I embrace and use my spiritual gifts?

This book also includes a 125-question Spiritual Gift Inventory test.

REVIEWS

J. D. Myers' title *What are the Spiritual Gifts?* is perfect and delivers in identifying spiritual gifts mentioned in the Bible and how to personally discover your gifts to help others. Those who grew up going to church are very familiar with the topic of spiritual gifts. I would encourage those who didn't grow up in the church to read as well if wishing God's help to make a difference in the lives of others through your talents, interests, skills, and abilities.

Those who grew up going to church want to understand more about gifts such as tongues, prophecy, etc. The book does a great job of discussing whether some gifts no longer exist and how we can understand such gifts. –Mike Edwards

Jeremy Myers pulls out all the distractions that keep us from understanding our spiritual gifts given to us from a loving God. –David DeMille

Why do we think spiritual gifts are a mystery? According to Mr. Myers, we shouldn't. In a simple presentation, he offers his view of the Spiritual Gifts, and some of the characteristics for each of them (with strengths and pitfalls). The book also suggests five simple ways of discerning your gift, including a test in the end. While a test can be useful, much more useful are the other ways, like asking yourself what you think other Christians should do more … –The Pilgrimm

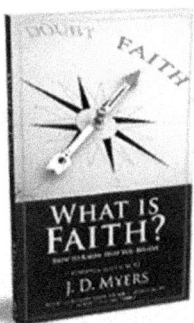

WHAT IS FAITH? HOW TO KNOW THAT YOU BELIEVE

You might know what you believe ... but do you know *that* you believe?

While many Christians know that they are supposed to believe, they don't know if they actually do believe.

Stop wondering if you have false faith, spurious faith, temporary faith, intellectual faith, or head faith instead of heart faith. All such terms are unhelpful and unbiblical, and cause many Christians to wonder if they have truly believed.

By reading this book, you will not only discover how faith works, but also how to know that you believe.

This book also answers some of your most pressing questions about faith, such as the relationship between faith and works, whether or not God gives the gift of faith, and how it is possible to be certain about your faith. This book also provides explanations for several key Bible passages about faith.

REVIEWS

Once again, Jeremy Myers brings clarity to a topic that many are confused about. Faith is such a difficult subject for some. Do I have enough faith? I have doubts, how does that affect my faith? What is child-like faith? Do I have little faith, small faith or great faith? Many Christians put faith in their faith. Jeremy does a wonderful job of explaining these concepts and more in this book. Having read, and listened to, many of Jeremy's books and podcasts, I can attest to his in-depth knowledge and proficient writing style. Whether you agree with all his points or not, you will come away with more knowledge and understanding after reading this book. This is a book that I would recommend all new Christians read and be used in discipleship classes. –Michael Wilson

I was privileged to receive an advanced copy and am happy to report that the book was enormously helpful. Having a firm foundation of knowing that you are fully loved and accepted by God is essential to spiritual growth, and in our day the greatest impediment to having this firm foundation is wondering, "Have I really believed?" Jeremy helps the reader answer this question. To any Christian who is unsure of your foundation, this book is for you! –K. E. Young

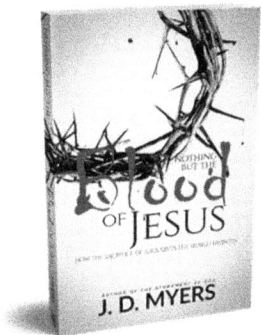

how these definitions provide clarity on numerous biblical texts.

REVIEWS

Building on his previous book, "The Atonement of God," the work of René Girard and a solid grounding in the Scriptures, Jeremy Myers shares fresh and challenging insights with us about sin, law, sacrifice, scapegoating and blood. This book reveals to us how truly precious the blood of Jesus is and the way of escaping the cycle of blame, rivalry, scapegoating, sacrifice and violence that has plagued humanity since the time of Cain and Abel. *Nothing but the Blood of Jesus* is an important and timely literary contribution to a world desperately in need of the non-violent message of Jesus. –Wesley Rostoll

My heart was so filled with joy while reading this book. Jeremy you've reminded me once more that as you walk with Jesus and spend time in His presence, He talks to you and reveals Himself through the Scriptures. –Reader

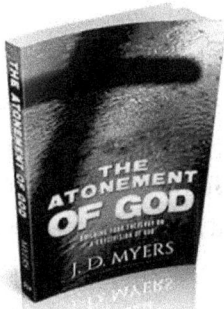

THE ATONEMENT OF GOD: BUILDING YOUR THEOLOGY ON A CRUCIVISION OF GOD

After reading this book, you will never read the Bible the same way again.

By reading this book, you will learn to see God in a whole new light. You will also learn to see yourself in a whole new light, and learn to live life in a whole new way.

The book begins with a short explanation of the various views of the atonement, including an explanation and defense of the "Non-Violent View" of the atonement. This view argues that God did not need or demand the death of Jesus in order to forgive sins. In fact, God has never been angry with us at all, but has always loved and always forgiven.

Following this explanation of the atonement, J. D. Myers takes you on a journey through 10 areas of theology which are radically changed and transformed by the Non-Violent view of the atonement. Read this book, and let your life and theology look more and more like Jesus Christ!

REVIEWS

Outstanding book! Thank you for helping me understand "Crucivision" and the "Non-Violent Atonement." Together, they help it all make sense and fit so well into my personal thinking about God. I am encouraged to be truly free to love and forgive, because God has always loved and forgiven without condition, because Christ exemplified this grace on the Cross, and because the Holy Spirit is in the midst of all life, continuing to show the way through people like you. –Samuel R. Mayer

This book gives another view of the doctrines we have been taught all of our lives. And this actually makes more sense than what we have heard. I myself have had some of these thoughts but couldn't quite make the sense of it all by myself. J.D. Myers helped me answer some questions and settle some confusion for my doctrinal views. This is truly a refreshing read. Jesus really is the demonstration of who God is and God is much easier to understand than being so mean and vindictive in the Old Testament. The tension between the wrath of God and His justice and the love of God are eased when reading this understanding of the atonement. Read with an open mind and enjoy! –Clare N. Bez

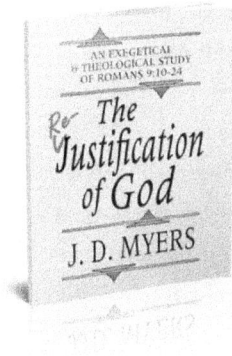

THE RE-JUSTIFICATION OF GOD: A STUDY OF ROMANS 9:10-24

Romans 9 has been a theological battleground for centuries. Scholars from all perspectives have debated whether Paul is teaching corporate or individual election, whether or not God truly hates Esau, and how to understand the hardening of Pharaoh's heart. Both sides have accused the other of misrepresenting God.

In this book, J. D. Myers presents a mediating position. Gleaning from both Calvinistic and Arminian insights into Romans 9, J. D. Myers presents a beautiful portrait of God as described by the pen of the Apostle Paul.

Here is a way to read Romans 9 which allows God to remain sovereign and free, but also allows our theology to avoid the deterministic tendencies which have entrapped certain systems of the past.

Read this book and—maybe for the first time—learn to see God the way Paul saw Him.

REVIEWS

Fantastic read! Jeremy Myers has a gift for seeing things from outside of the box and making it easy to understand for the rest of us. The Re -Justification of God provides a fresh and insightful look into Romans 9:10-24 by interpreting it within the context of chapters 9-11 and then fitting it into the framework of Paul's entire epistle as well. Jeremy manages to provide a solid theological exegesis on a widely misunderstood portion of scripture without it sounding to academic. Most importantly, it provides us with a better view and understanding of who God is. If I had a list of ten books that I thought every Christian should read, this one would be on the list. –Wesley Rostoll

I loved this book! It made me cry and fall in love with God all over again. Romans is one of my favorite books, but now my eyes have been opened to what Paul was really saying. I knew in my heart that God was the good guy, but J. D. Myers provided the analysis to prove the text. ... I can with great confidence read the difficult chapters of Romans, and my furrowed brow is eased. Thank you, J. D. Myers. I love God, even more and am so grateful that his is so longsuffering in his perfect love! Well done. –Treinhart

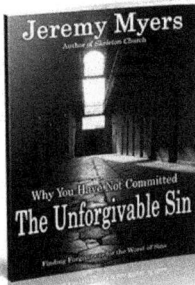

WHY YOU HAVE NOT COMMITTED THE UNFORGIVABLE SIN: FINDING FORGIVENESS FOR THE WORST OF SINS

Are you afraid that you have committed the unforgivable sin?

In this book, you will learn what this sin is and why you have not committed it. After surveying the various views about blasphemy against the Holy Spirit and examining Matthew 12:31-32, you will learn what the sin is and how it is committed.

As a result of reading this book, you will gain freedom from the fear of committing the worst of all sins, and learn how much God loves you!

REVIEWS

This book addressed things I have struggled and felt pandered to for years, and helped to bring wholeness to my heart again. –Natalie Fleming

A great read, on a controversial subject; biblical, historical and contextually treated to give the greatest understanding. May be the best on this subject (and there is very few) ever written. – Tony Vance

You must read this book. Forgiveness is necessary to see your blessings. So if you purchase this book, [you will have] no regrets. —Virtuous Woman

Jeremy Myers covers this most difficult topic thoroughly and with great compassion. —J. Holland

Wonderful explication of the unpardonable sin. God loves you more than you know. May Jesus Christ be with you always. —Robert M Sawin III

Excellent book! Highly recommend for anyone who has anxiety and fear about having committed the unforgivable sin. —William Tom

As someone who is constantly worried that they have disappointed or offended God, this book was, quite literally, a "Godsend." I thought I had committed this sin as I swore against the Holy Spirit in my mind. It only started after reading the verse about it in the Bible. The swear words against Him came into my mind over and over and I couldn't seem to stop no matter how much I prayed. I was convinced I was going to hell and cried constantly. I was extremely worried and depressed. This book has allowed me to breathe again, to have hope again. Thank you, Jeremy. I will read and re-read. I believe this book was definitely God inspired. I only wish I had found it sooner. —Sue

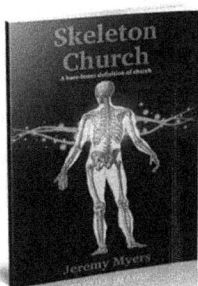

SKELETON CHURCH: A BARE-BONES DEFINITION OF CHURCH (PREFACE TO THE CLOSE YOUR CHURCH FOR GOOD BOOK SERIES)

The church has a skeleton which is identical in all types of churches. Unity and peace can develop in Christianity if we recognize this skeleton as the simple, bare-bones definition of church. But when we focus on the outer trappings—the skin, hair, and eye color, the clothes, the muscle tone, and other outward appearances—division and strife form within the church.

Let us return to the skeleton church and grow in unity once again.

REVIEWS

I worried about buying another book that aimed at reducing things to a simple minimum, but the associations of the author along with the price gave me reason to hope and means to see. I really liked this book. First, because it wasn't identical to what other simple church people are saying. He adds unique elements that are worth reading. Second, the size is small enough to read, think, and pray about without getting lost. –Abel Barba

In *Skeleton Church*, Jeremy Myers makes us rethink

church. For Myers, the church isn't a style of worship, a row of pews, or even a building. Instead, the church is the people of God, which provides the basic skeletal structure of the church. The muscles, parts, and flesh of the church are how we carry Jesus' mission into our own neighborhoods in our own unique ways. This eBook will make you see the church differently. –Travis Mamone

This book gets back to the basics of the New Testament church—who we are as Christians and what our perspective should be in the world we live in today. Jeremy cuts away all the institutional layers of a church and gets to the heart of our purpose as Christians in the world we live in and how to affect the people around us with God heart and view in mind. Not a physical church in mind. It was a great book and I have read it twice now. –Vaughn Bender

The Skeleton Church … Oh. My. Word. Why aren't more people reading this!? It was well-written, explained everything beautifully, and it was one of the best explanations of how God intended for church to be. Not to mention an easy read! The author took it all apart, the church, and showed us how it should be. He made it real. If you are searching to find something or someone to show you what God intended for the church, this is the book you need to read. –Ericka

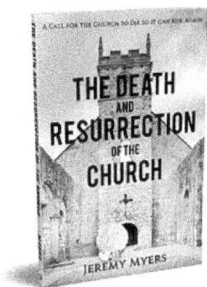

THE DEATH AND RESURRECTION OF THE CHURCH (VOLUME 1 IN THE CLOSE YOUR CHURCH FOR GOOD BOOK SERIES)

In a day when many are looking for ways to revitalize the church, Jeremy Myers argues that the church should die ... so that it can rise again.

This is not only because of the universal principle that death precedes resurrection, but also because the church has adopted certain Satanic values and goals and the only way to break free from our enslavement to these values is to die.

But death will not be the end of the church, just as death was not the end of Jesus. If the church follows Jesus into death, and even to the hellish places on earth, it is only then that the church will rise again to new life and vibrancy in the Kingdom of God.

REVIEWS

I have often thought on the church and how its acceptance of corporate methods and assimilation of cultural media mores taints its mission but Jeremy Myers eloquently captures in words the true crux of the matter—that the church is not a social club for do-gooders but to disseminate the good news to all the nooks and crannies in the world and particularly and primarily those bastions in the reign of evil. That the "gates of Hell" Jesus pronounces indicate that the church is in an offensive, not defensive, posture as gates are defensive structures.

I must confess that in reading I was inclined to be in agreement as many of the same thinkers that Myers riffs upon have influenced me also—Walter Wink, Robert Farrar Capon, Greg Boyd, NT Wright, etc. So as I read, I frequently nodded my head in agreement. –GN Trifanaff

The book is well written, easy to understand, organized and consistent thoughts. It rightfully makes the reader at least think about things as … is "the way we have always done it" necessarily the Biblical or Christ-like way, or is it in fact very sinful?! I would recommend the book for pastors and church officers; those who have the most moving-and-shaking clout to implement changes, or keep things the same. –Joel M. Wilson

Absolutely phenomenal. Unless we let go of everything Adamic in our nature, we cannot embrace anything Christlike. For the church to die, we the individual temples must dig our graves. It is a must read for all who take issues about the body of Christ seriously. –Mordecai Petersburg

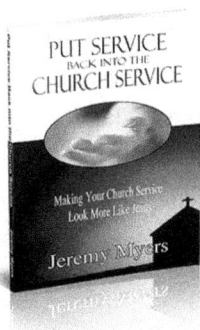

PUT SERVICE BACK INTO THE CHURCH SERVICE (VOLUME 2 IN THE CLOSE YOUR CHURCH FOR GOOD BOOK SERIES)

Churches around the world are trying to revitalize their church services. There is almost nothing they will not try. Some embark on multi-million dollar building campaigns while others sell their buildings to plant home churches. Some hire celebrity pastors to attract crowds of people, while others hire no clergy so that there can be open sharing in the service.

Yet despite everything churches have tried, few focus much time, money, or energy on the one thing that churches are supposed to be doing: loving and serving others like Jesus.

Put Service Back into the Church Service challenges readers to follow a few simple principles and put a few ideas into practice which will help churches of all types and sizes make serving others the primary emphasis of a church service.

REVIEWS

Jeremy challenges church addicts, those addicted to an unending parade of church buildings, church services, Bible studies, church programs and more to follow Jesus into our communities, communities filled with lonely, hurting people and BE the church, loving the people in our world with the love of Jesus. Do we need another training program, another seminar, another church building, a remodeled church building, more staff, updated music, or does our world need us, the followers of Jesus, to BE the church in the world? The book is well-written, challenging and a book that really can make a difference not only in our churches, but also and especially in our neighborhoods and communities. –Charles Epworth

I just finished *Put Service Back Into Church Service* by Jeremy Myers, and as with his others books I have read on the church, it was very challenging. For those who love Jesus, but are questioning the function of the traditional brick and mortar church, and their role in it, this is a must read. It may be a bit unsettling to the reader who is still entrenched in traditional "church," but it will make you think, and possibly re-evaluate your role in the church. Get this book, and all others on the church by Jeremy. – Ward Kelly

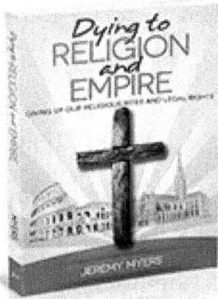

DYING TO RELIGION AND EMPIRE (VOLUME 3 IN THE CLOSE YOUR CHURCH FOR GOOD BOOK SERIES)

Could Christianity exist without religious rites or legal rights? In *Dying to Religion and Empire*, I not only answer this question with an emphatic "Yes!" but argue that if the church is going to thrive in the coming decades, we must give up our religious rites and legal rights.

Regarding religious rites, I call upon the church to abandon the quasi-magical traditions of water baptism and the Lord's Supper and transform or redeem these practices so that they reflect the symbolic meaning and intent which they had in New Testament times.

Furthermore, the church has become far too dependent upon certain legal rights for our continued existence. Ideas such as the right to life, liberty, and the pursuit of happiness are not conducive to living as the people of God who are called to follow Jesus into servanthood and death. Also, reliance upon the freedom of speech, the freedom of assembly, and other such freedoms as established by the Bill of Rights have made the church a servant of the state rather than a servant of God and the gospel. Such freedoms must be forsaken if we are going to live within the rule and reign of God on earth.

This book not only challenges religious and political liberals but conservatives as well. It is a call to leave behind the comfortable religion we know, and follow Jesus into the uncertain and wild ways of radical discipleship. To rise and live in the reality of God's Kingdom, we must first die to religion and empire.

REVIEWS

Jeremy is one of the freshest, freest authors out there—and you need to hear what he has to say. This book is startling and new in thought and conclusion. Are the "sacraments" inviolate? Why? Do you worship at a secular altar? Conservative? Liberal? Be prepared to open your eyes. Mr. Myers will not let you keep sleeping!

Jeremy Myers is one or the most thought provoking authors that I read, this book has really helped me to look outside the box and start thinking how can I make more sense of my relationship with Christ and how can I show others in a way that impacts them the way that Jesus' disciples impacted their world. Great book, great author. – Brett Hotchkiss

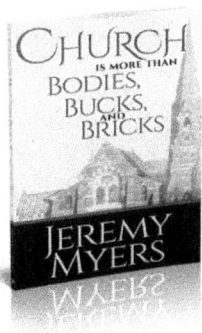

CHURCH IS MORE THAN BODIES, BUCKS, & BRICKS (VOLUME 4 IN THE CLOSE YOUR CHURCH FOR GOOD BOOK SERIES)

Many people define church as a place and time where people gather, a way for ministry money to be given and spent, and a building in which people regularly meet on Sunday mornings.

In this book, author and blogger Jeremy Myers shows that church is more than bodies, bucks, and bricks.

Church is the people of God who follow Jesus into the world, and we can be the church no matter how many people we are with, no matter the size of our church budget, and regardless of whether we have a church building or not.

By abandoning our emphasis on more people, bigger budgets, and newer buildings, we may actually liberate the church to better follow Jesus into the world.

REVIEWS

This book does more than just identify issues that have

been bothering me about church as we know it, but it goes into history and explains how we got here. In this way it is similar to Viola's *Pagan Christianity*, but I found it a much more enjoyable read. Jeremy goes into more detail on the three issues he covers as well as giving a lot of practical advice on how to remedy these situations. –Portent

Since I returned from Africa 20 years ago I have struggled with going to church back in the States. This book helped me not feel guilty and has helped me process this struggle. It is challenging and overflows with practical suggestions. He loves the church despite its imperfections and suggests ways to break the bondage we find ourselves in. –Truealian

Jeremy Meyers always writes a challenging book ... It seems the American church (as a whole) is very comfortable with the way things are ... The challenge is to get out of the brick and mortar buildings and stagnant programs and minister to the needy in person with funds in hand to meet their needs especially to the widows and orphans as we are directed in the scriptures. –GGTexas

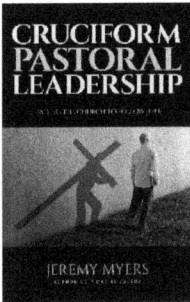

CRUCIFORM PASTORAL LEADERSHIP (VOLUME 5 IN THE CLOSE YOUR CHURCH FOR GOOD BOOK SERIES)

The final volume in the *Close Your Church for Good* book series look at issues related to pastoral leadership in the church. It discusses topics such as preaching and pastoral pay from the perspective of the cross.

The best way pastors can lead their church is by following Jesus to the cross!

ADVENTURES IN FISHING (FOR MEN)

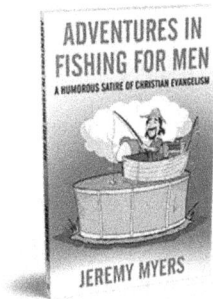

Adventures in Fishing (for Men) is a satirical look at evangelism and church growth strategies.

Using fictional accounts from his attempts to become a world-famous fisherman, Jeremy Myers shows how many of the evangelism and church growth strategies of today do little to actually reach the world for Jesus Christ.

Adventures in Fishing (for Men) pokes fun at some of the popular evangelistic techniques and strategies endorsed and practiced by many Christians in today's churches. The stories in this book show in humorous detail how little we understand the culture that surrounds us or how to properly reach people with the gospel of Jesus Christ. The story also shows how much time, energy, and money goes into evangelism preparation and training with the end result being that churches rarely accomplish any actual evangelism.

REVIEWS

I found *Adventures in Fishing (For Men)* quite funny! Jeremy Myers does a great job shining the light on some of the more common practices in Evangelism today. His allegory gently points to the foolishness that is found within a system that takes the preaching of the gospel and tries to reduce it to a simplified formula. A formula that takes what should be an organic, Spirit led experience and turns it into a gospel that is nutritionally benign.

If you have ever EE'd someone you may find Myers' book offensive, but if you have come to the place where you realize that Evangelism isn't a matter of a script and checklists, then you might benefit from this light-hearted peek at Evangelism today. –Jennifer L. Davis

Adventures in Fishing (for Men) is good book in understanding evangelism to be more than just being a set of methods or to do list to follow. –Ashok Daniel

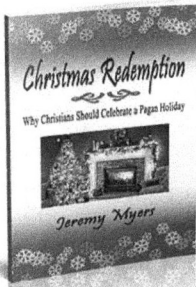

CHRISTMAS REDEMPTION: WHY CHRISTIANS SHOULD CELEBRATE A PAGAN HOLIDAY

Christmas Redemption looks at some of the symbolism and traditions of Christmas, including gifts, the Christmas tree, and even Santa Claus and shows how all of these can be celebrated and enjoyed by Christians as a true and accurate reflection of the gospel.

Though Christmas used to be a pagan holiday, it has been redeemed by Jesus.

If you have been told that Christmas is a pagan holiday and is based on the Roman festival of Saturnalia, or if you have been told that putting up a Christmas tree is idolatrous, or if you have been told that Santa Claus is Satanic and teaches children to be greedy, then you must read this book! In it, you will learn that all of these Christmas traditions have been redeemed by Jesus and are good and healthy ways of celebrating the truth of the gospel and the grace of Jesus Christ.

REVIEWS

Too many times we as Christians want to condemn nearly everything around us and in so doing become much like the Pharisees and religious leaders that Jesus encountered. I recommend this book to everyone who has concerns of how and why we celebrate Christmas. I recommend it to those who do not have any qualms in celebrating but may not know the history of Christmas. I recommend this book to everyone, no matter who or where you are, no matter your background or beliefs, no matter whether you are young or old. –David H.

Very informative book dealing with the roots of our modern Christmas traditions. The Biblical teaching on redemption is excellent! Highly recommended. –Tamara

This is a wonderful book full of hope and joy. The book explains where Christmas traditions originated and how they have been changed and been adapted over the years. The hope that the grace that is hidden in the celebrations will turn more hearts to the Lord's call is very evident. Jeremy Myers has given us a lovely gift this Christmas. His insights will lift our hearts and remain with us a long time. –Janet Cardoza

I love how the author uses multiple sources to back up his opinions. He doesn't just use bible verses, he goes back into the history of the topics (pagan rituals, Santa, etc.) as well. Great book! –Jenna G.

JOIN JEREMY MYERS AND LEARN MORE

Take Bible and theology courses by joining Jeremy at
RedeemingGod.com/join/